THE DEMONIC COMEDY

SOME DETOURS IN THE

BAGHDAD

OF SADDAM HUSSEIN

PAUL WILLIAM ROBERTS

FARRAR, STRAUS AND GIROUX / NEW YORK

Farrar, Straus and Giroux
19 Union Square West, New York 10003

Copyright © 1997 by Paul William Roberts
Printed in the United States of America
Designed by Tannice Goddard
First published in 1997 by Stoddart Publishing Co. Limited, Canada
First American edition published in 1998 by Farrar, Straus and Giroux

Library of Congress Cataloging-in-Publication Data
Roberts, Paul William.
    The demonic comedy : some detours in the Baghdad of Saddam Hussein
/ Paul William Roberts. — 1st American ed.
        p.   cm.
    Includes excerpts previously published in the May, 1991 issue of
Saturday night, and the May, 1996 issue of Harper's.
    Includes bibliographical references (p.   ) and index.
    ISBN 0-374-13823-0 (alk. paper)
    1. Persian Gulf War, 1991—Personal narratives, Canadian.
2. Roberts, Paul William—Journeys—Iraq—Baghdad.   3. Baghdad
(Iraq)—Description and travel.   I. Title.
DS79.72.R64   1998
956.7044'2—DC21   98-20558
                                                                              CIP

for
Elijah & Arabella

Let the beauty we love be what we do.
There are hundreds of ways to kneel and kiss the ground.
— JELALUDDIN RUMI

Contents

Acknowledgments

In Nelson Doucet, I am fortunate to have the kind of publisher that most writers only dream of; he is indeed this book's onlie begetter. I wish there were a more effective gesture of gratitude. I have also been lucky to find myself in the hands of the two finest magazine editors in North America: Anne Collins and Lewis H. Lapham. Without their encouragement and money none of the following contents would have been possible; and without Anne's credit card I'd still be pumping Iraqi oil from the earth by hand.

Without Lufthansa German Airlines and their public relations director, the mysterious Chris Wendland, the nearest I'd have got to Baghdad would probably have been Halifax. My thanks also to Himo Mansur of Canadian Travel Abroad Ltd. for his invaluable assistance in times of need.

To that amazing one-woman force of culture Lorraine Monk I owe a more organized existence, a good deal of single malt, much wisdom, more critical insight, and an appreciation for the frozen image that is anything but cold. She also introduced me to the Bank of Nova Scotia's Anita B. Filipe, the only bank manager who's ever wanted to meet me . . . and, while I don't understand what she says, what she *does* makes eminently good sense.

As always, without the wise Don Di Marco Gabel I'd be *riding* Cruise missiles, not writing about them. And now his son, Lorien Gabel of Interlog Internet Services, has begun providing the other pillar supporting my shaky life. Malcolm J. Kaswan of New York has been a mighty and sheltering rock, too — even though I ask for herring from the bottom of the barrel — his quicksilver wit and penetrating insights are deeply appreciated. For his unerring literary sensibility, inimical humor, and deeply cherished friendship, I thank Norman Snider.

Without Nagui Ghali, the Middle East would often lack heart, I'd rarely have breakfast, and the Internet's bandwidth would double. Without the Phantom of Stoddart, Patti McCabe, I'd have never been forced to hide from Uma Thurman. With Donald G. Bastian's conscience as my god, I never worried about missed deadlines and, after he provided Lynne Missen, I never worried about missed lines either. My literary agent, Mildred Marmur of New York, has been constantly wrestling wolves from my door and descrying new horizons, in spite of her husband's tragic death. I thank her exceedingly.

Without the late Allen Ginsberg I would not have understood how a tender heart can be man's greatest contribution to the world. I miss him. Without the late Timothy Leary I would not have seen for myself what saves us from ourselves.

For our strange and wild journey to the shores of Atlantis together, and for wisdom tempered by genius and God's own black humor, I thank John Anthony West, America's answer to the Nasruddin stories. To those whose letters light up my basement with humor, humanity, intrigue, and verve — Leatha F. Holloway of Florida, Sjorje Green of Australia, and Vicki Hiatt of Dreamworks — I can only say that you make me inclined to believe the written word has a future.

Alexander Epstein, lawyer, one-man global peace mission and tireless humanitarian, makes me believe the human race has a future. As always, he is a great inspiration, and an example that should shame us all.

Richard Sparks of "Hollywood" especially deserves my deepest consolation and to know that the answers he's seeking are: "petroleum jelly; she looks much older in make-up; a good broad-spectrum antibiotic; and, yes, but he's a poor marksman." To Lord and Lady Abydos, Rand and Rose Flem-Ath, I'd like to say *Mnest-ya kve chuhha abonid*, but I'll have to settle for *Upwards and On to Six Thousand Degrees*. Daniel Lynch made no contribution to this book; nor did Steven Alix — but Isabel and Alison made up for their inutility, and their friendship makes for far more.

I would like to thank Bob Dylan, elusive acquaintance, invisible collaborator, and Last Poet, for singing "Masters of War" to an audience at the 1991 Emmy Awards more concerned with hair, bosoms, fame, and wealth than the bombs their government was then dropping on Baghdad. It was a sad reminder that rock music once used to mean something.

Lastly yet far from leastly, I must thank the family that has put family into someone unfamiliar with the thing: Constance, Dorothy, David, Ray, Marino, Nelda, Rudy, Margie, Elvi, and Kiki. And then there's Tiziana Buttignol (*oreed taani diblet' za-waag al-aanisa' min-fadlak*) who has taught me how to be human. Thank you.

IRAQ: A TIMELINE

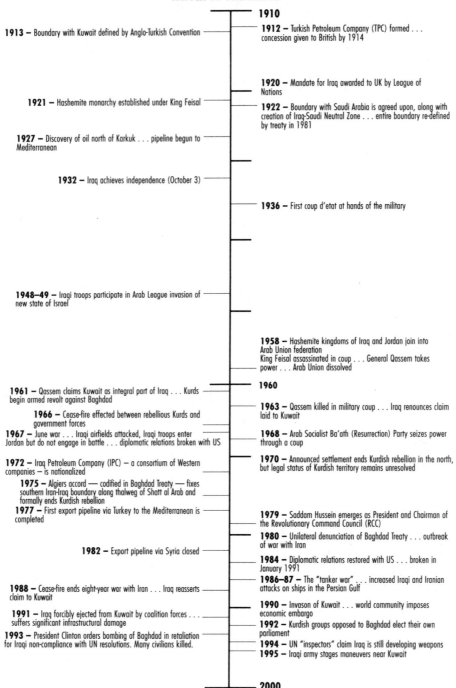

1910

1913 – Boundary with Kuwait defined by Anglo-Turkish Convention

1912 – Turkish Petroleum Company (TPC) formed . . . concession given to British by 1914

1920 – Mandate for Iraq awarded to UK by League of Nations

1921 – Hashemite monarchy established under King Feisal

1922 – Boundary with Saudi Arabia is agreed upon, along with creation of Iraq-Saudi Neutral Zone . . . entire boundary re-defined by treaty in 1981

1927 – Discovery of oil north of Karkuk . . . pipeline begun to Mediterranean

1932 – Iraq achieves independence (October 3)

1936 – First coup d'etat at hands of the military

1948–49 – Iraqi troops participate in Arab League invasion of new state of Israel

1958 – Hashemite kingdoms of Iraq and Jordan join into Arab Union federation
King Feisal assassinated in coup . . . General Qassem takes power . . . Arab Union dissolved

1961 – Qassem claims Kuwait as integral part of Iraq . . . Kurds begin armed revolt against Baghdad

1960

1963 – Qassem killed in military coup . . . Iraq renounces claim laid to Kuwait

1966 – Cease-fire effected between rebellious Kurds and government forces

1967 – June war . . . Iraqi airfields attacked, Iraqi troops enter Jordan but do not engage in battle . . . diplomatic relations broken with US

1968 – Arab Socialist Ba'ath (Resurrection) Party seizes power through a coup

1972 – Iraq Petroleum Company (IPC) – a consortium of Western companies – is nationalized

1970 – Announced settlement ends Kurdish rebellion in the north, but legal status of Kurdish territory remains unresolved

1975 – Algiers accord — codified in Baghdad Treaty — fixes southern Iran-Iraq boundary along thalweg of Shatt al Arab and formally ends Kurdish rebellion

1977 – First export pipeline via Turkey to the Mediterranean is completed

1979 – Saddam Hussein emerges as President and Chairman of the Revolutionary Command Council (RCC)

1980 – Unilateral denunciation of Baghdad Treaty . . . outbreak of war with Iran

1982 – Export pipeline via Syria closed

1984 – Diplomatic relations restored with US . . . broken in January 1991

1986–87 – The "tanker war" . . . increased Iraqi and Iranian attacks on ships in the Persian Gulf

1988 – Cease-fire ends eight-year war with Iran . . . Iraq reasserts claim to Kuwait

1990 – Invason of Kuwait . . . world community imposes economic embargo

1991 – Iraq forcibly ejected from Kuwait by coalition forces . . . suffers significant infrastructural damage

1992 – Kurdish groups opposed to Baghdad elect their own parliament

1993 – President Clinton orders bombing of Baghdad in retaliation for Iraqi non-compliance with UN resolutions. Many civilians killed.

1994 – UN "inspectors" claim Iraq is still developing weapons

1995 – Iraqi army stages maneuvers near Kuwait

2000

PART ONE

The Paradise
1990

At that point — I would have you see — the force
to which one yielded mingles with one's will;
and no excuse can pardon their joint act.
Absolute will does not concur in wrong;
but the contingent will, through fear that its
resistance might bring greater harm, consents.
— DANTE, *Paradiso* IV 37

Future wars will be as ferociously ideological as the old wars of religion.
— ALDOUS HUXLEY, *Ends and Means (1937)*

The Bogeyman will never leave until you can
laugh in his face.
— OLD WELSH SAYING

THE FIRST & SECOND NASSER

My journal entry reads "Feb 15, Cairo. Saddam's boy (mugged). Tomorrow 11:30 — meet Boutros-Ghali. . . ."

The boy lay bleeding in an alley, his mouth contorted by a dozen kicks and punches into an ironic grin that seemed to say, "I showed 'em." His assailants — there were perhaps ten of them — broadcast a mirthless edgy laughter, still ready to put the boot in again, should the situation warrant it.

Now, I'm no hero, but I do have a sense of justice — I have righteous indignation to spare, in fact — and it was this vague little instinct that made me stand between them and the bloody boy, arms raised in a gesture of what I hoped was abject pacifism, searching for some Arabic *mots justes*: "Enough! Okay? Leave him alone . . ."

One of them — a very big bastard — assessed me, assessed my potential as a victim, and glanced back to his colleagues for second opinions. He received none, mercifully. Instead, their looks said, "We've done enough without including the Ferengi. Let's make dust . . ."

"What's the problem?" I wanted to know what kind of richly deserved retribution I might be interfering with.

The big bastard reached down and scooped up a large ball of torn paper, throwing it at my feet in an oddly childish fuck-you gesture. I picked it up cautiously, smoothing the jagged mass open until most of a poster bearing the image of Saddam Hussein quivered between my hands in the evening breeze.

"Saddam Hussein bullsheet!" he snarled.

I was inclined to agree, and the wild-eyed pack eagerly picked up this assent, backing off until they could reasonably turn and run with dignity.

The boy — he was only sixteen or so — got up without my help, wiping blood onto the sleeve of his gelabia. It wasn't serious, it wasn't like running into some home boys who wanted your Reeboks, or some British soccer fans who found your face offensive. Egypt's a civilized place.

"You okay?"

"Beeg sheets," he replied, looking angrily down the vespertine alley at shadows and memories. "Saddam he weel be second Nasser! Then they weel change the words . . ."

He brushed my help aside, striding lopsidedly off alone.

By April 1990 I had been in Egypt several months, researching the book that came to be called *River in the Desert*. It was my second visit to the country, and my acquaintances there now ranged from cabinet ministers, through Bedouin nomads, art critics, Sufi mystics, small businessmen, and cab drivers, to rural fellahin and Islamist fundamentalists. However, it was my fifteenth visit to an Arab nation; I had many Arab friends, so I felt reasonably attuned to Arab attitudes, ethics, ideas, politics, aspirations, and even, to some extent, the often balefully enigmatic Arab soul.

In February 1990, Boutros Boutros-Ghali, then Egypt's foreign minister, had told me that the cause of most Arab problems and misunderstandings — and he spoke authoritatively since he'd recently written a book on Arab disputes — lay in geography. "The Arab nations," he said, were "an archipelago: islands in a sea of sand. Drive from Paris to Moscow, and you never leave civilization. Yet from here to Benghazi, and from Benghazi to Tripoli, and from Tripoli to . . . it's just sand. There's no continuity of culture, thus no continuity of action or thought . . ."

What was this buzz on the street about Saddam Hussein?

The answer: "He has a big stick. Arabs appreciate a man with a big stick."

Was he really positioning himself to be the second Nasser, though?

Boutros-Ghali shrugged. They were big shoes to fill. But Iraq had the second largest deposits of Arab D-grade oil — the finest — on earth, and it was ultimately oil that determined how big a stick any Arab leader could have. Oil and an attitude toward Israel.

But how receptive to a new Nasser — a revived dream of the United Arabia — were Arabs these days? The image of the bloody boy hovered over this conversation, and I persisted with questions that then had no answers. I must have been a nuisance, because I managed to get myself invited along with the Egyptian delegation to attend the Arab Summit to be held in Baghdad, May 1990.

ROCKED IN THE CRADLE OF CIVILIZATION

"Iraqi womans all are wars," announced Ahmed, who had the window seat in our Air Egypt jet.

"Wars?"

He was a kind of undersecretary in the Commerce ministry, I learned, and seemed to have very little in the way of work ahead of him in Baghdad — unless you count getting laid as toil.

"*Hoo-rezz!*"

"Why are they whores?"

He looked at me pityingly: surely I knew what made women whores?

"They making always zigzig with men-not-the-husbands . . ."

"Oh. All of them?"

"*Ayah!* Most, man, most! What-is-it-you-wanting-more?"

"Huh?"

"Sticking with me, my brother. The Ahmed-I will be the-showing-you . . . Baghdad is poono-grop!"

"Poonogrop?"

"*Aiwa!* Betting-you-buttock-dollaris . . . We will being for the far-out-time, us!"

And so we were.

Lest anyone think me guilty of chauvinistic attitudes toward the English-challenged of this world, my Arabic is infinitely more risible than any of the many utterances with which Ahmed — and others — daily entertained me. Misunderstandings and slapstick etiology were the very warp and woof upon which the fabric of our days in Iraq was woven; to omit them would relegate much that happened in the twisted, resonant labyrinths of conversation to a synaptic Twilight Zone.

Instead of Customs and Immigration, Iraqi authorities felt that what you really needed on disembarking from an international flight was a stand-up buffet lunch n' cabaret, with jugglers and a species of Elvis impersonator clad in red sequins. This man had an unusual name — Mekwip, perhaps — and bestrode a white dais on wheels that was propelled around the Customs and Immigration buffet area at an alarming speed by two goblin-like boys in green taffeta. Mekwip kept his balance by keeping his feet a yard and a half apart, while he crooned through a radio mike to the accompaniment of a band some distance away and crammed — all ten of them — on top of what might well have been a desk swathed in orange and green crepe paper. They looked like wax exhibits in a museum of musical instruments: one strummed a white Fender Stratocaster, one some kind of lute, another played a vast pearl-inlaid accordian, another the oud, while the rest clapped their hands or battered away at various kinds of drum.

"Taaap-whaam, mea-paturaaanappa!" hollered Mekwip.

"Big star," Ahmed informed me. "Big-gest star! Iraqi roller-rock music," he added, as if I might otherwise have suspected it was Syrian hip-hop or Yemeni Blue Grass.

"Welcome to Iraq," said a woman wearing so much eyeliner she appeared to be staring out from behind the fissures in a coal face. "You are from Morocco?" Her clothes were probably conspired upon and conjured forth by the same gang guilty of Barbie's less restrained party outfits: everything was fried in gold, dazzled by sequins, or adrift in wreathes of chiffon.

"No . . . er . . ."

"Too bad."

"What?"

"Moroccan men only are welcome here." She pressed a palm either to her heart or her left breast, then clicked away proudly on heels like knitting needles.

"E-jeeptisss?" This was a man who appeared to be wearing a fair bit of makeup himself, along with a suit of puce, apricot, and white checks that was large enough and more than sufficiently flamboyant to have been an heirloom from Bozo the Clown.

"Here-for-we, us!" shouted Ahmed — unnecessarily, since I was right beside him.

"How are kebabisss?" asked Bozo's heir, again producing that curious hissing noise with which he terminated all sentences. "And tabouli is goodisssss?"

"Great . . ."

"And Iraq people singerisssss?"

"Fab. Just fab. Really."

"Goodissss. Now, we are proceeding to Security Checkisssss."

"Please, good-sir," Ahmed now protested, looking back somewhat forlornly at the removable feast. "We are the-waiting-here-minutes, yes? For to enjoys-party after many-houred flightings."

"Why don't you speak Arabic, Ahmed?"

"They here the not-understanding-it-them."

"Oh."

"Iraqi accenting is for-make-the-goats-sicking . . ."

The vast majority of Arab men consider their own personal forms and dialects of Arabic to be the only true and perfect ones. Many even seem to prefer conversing in a (sometimes very) foreign tongue rather than exposing the precious mother one to a risk of pollution and ridicule by proximity to rabble-babble.

"Security goingissss! Plissss!!" hissed Bozo. This time, however, he was more forceful — more snoop than boob. Heir to the mournfully savage, cruelly satiric Court Jester, the clown — particularly the faintly sinister, Felliniesque clown — is an ideal disguise for undercover police officers.

Security was behind a hospital ward-like screen a few yards down a dead-end corridor. It definitely wasn't as much fun as the buffet n' cabaret. It was my first up-close glimpse of "Them," however.

There's not much that is secret about Iraq's Secret Police, the feared Mukhabarat. Its officers all have moustaches as much like Saddam's luxuriant broom of a growth as they can manage (and most Iraqi men can manage a reasonably prodigious facsimile). Not all of them, however, wear uniforms: like men who are used to uniforms and *should* be wearing uniforms, they are, in fact, wearing uniforms by *not* wearing uniforms. They might as well have been perched on white stallions and clad in gold-trimmed scarlet, with plumed hats and jingling spurs, for all the inconspicuousness they managed to achieve.

But men in the cattle-prod, thumb-screw and rack business — the late-night-visit, sudden-disappearance, and amateur surgery game — don't want to be inconspicuous, and they certainly don't crave civilian individualism. There's safety in numbers: it dilutes the bad karma — and it tends to deter from ideas of vengeance those relatives of the man you gave some non-elective proctological procedures to last week, before feeding him alive to starving rottweilers. Having a bottle broken inside your rectum is not supposed to be pleasant, of course (you can't get the pieces out), but it must seem especially unpleasant when no reason for this savage indignity is ever offered by the authorities inflicting it. No charge is ever laid, because no crime has been committed. Everyone knew "that suspects always existed, even for crimes that had not yet been committed."[1] Saddam himself had spelled it out back in 1978:

> The revolution chooses its enemies, and we say chooses its enemies because some enemies are chosen by it from among the people who run up against its program and who intend to harm it. The revolution chooses as enemies those people who intend to deviate from its main principles and starting points.[2]

This was everyday life in Baghdad. This was *normal*.

Random violence and arbitrary cruelty keep the masses in line before they've done anything to merit punishment, in order that they will never want to merit it. This was an atheist state's version of hellfire and damnation, developed — and on an epic level — by the ex-priest, Josef Stalin. Saddam's secular Inquisitors had been trained by the East German secret police, so they knew the theory behind this practice. A few had to be sacrificed for the good of many, and this was best achieved through fear. Just as no one ever returned from hell, from the demons with pitchforks and the vats of boiling sulfur, so no one ever returned from the covert human abattoirs, from the hooks, wires, and grotesque parodies of internal medicine with which the Mukhabarat purged their compatriots of sin. Through such a perpetual Inquisition they maintained an orderly society. Those who see cruelty and silence in the face of barbaric injustice as a tragic flaw in many Arab societies would do well to remember that Saddam Hussein's regime was modeled on those of Stalin and Hitler; it has no parallel in the Arab world.

What went on behind the windowless walls of Mukhabarat bastions was bad enough — it could take a week or more to die from bowels lacerated by shards of broken glass — but what was rumored to go on there was even worse. All day long, the average Iraqi was being eaten alive by his own imagination; at night, it was by dreams.

But all of this was more rumor and hearsay back in 1990 than it was conventional wisdom or documented fact. There were many reports from various agencies that Saddam had created a living hell for his countrymen, but these were regarded with a degree of suspicion as likely products of Israeli propaganda. The truth, however, was far worse than almost anyone outside Iraq suspected: the place was an interactive psychological horror movie, one moving from an R- to an XXX-rating, too. And the agents of this repellent animated nightmare were the men with moustaches: the Mukhabarat.

"Papers," one demanded, holding out his hand without looking at me.

They had some serious equipment behind their screen: sniffing machines, X-ray machines, scanners of some other sort, and state-of-the-art computers. My papers created bafflement.

"Not Egypt passport," a moustache stated, holding my British passport as if it were smeared with snot.

The Egyptians, however, had Security with their delegation too, and soon Iraqi Security faced Egyptian Security, making it clear that there was not much in the way of international brotherhood for those in Security.

Egyptian Security looked more like a team of cruel accountants, though. They had no moustaches but they did have authority. They even had authorizations — one of them clearly mine, with photocopied passport pix, stamps, signatures, and official calligraphy festooned all over it like doodling. Iraqi Security now had my baggage, which they electronically sniffed, scanned, zapped, then searched manually, hauling out clothes as if clearing a blocked drain, scrutinizing medicines and toiletries — including, much to my shame, a dozen sewing kits and some thirty-odd mini-soaps from the Ramses Hilton in Cairo.

"Imodium," said a moustache, rattling a cylinder of bluish capsules at me.

I nodded apologetically.

"For loose bow-well," he announced.

I nodded again. Yes, Iraq! my bowels are loose!

"May you have firm bow-well in Iraq, dear sir." He tossed the Imodium back.

"Thank you." I wondered if it was, perhaps, a traditional greeting.

Two tape recorders and three cameras were more of a problem than loose bowels, though: he wanted them, I could tell. So could Egyptian Security, evidently, for there ensued a bitter exchange during which the words "Sony" and "Nikon" were mentioned frequently. The man settled for two packs of Marlboros.

"WELCOME TO IRAQ: CRADLE OF CIVILIZATION"

It was written like a subtitle along the bottom of a mural inside the airport Arrivals area. The entire sweep of Iraqi history seemed to be covered by this one gigantic image, which began, far to the left, with Nebuchadrezzar proudly surveying his victorious troops as they marched through Babylon, the capital, raising swords in salute and leading prisoners in chains. You could tell these prisoners were Jews captured after the fall of Jerusalem because they all looked so much like Der Stürmer caricatures they might as well have been exclaiming "Oi Vay!" while wearing yellow Stars of David, phylacteries, and yarmulkes.

About halfway along the mural, a similar scene was repeated, but this time in the new capital of Baghdad, with Caliph al-Mansūr view-ing a military parade that included prisoners who were all wearing either the national dress of Turkey or Persia and looked as if they'd been ambushed on their way to perform at a folk dancing festival. Some had fallen to their knees before the caliph, presumably begging for an amnesty to dance first, then die — a leniency that, judging by al-Mansūr's stern, beetle-browed frown, they were not likely to receive.

Finally, taking up a good quarter of the mural's right end, there were scenes of Saddam's own struggle, culminating with a march of uniformed clones saluting their leader with raised rifles and leading in chains what were, evidently, the same prisoners captured by previous armies but now wearing army uniforms or ayatollahs' robes. All that had really changed in a few millennia, it seemed, were hats: from the towering mitered crowns of ancient Babylonian kings, this headgear timeline progressed through the jeweled silk turbans of the caliphs to the humble military beret of Saddam.

If this were the cradle of civilization, its baby must have fallen out and cracked its skull, or else endured a momentously battered childhood, since it had definitely become a very disturbed adult . . .

Right outside the terminal there were several brand-new coaches waiting, all of them swathed in banners reading either "Baghdad Summit '90" or some hyperbolic encomium relating to President Saddam Hussein in one of his various avatars — such as "Father of the Nation" or "Hero of the Revolution." Like God, he had many names, many roles, many attributes. Accordingly, Iraq possessed many large pictures of him. From a coach so cold with conditioned air that my breath turned to frost on its darkened windows, I watched as Baghdad and its generous allotment of Saddam's many gargantuan selves unfolded above and beyond broad, clean, and, most of all, new boulevards. Beside me, Ahmed watched our tour guide, Mari, a handsome thirty-something green-eyed brunette, who wore a black sheath of dress in one of those fabrics whose elasticity is so formidable that garments can actually be a size or two smaller than the wearer's own skin. She rustled up and down the aisle, pointing out landmarks, leaving a humid breeze of musky perfume in her wake.

"Christian women, she," Ahmed told me.

There are many Christians in Iraq, mainly Nestorians (Eastern Orthodox) but not necessarily; and there are also many people with pale brown, red, or even blonde hair, green or blue eyes — Christian and Muslim alike.

"Christian womens all-the-whores," stated Ahmed.

"Thanks."

He stuttered in horror, realizing what he'd said. "N-n-not the wife-and-mother-you, my friend. Allah! Forgeeve me, friend. I ignorant speaking-me . . ."

"True."

"But this . . ." He gestured helplessly at Mari, who had bent to retrieve her ballpoint at this juncture, her butt suddenly an inch from Ahmed's nose like some shadowy questionable life-form from the XXX-rated abyss, a Thing whose sole feature was a shallow cleft framed by a V of ridged sinew.

It did seem to be deliberate.

And it was about the most exotic sight I'd noticed so far in Baghdad, which is not a very exotic place, despite its reputation. It had dawned on me everyone well-known and widely associated with the city was actually fictional: Ali Baba, Aladdin, Sinbad, Scheherazade and her many Nights. Who, then, are the eminent nonfictional Baghdadites? Besides the founding caliphs, al-Mansūr and al-Rashid (who was also patron of the 1,001 Nights), there aren't any. And there isn't even a central bazaar, no mysterious *souk* stacked with glittering gold, ablaze with intrigue and the swirling sheen of handmade silk rugs. What's more, there never has been a bazaar: al-Mansūr's religious convictions decreed all trade had to take place beyond the city walls. Iraqis don't make carpets, either, so any for sale in Baghdad or elsewhere would generally be from Turkey or Iran.

Phenomenally great PR is what Baghdad must have had for centuries now; thus it comes as no surprise to find that the Saatchi brothers — those London-based global advertising and marketing wizards whose media campaigns won Margaret Thatcher two elections — were born in the city. Like many Jewish families in Arab countries (although there are partial exceptions such as Syria and Morocco), the Saatchis left Baghdad after the Suez crisis, when the future of the relationship between Western neo-imperialism and the Arab world was first revealed as one of a quintessential inequality predicated by ad hoc pro-Zionism.

They were the lucky ones. When the revolutionary Ba'ath regime — a kind of Arab Nazi Party — came to power in July 1968, no Jew left in Iraq was safe. In the wake of the Arabs' massive defeat by Israel during the Six Day War of 1967, a state of shocked disbelief traumatized political life across the Middle East. Why had it happened? What should the Arab response be? In the states bordering Israel, this latter question was answered by fostering Palestinian movements. But Iraq is a little too far from Israel for such a response to have seemed adequate, so the Ba'athi came up with something just as concrete and yet also uniquely their own. Indeed, it can be argued that the path to the Ba'athist regime's installation as supreme rulers of Iraq led through the door of anti-Semitism, which they first opened two months after the war, on September 6, 1967, during a huge demonstration against the old 'Aref regime.

In a series of passionate, angry speeches to dazed crowds, Ba'athist leaders demanded that immediate action be taken against all local agents of Zionism and imperialism. This struck the match that relit a torch extinguished in Iraq many years earlier in the political arena: the concept of a fifth column scapegoat capable of taking all the blame for a devastating war, and being justifiably punished for it, too. Parallels with Hitler's Germany are inescapable, and like the German Jews, Iraq's once-flourishing Jewish community had also played a long and important role in its country's history, making a contribution to the national culture disproportionately greater than that of any other minority.

Officially, the count of Iraqi casualties during the six days of fighting against Israel was ten soldiers dead and around thirty wounded.[3] "In these modest numbers," Samir al-Khalil, one of Iraq's pre-eminent intellectual voices in exile, comments:

> the awesome reach of a pan-Arabist reference system was powerfully displayed. The ghosts of tens of thousands of Egyptian, Syrian, Jordanian, and Palestinian casualties, to say nothing of the occupation of territories, the collapse of whole armies, and the destruction of equipment — all of this was summoned up in the fantasies of ordinary men and women as the responsibility of Iraq's tiny Jewish community, whose near-total withdrawal from all facets of public life dated back to the 1940s. . . . The two main outbreaks of anti-Semitism in modern Iraqi politics (1941, 1967–70) are both firmly associated with the ascendancy of pan-Arabism; attacks on the Jewish community have not come from the Communist party, Iraqi nationalist currents, or even the traditional confessional leaders.[4]

Before long, ideological assertions became a hideous reality, as a
Ba'athist regime began to further demonstrate its talent at manipulation
of symbols — but now from the position of official government. What
better symbolized the insidiously all-pervasive presence of imperialism
than the commodity most widely associated with it? Thus it was that the
Iraqi branch of the Coca-Cola Company had its offices raided and its
owner-president, along with his general manager, driven away wearing
blindfolds and handcuffs. Both were Muslim. Several weeks later the
president's mutilated corpse and a manager reduced to gibbering
insanity were returned to their respective families. Coca-Cola was
nationalized. The Americans didn't like this, and they weren't about to
forget it quickly, either. But Iraq was suddenly providing a bewildering
array of distractions that made desecration of the National Beverage
pale by comparison.

Three months after gaining power, on October 9, 1968, the government announced that it had cracked a major Zionist spy ring in the
port city of Basra on the Persian Gulf coast. Seventeen "spies" were
flown to a military base in Baghdad, then driven to an interrogation
center. Over the next month, arrests mounted, then on November 25,
Iraqi artillery units based in Jordan opened fire in their latest useful
contribution to the improvement of an Arab-Israeli dialogue. On
December 4, Israel expressed its own thoughts about Iraq with a
lightning air strike. Official figures list casualties as sixteen dead, thirty
wounded, but persistent rumors had it that these numbers were
whopping underestimates. The next day in Baghdad, there was a huge
demonstration organized by the government and led by party officials,
as well as a fair-sized contingent of imported Palestinian guerrillas.
Some forty thousand people marched from Liberation Square toward
the Presidential Palace, carrying along with them the coffins of dead
soldiers. In a characteristic two-hour harangue, broadcast live on Iraqi
television, President Ahmad Hassan al-Bakr addressed the crowd, pin-
pointing the role of "a rabble of fifth columnists and the new supporters
of America and Israel" in attacks on the Iraqi army:

> They aim to create malicious rumor and disturbances, employing for
> this end killings, sabotage, and undertaking operations behind the
> front lines of our heroic army . . . with the intention of keeping us

preoccupied from the great battle with the Zionist enemy. . . . We shall strike mercilessly with a fist of steel at those exploiters and fifth columnists, the handmaidens of imperialism and Zionism.[5]

Like any other pop rhetorician and crowd hustler, Bakr yelled out every now and then: "What do you want?" To which the well-orchestrated answer would come roaring back: "Death to the spies! Execution of spies, all the spies! Execution now!"

On December 14, Iraqi television presented an interview between a senior party official and two Muslim accomplices in the alleged espionage activities at Basra. The pair swiftly confessed their guilt and abject remorse, then told their story, in which Jews starred as prime movers and central villains — although a pinch of Muslims and a smattering of Christians were added to the brew for flavor and credibility's sake. This confession did not go unrewarded, either: the public prosecutor requested the court to commute the duo's death sentence to one of life imprisonment. They should be out by 2020 — if they've behaved themselves.

The seventeen "spies" were brought to trial on January 5, 1969. Thirteen of them were Jews. The tone of this trial was set from day one, yet no doubt the defendants had felt little reason for optimism long before this. But when your own counsel introduces himself to the court by apologizing to the prosecutor for having to defend spies, and then even states for the official record that he "would not like to see the traitors go unpunished," you can be fairly sure that you haven't hired the Dream Team.

The trial was a pig circus from start to finish, but a devilishly cruel and cunningly orchestrated one. The defendants were seemingly offered at least the form of a fair trial, each of them allowed to shuffle forward after charges were read out to mumble "not guilty" on each count. As this charade proceeded, Iraqi media demonstrated their objectivity and their independence from the interests of the status quo in an admirably unequivocal fashion: peals of derisive laughter rang out from the press's benches as each defendant registered his plea.

As occurred during the O. J. Simpson criminal trial, the very publicity of this spectacle masked the erasure of the public as a self-consciously independent entity. The media whipped themselves into a feeding frenzy. The cryptic initials — never any names — of fifth columnists still at large and now being asked to turn themselves in regularly interrupted radio broadcasts and flashed across television screens. A spate of car bombings cranked up the emotional pitch of public red alert, until vigilance reached such a finely tuned state that bombings were announced in the newspapers before they actually occurred. The result was that the dragnet spread almost invisibly, like a spider's web, and the number of spies it ensnared grew daily larger.

The bodies of the Basra Seventeen were left hanging from their scaffolds in Liberation Square some seventy yards apart, a distance that increased "the area of sensual contact between mutilated body and mass. . . ."[6] Estimates place the size of enthusiastic crowds that came to view the swaying corpses in central Baghdad as high as five hundred thousand.[7]

For twenty-four hours a carnival atmosphere prevailed, orchestrated by President Bakr. Along with other party notables, he came to address the people against a backdrop of hideously maltreated cadavers, which, although long dead, were still pelted with stones, pummeled with hoes and rakes, spat upon, and smeared with excrement by the chanting mob. In one speech, Salah 'Umar al-'Ali, minister of guidance, even promised more of the same free entertainment: "Great Iraqi people! This is only the beginning! The great and immortal squares of Iraq shall be filled up with the corpses of traitors and spies! Just wait!"[8]

They didn't have to wait very long, either; but the general public's enthusiasm for Ba'athism's brave new world grew increasingly reserved as the realization that no one was safe kicked in and fear took hold of them. For the trials that followed were largely of Christians and Muslims, then of just Muslims, and after that of Ba'athi Muslims, as the party, having purified Iraq's people, turned upon itself. Those who wonder what really happens when a serpent starts to devour its own tail should be more observant: the head stops biting when it starts to feel the pain itself. After all, purgatory isn't Hell and purgation should stop short of suicide.

Out of this frenzy of purification emerged, in pristine shape, Saddam Hussein al-Takriti — in much the same manner as Josef Stalin's power-base was consolidated by the Bolshevik purges in Moscow, 1936–38. It is tyranny's trademark to erase what came before, lest anyone trace the road back and realize that the present has become far, far worse than anything in the past. The dictator's tools are a present terror that creates mass amnesia in the interests of a promised future — one that remains all promise and no future.

Thus everything — from roads to hotels, cigarette brands, boroughs, buildings, and boats — amply demonstrated that, beyond the caliphs Mansūr and Rashid, there had been no one worth naming anything after until Saddam came along. What little was not now named after him was named after them. Centuries of struggle and human aspiration were erased as schools adopted the new curriculum, and education itself became just another brutal clumsy tool of a political machine increasingly bent on shaping reality in its own image.

From the Saddam International Airport, heading down the Saddam Freeway, past Saddam City and the Saddam Water Purification Plant, we sped by Saddam institutes, Saddam housing estates, Saddam boys' clubs, Saddam sports arenas, Saddam hospitals, Saddam cafés, and, of course, dozens of Saddam billboards, statues, mosaic walls, and monster outdoor portraits. A banner some three hundred feet long that spanned the highway at one point — probably for the summiteers' benefit — welcomed us to "The Iraq of Saddam Hussein." This proprietorial touch had something very Hollywood about it, like "Wes Craven's Halloween."

Beyond the ring road, everything was modern — yet in that seventies' Vulcan-V-Bomber Disco style. Had the structures on all sides been people, they would have been white-suited John Travoltas strutting their stuff, flared pants flapping, the Vitalis sheen of perfect hair glinting in the sunlight. *Stayin' alive, stayin' alive . . .* It could be Baghdad's theme song now — but for other reasons. In Baghdad, disco was still alive, though, still groovy — or so the Saddam Discotheque seemed to indicate.

"As you weel no-teece," Mari was telling us, "the Ee-raq of Saddam Oo-sayanne iss veree mod-erne. Veree mush a-pard of this twen-tee-eth senshry. A senshry of thee Ar-ab and off Saddam Oo-sayanne his-self . . ."

"She-the one hot-baby, she is . . . ," drooled Ahmed. He gently patted my knee. "We having for us the large time-party, yes?"

"Time party?"

Someone had told me that Saddam held onto power with a reign of terror unequaled in history. Or perhaps in the history of Iraq? Maybe it was the reins of power he held onto with unequaled terror? I forget. But Baghdad did not immediately strike me as a city quaking under the yoke of a psychopathic monster. I asked Ahmed about this, but he merely replied that the iron hand required of rulers is usually sheathed by a velvet glove. At least, I think that was what he wanted to say. Iron hand, big stick, velvet glove — whatever it was that Saddam had at the end of his arm, many Arabs approved of it.

We turned off a broad boulevard into the walled compound of some prosperous mega-corporation's headquarters. A neo-Stalinesque sky-scraping edifice in high-grade concrete soared up from acres of elaborately manicured gardens and a warren of small roads, each with its own barrier and mini guard post.

"What's this?" I asked. "A corporate statement by the national oil and strobe lighting conglomerate?"

"Astro-blighting?"

It was the Al Rashid Hotel, in fact, an establishment that, in the five-star world of gleaming international hotels, was a good seven stars — if not more. It looked almost unnecessarily lavish, and it barely resembled a hotel until you'd entered the main doors, then crossed a massively empty lobby-like space that led, after another regal set of doors, to the real lobby. There were elevators in the ante-lobby, but they were not for hotel guests, I later noticed. There was something distinctly odd about this arrangement.

"You find Iraq very impressive," a bellboy told me.

"Do I?"

"You were expecting a backward place, I think? But you find instead a place finer than any in the West."

I asked him how he knew this — had he visited the West?

"We learn this in college," he replied. "Our educational system is extremely advanced. West is in the klein."

"The what?"

"No 'what.' Klein . . . your greatest philosopher, Oz-Whirled Spangler, he has said so in his great book, *The Klein of the West*. Am I not right?"

"Oh . . . do people still read Spengler?"

"You have not read Spangler's *The Klein*?"

"It wasn't on any reading list I saw . . ."

He nodded sagely, then, evidently pleased by this encounter, reminded me that Iraq's educational system was extremely advanced, with books in the library.

"Books!"

"Yes. Books! And of course many gasjets."

"Gasjets?"

The room was astoundingly opulent.

"See," said the bellboy, pressing a button on the bedside table.

The curtains opened. Other buttons, other "gasjets," opened or fired up other aspects of the room.

"Which one unpacks my cases?"

"Alas, you will have to perform that task yourself. But this one is for to open your whore drobe."

"How convenient!" It sounded like prostitution's answer to the mini-bar.

I handed him ten dinars — about two dollars back then — but he recoiled from the notes as if they were aflame.

"It is not necessary," he explained. "Here we have exceptional salaries, and all things we need are provided. This is a *rich* country."

This is a rich bathroom, I told myself, wallowing in soap and steam and marble, until a knocking on the door forced me to don a bathrobe made of terry cloth like astrakhan and see who was there.

Ahmed.

Making the universal sign of silence with forefinger to lips, he pushed me back into the room, then proceeded to point out various spots on the wall and, forcing me down on all fours, beneath furniture.

Back out in the corridor he managed to convey that the room was heavily bugged — so I should —

"What? Not lounge around nude?"

"Not the joking-make Saddam-of," he advised. "Beeg mistook."

Back in the room alone, I stared at a black spot near the top edge of a painting depicting wild horses on the run.

"Club sandwich and mineral water, please," I told it.

THE TIME PARTY

Our first official function was a cocktail party without cocktails:

His Excellency the Hon. Minister for
Culture Invites

To a Cocktail Party for Celebrating of
Revolutionary Art Forms by
The Great Iraqi Artisans & Poets
In Lobby of Saddam Art Center

PLEASE TO NOTE THAT NO ALCOHOLICS
BEVVERAGES WILL BE SERVED AND
HORSE DOEVERS AT SIX P.M.

The space for my name had been left blank, although an envelope containing the invitation bore it. I suddenly pictured waiters refusing to serve cherry brandy: "It is an alcoholic's beverage, sir."

"What is being-this-one?" inquired Ahmed, pointing to "Horse Doevers."

"Flanks of Arab stallion?"

He cast me a worried glance. "Is simple-peoples, the Iraq-people. Too-much the-simple . . ."

Egyptians appear to have been taught that most other Arabs are primitive folk, untutored in the ways of civilization and much given to alien manners, strange foods, loose women. One must be careful with them. As he later told me — after I'd confessed to joking — Ahmed imagined he'd find a couple of old carthorses turning on a spit over beds of glowing charcoal in the Saddam Art Center's lobby.

But there had been a change of plans. The party was relocated to the Saddam War Memorial, according to Omar, who described himself as our liaison — he pronounced it "lesion" — and seemed to recognize Ahmed and me the moment we appeared in the lobby, although it was the first time I'd certainly ever seen him.

He was one of those drivers who feel it necessary to make frequent eye contact with passengers, as if making sure they haven't leapt out or died of boredom. He had a similar approach to Baghdad's rush-hour traffic, too, only applying his brakes when the vehicle ahead had proved beyond all reasonable doubt that it wasn't a hallucination. The case for traffic lights, however — *fact or fiction?* — had been settled long ago, it appeared, and he was not a believer. As other cars groaned and squeaked to a stop, he would react with an atheist's scorn, honking at them furiously as he lurched and wove by, plunging into the turbulent river of intersecting rubber and metal that now flowed crosstown on either side of us. Occasionally, when faced with this sudden pincer attack, he'd emit a howl of outraged disbelief, like someone turning into a herd of migrating iguanas: what the hell were they doing here?

"Iraq is beautiful country, yes?" he stated, launching into a hymn of praise for Saddam's glorious achievements that sounded more like a sales pitch to countries shopping for a reliable dictator.

"We have democracy here," Omar assured me. "Although people saying we are not."

"Why are they saying that?"

"O, my-Godness! Looking-you her!" Ahmed, sitting up front, was like a man trying to watch several games of tennis simultaneously, as he scanned the side and crosswalks for babes. "O-O-O, Ohhhh-my . . . G —"

"Don't get whiplash."

"What is this wee plash?" asked Omar. "It is democracy?"

An ad I'd once seen in England for MISTRESS WHIPLASH suddenly flickered into my mind. It read: "Only Sincere Students of Pain Need Apply." The Mistress now had Saddam's head, though, and I briefly wondered if it was possible that Iraqis were sincere students of pain, dedicated masochists to whom cruel servitude was the only true democracy.

"The reason they say that, Omar, is because your president wasn't elected and you have no official opposition parties. It may seem a quibble, I know, but we Westerners are a spoiled lot."

"Saddam he is *elected*!" His voice soared into a warbling treble. "What is this bull's sheet, *not elected*?"

"Who elected him?"

"Revolutionary Council is *electing* him."

"How is the Revolutionary Council elected?"

"Saddam he is *personally* choosing them," replied Omar, with pride.

"Oh, well, sorry then: that sounds pretty democratic to me."

He grunted satisfaction. "Yes. People they not understanding Iraqi way. They are too much jealous that we have now the most advanced nation on earth."

"I thought Turkey was the most advanced nation on earth."

"Turkey *bull*-sheet!" he spat (cheap sarcasm was wasted on him). "Turkey people big liars-all. Always they try for make wars. Big bull-sheet Turkey."

"What about Iran? They have a revolutionary government, too."

He literally spat through the window right into an adjacent car. "Iran! Phaaaat! Iran big goddam bull-*sheeeet*! Irani people they like sheeps, like dogs! They speet in the face of Iraqi people."

"So do you."

"*What* you say?"

"That was a bad war. How many Iraqi soldiers died?"

Omar kept turning round to face me as if his neck mechanism had blown a fuse. "What Iraq soldier *dying*? Hmmm? *Who* tell you this?" He was really angry now.

"Everyone knows that both sides suffered terrible losses. Khomeini was sending children to the front line by the end."

"No Iraqi children *fighting*. Where you hearing *this*? You Western press reporting *bull-sheet*! America *bull-sheet*! Israeli people *bull-sheet* people! Iraqi army is just protect our country and defend for our friend country, Kuwait. America *no help* America-friend. America too much fear bull-sheet ayatollah . . . America no help good-friend Shah of Irani. Only *Saddam* he not fear Irani. Iraqi people army fighting for *defend* America, *defend* Kuwait. Iraqi people good friend to America. But you people too much *jealous* for we *advanced* nation. America —" He was spluttering with fury now.

"America's bullshit?" I offered, wondering if I ought to ask him which countries weren't bullshit.

Omar swung the car through four lanes and jammed on his brakes at the sidewalk. I thought he was about to jump out and beat me up. Instead, however, he poked the radio on. A big marching band was playing at slightly the wrong speed. Ahmed turned, gritting his teeth at me and rolling his eyes theatrically.

The music stopped abruptly and a *basso profundo* voice rumbled into a sort of inconclusive melody without accompaniment for about fifty seconds, then paused. Omar killed the radio and took off like a skeet, hurtling diagonally across the boulevard and up a ramp onto a completely empty highway. I was confused.

"Who was that on the radio?"

"It nothing," Omar muttered.

"Oh. Okay. How come this road is empty and all the others look like a gold rush?"

"No goll drush! This special road for you!"

"For me?" The highway to Hell, maybe?

"Look!" Omar commanded, pointing through his window.

In the distant shimmering haze of Baghdad's dusty humidity appeared what looked like a hundred-foot-high egg made of turquoise cloisonné.

"Jesus! What is that? The Easter Bunny's personal stash?"

"Saddam War Memorial," sighed Omar, as if some epic quest had finally ended at its goal. "The price: four billion dollars!"

"That's a little out of my range, Omar. Besides, I'd never get it home. But thanks anyway."

"No-no-no . . . not gift for you. Tctch!" The sound was supposed to convey an advanced and civilized man's exasperation at being forced to deal with idiots. "Saddam he give to country this memory for the brave Iraqi soldier who die for defending of nation."

"So at least *one* did die then?"

"Yes. Tctch! This for unknowing soldier grave."

The tomb of the Unknowing Soldier: he never knew what hit him . . .

"We this Unknowing-tomb-soldier in Cairo," Ahmed announced unexpectedly.

"Bull-*sheet!*" yodeled Omar. "In Cairo you having big slum beggar and everywhere dirt. Ejeept *bull-sheet!* You not having Saddam Unknowing Soldier memory. You talking *bull-sheet!*"

"Mubarak-president he is-making-is for wars memorying. He —"

Omar spat again. "Mubarak *bull-sheet!* Sadat president *bull-sheet!* They are give *nothing* to you people. Ejeept people they all too much *poor* people. They all no-jobs, no-houses, no businessing. And —" He reached into the glove compartment and hefted out a plastic bag of dates. "Ejeept date for *dog foodings*. Iraqi date . . ." He plucked one out and popped it into his mouth. "Iraqi dates is bestest date on these world." He sighed sensually.

"You true-you," agreed Ahmed. "I am *too much* liking-for the date-Iraq. You right-is, friend. Iraq date too-good."

Omar then graciously handed round the bag of Iraqi dates — which, in fact, are up there with the best dates money can buy. Ahmed and I soon also sighed with sensual satisfaction.

"You, I the good-friend now. Yes? No fight, yes? Just good date and good friend . . . like one families, I think. Is it so?"

The three pals, arm in arm, walked across acres of shimmering white marble toward the world's biggest Easter egg. It was actually two halves of an egg, offset vertically so that from certain angles it appeared to be one whole egg. Cunning. One day there'll be a large island where all the architects in the world who've been afflicting us with giant war memorial eggs can be exiled for life to fight it out with each other and leave the designing of human spaces to humans able to define the terms "harmony" and "proportion" in ten words or less.

"This Italy mar-*bool*." Omar did a sort of curtsy at the ground.

I wondered if Italy had any marble left after filling this mammoth order. Only the Taj Mahal provided any sort of competition to the Saddam War Memorial's *Guinness Book of Records* entry: most marble used in a single building project solely for the purpose of impressing visitors. Both structures were built by leaders as tombs for the love of their lives, too.

Like all military dictators, Saddam was forced to make frequent and generous protestations of undying love to the army that kept him in power. Four billion dollars was certainly generous, but I wondered whether the army wouldn't have preferred a cash bonus to the egg. Even if a million strong — as they were rumored to be — Iraq's soldiers would have still received around a year's extra salary each.

The Saddam Big Egg stood at the edge of Saddam City, a slum area bulldozed to create low-cost housing for the poor and a boom market for concrete. Like many such projects, it was predestined to become a slum area once more, as the concrete disintegrated and a new regime felt no compunction to renovate a showcase of the old one.

Omar evidently lived in Saddam City, which, to hear him tell it, though, was the Beverly Hills of Baghdad. His house boasted a kitchen, a bathroom, a bedroom, and even a "room of eatings." I wondered what features his previous home had offered.

"I living with house of wife her mother," he told us. "With wife and childrens five."

"The mother-in-law, yeah. That can be a nightmare all right."

"And wife her brother who have one good wife with ten childrens . . ."

"Jeez!"

"Then he also second wife with her three childrens."

I wrestled with the arithmetic. That Old Lady had more room in her shoe.

"Twenty-four people! It probably wasn't a very big house, either. Was it?"

He looked puzzled.

"No this twenny-four . . ."

It was actually thirty-two when you added various aunts, uncles, and sisters. And by the sound of it, the place wasn't a very big hut. Or sock.

If Saddam had rescued me from that, I thought, I'd believe the sun shone out of his holster, too — as Omar clearly did. He wasn't kidding about the new housing being low cost, either: his place set him back around five bucks a year. Initially, I'd asked what percentage of his income went on rent and had taken the lengthy interval of contorted brows and frenzied finger-counting that preceded his answer as a sign that what Saddam gave with one hand he took back with the other — the one that wore the velvet glove and held the big stick, presumably. But it turned out that Omar had trouble with fractions and percentages. So do I, which is why we simply multiplied the rent by a hundred and, finding it far less than a hundredth of his income, left it at that. The rent was so little that I'm not even sure whether the government bothered to collect it.

Like Big Egg, Saddam City was a product of the Oil Boom Years — the days when Saudi sheikhs were Allah's gift to casino owners and Cartier's, when Colonel Gaddafi had his Bedouin robes made by Yves St. Laurent and planned to irrigate the Sahara Desert, and when Saddam Hussein injected new life into Soviet armaments industries while, at home, becoming Daddy Warbucks to Little Orphan Araby. Those days were gone now, though, and the Leader had something else up his sleeve. But what was it? An even bigger stick, perhaps?

"Maybe he taking Kuwait and Saudi for Iraq," suggested Omar, laughing raucously.

"America wouldn't like that."

"America *bull-sheet!*"

"Oh yeah, I forgot that. Calm down, Ome. We're one big happy family, remember?"

"You good friend," Omar confessed. "All good friend here. I am *too much* liking for you."

The dates came out again, peace returned to the Middle East, and we walked into the cool shadows of Big Egg, whose shadows were all the more cool due to a fountain that blew jets of sparkling water fifty feet up between its concave halves. It was like entering the Blue Giant's bladder.

Without warning, a military band concealed behind the Egg's curving walls of turquoise tile launched into what could have been Sousa's version of "For He's a Jolly Good Fellow."

The crowd of delegates ahead of us vanished from sight near the fountain. One minute they were there, the next they weren't — and there was no hiding place out on the burning plain of finest Italian marble surrounding us. Behind, V-formations, blocks, lines, and other varieties of delegate groupings were closing in. It looked like the pursuit of a couturier's army, The Royal Hi-Fashion Corps & Combined Special Hair Services. I suddenly felt heinously under-dressed. Everyone except Omar, Ahmed, and me was wearing either the kind of tuxedo that appears to be made from burnished gun metal, or Lawrence of Arabia's dress uniform.

Way behind this advance guard came what must have been its secret weapon: forms like ghosts hewn from darkness itself zigzagged in tight little batches as if they were one entity that owned several different bodies all joined at the hip. As the heat-haze with its wobbling distortions of form retreated behind this new menace, it was obvious that they were wives sentenced to life in veil with no chance whatsoever of parole.

"The invite said nothing about 'Black Tie,'" I protested. "I thought it was an art show? At an art gallery . . . ?"

"Blagg Thai?"

But no one except me minded, though. So I didn't mind either.

Next to the fountain's wall were curving stairs leading down to some kind of lower level. The place was actually a windowless version of one of those Man-hattan apartments you see in *Architectural Digest*: all art and space, no furniture. There was a receiving line of generals and generals' wives standing where the fountain's real source lay. Whatever powered those mighty jets trembled beneath the marble; ozone filled the air, as did an aura of chilled respite from the sweating mortals' world above.

"Where you are from?" inquired a clerkly colonel.

"Toronto."

"Morocco?"

"No, Toronto."

But I was from Morocco as far as he was concerned, and this was announced as I began shaking the line of hands. All of the generals had British public school accents.

"His Majesty, King Hassan, is here?" asked one.

"Probably."

"Jolly good."

White-coated waiters ferried trays of mini kebabs, hummus, and pita bread back and forth. Ahmed was accosted by one of his delegation, and Omar escorted me to a table serving nationalized Coca-Cola.

"This for Muslim-drink," he said.

"Yes, I'd gathered that."

"You like the whiskey, I think?"

"True."

He unleashed a volley of Arabic at one of the servers, who reached behind him and produced a bottle of Chivas Regal, filled two tumblers with it, and handed us one each.

"Whiskey good," said Omar.

"Cheers."

"This Iraqi art." He gestured toward a wing of the subterranean apartment that opened out ahead. It looked more like a warehouse than an art gallery, with canvases propped against walls and plaster sculptures piled between them.

Soon an Iraqi artist named Thomas was explaining why Iraqi art seemed only to have one subject: Saddam Hussein.

"It is like your Symbolist Movement."

"It is?"

"Yes. Saddam symbolizes the spirit of the new Iraq."

"I see. But if you didn't know who he was you wouldn't get that, would you?"

"Everyone in Iraq knows who Saddam Hussein is," replied Thomas, somewhat astonished by my stupidity.

There were busts, portraits, and various scenes in which Saddam featured as leader of men or godlike being observing the actions of mortals. Thomas's own work was embarrassingly awful: huge canvases teeming with clunky figures, lacking all sense of proportion and even any knowledge of perspective. I asked if this primitivism represented a school of Iraqi art, but he didn't know what I was talking about.

"Well, see that figure behind the group there? He should be smaller, because he's farther away, right? Yet he's *bigger* . . ."

"He is in front, not behind."

"Why's that arm over his leg, then?"

There was no denying this, and Thomas peered at his own painting in wonder, striving to come up with an answer. I asked if there were artists who disapproved of Saddam and painted their disapproval.

"*Everyone* they approve of Saddam."

"There must be *some* who don't."

"No."

"Must be *one*."

"No."

I told him it was unusual to see artists supporting the status quo, whatever it was, but just got a lecture on Western decadence. Art that didn't serve the state was useless and decadent. Totalitarian regimes produce art, it seems, but not artists. Saddam was evidently a big sup-porter of the arts: he owned a number of Thomas's paintings.

I managed to slip away and mingle. The place was packed by now, and more guests were still arriving, most of them dressed for an Arabian Nights gala theme ball.

The air-conditioning, which had earlier maintained the tempera-ture at that of a meat safe, had now either been turned down by request or it had packed up altogether, because the place was stifling in spite of its lobby fountain. Unlike most of Iraq, Baghdad has humid-ity, due to the Tigris River and surrounding swamplands. It also has mosquitoes, a sizable contingent of which had by now crashed the party. Few of the human guests seemed familiar with either humidity or mosquitoes.

"I hope we resolve this problem between Iraq and Kuwait — that's all," said a man who turned out to be Tunisia's minister of finance, when I asked him what he hoped the Summit would achieve.

I'd vaguely heard about a dispute over border territory between the two states, but nothing to indicate it was a major problem.

"The Kuwaitis are very arrogant," stated the Minister. "The area in question is clearly part of Iraq. But that's beside the point. They are drilling diagonally into Iraqi oil even across the current border. That is unconscionable. My God! It's wet down here."

He mopped his dripping brow and tugged at a starched shirt collar damp with sweat. I swatted a fat mosquito on my wrist, leaving it squashed in a pool of blood.

"Tccch! What's happened to the air? Excuse me a moment." He squeezed off through crowds of similarly perspiring, swatting people.

A blonde woman, who looked as if her long career in the entertainment business was finally winding down, asked me to "loan" her a cigarette. The black sequins swathing her formidable prow scratched my wrist as I attempted to offer her a light.

"Ridiculous!" she snorted, serpents of smoke diving to freedom from her nostrils. "Look how many people they have crammed down here!"

I learned she was the wife of the Syrian ambassador's doctor.

"He's actually President Assad's doctor," she added conspiratorially. "But don't tell anyone. Leaders aren't supposed to need doctors."

"I understand."

Perhaps her husband specialized in the treatment of dictators, since before his current practice he'd been Gaddafi's personal physician. What was that like?

"Charming man, of course. But quite mad. Don't tell anyone!"

"I won't." I wanted to add: because they already know . . .

"He's an addict," she elaborated.

"Addict?"

"Pills. To wake him up, to calm him down, to put him to sleep. In between, he's perfectly charming, though. Perfectly."

I wondered when "in between" might be.

"Around lunch," she replied. "My husband told him he should quit.

That's why we're in Syria now."

They were from Lebanon, but "you can't live there anymore. He's writing a history of the world, you know?"

"Your husband?"

"No, no. He doesn't even like writing prescriptions. Gaddafi. Yes. He used to read us sections from it. Interesting. A little biased, though — in my opinion."

"Biased. Really?"

"But interesting. Did you know that Shakespeare was an Arab?"

"No, I didn't. The playwright Shakespeare?"

"Of course, it's obvious when you think about it . . ."

"It is?"

"His *name*, darling! Shiekh Spiero: it's an Arab name."

"That's what Gaddafi says?"

"Of course! They're all Arab stories, too: Romeo and Juliet, Hamlet, Aladdin . . ."

"*Aladdin*?"

"And Sinbad the Sailor, and . . ."

"What about Richard III?"

"I don't think that's Shakespeare, darling. You're confused."

"Maybe. Must be the heat?"

By now the pressure of bodies on all sides was getting a little much for me. I regretted knocking back the scotch so quickly: it felt like a lake of sulfur in my guts. So I excused myself, saying I needed some air. She said she'd join me, trying to dab the perspiration reaching her eyes without smudging the teaspoon of mascara around them or the lash-enhancer that made it look as if she had sooty quills sprouting from her eyelids. But we quickly found we couldn't move an inch in any direction. Whichever way I pushed, seeking an exit, a far more powerful force pushed back angrily. I could feel the man beside me's stomach rumbling through my elbow. There was more room in a Tokyo subway train during rush hour. And far more air.

The doctor's wife was beginning to look the way I felt: her face had turned the color of a turkey's jowls, and she was inhaling deeply.

"Oh, darl —" she began to say.

Then her eyes rolled back and her head lolled forward, mouth open. A wobbling pendant of drool swung from her crimson lower lip for some seconds, before plopping onto my chest.

"She's fainted!" I told Prince Faisal, or whichever potentate stood behind me.

"*La. Shukran,*" he said. "No thanks."

There was no danger of her falling, although I could feel the odd sequin snap against me as gravity strove to claim her. I tapped the shoulder of another man, raising my voice.

"Shusssh!" he hissed back.

Suddenly a military band nearby began to blast out the National Anthem, and a blaze of television camera lights revealed a cohort of soldiers escorting someone across the distant lobby area. A pressure wave sent all of us gliding back several inches together in one mass. There were groans and squeaks from near and far. Without warning, I burped up a lumpy mouthful of what tasted like scotch and ear wax, which I was obliged to swallow again.

As the band came to a clumsy end, with wails and thumps trailing off tunelessly, a tapping of microphones and some ear-torturing feedback preceded a voice introducing General Somebody, who was evidently Iraq's Minister of Culture.

"Majesties, Royal Highnesses, and honorable delegates," boomed the Minister, "on behalf of President Saddam Hussein, I welcome you to the —"

At this point, the microphone cut out, milliseconds before the lights died. Being underground, the place was not just dark, it was utterly, totally pitch black. A hushed silence was followed by cries of reassurance and groans of despair. It crossed my mind that Saddam was about to exterminate most of the Arab world's leadership with one devilish blow. That was why the venue had been changed. Surely he didn't imagine this could be the route to reviving the dream of a United States of Arabia led by himself?

"Power is out!" someone usefully informed us.

Then an emergency lighting system cast a jaundiced glow over mayhem before fading back into blackness as its batteries were drained.

In the West panic would probably have effervesced into a lethal stampede by now. But most of those present were all too familiar with power cuts. For all I knew, they'd experienced many a moment like this before and weren't unduly bothered by what was many people's worst nightmare come true. I tried consoling the doctor's wife, my breath a blistering combo of skunk squirt, distillery, and cat pee. But all I could hear from her was the odd "Uhhh-Oh," which trailed off into a bubbling fusion of snore and purr.

A vague yet distinct movement forward indicated exodus had begun.

After half an hour of sweltering and Stygian heaving and groaning, to the constant refrain of "No pushing!" and "Calm, everyone," I reached the end of the lobby by the fountain (no longer gushing) that led toward the stairs back up to Life. Here there was not only light but also, very suddenly, too, space. I felt the doctor's wife and everyone else fall away — it was like being a moth suddenly freed from the cocoon — and only stabbing cries of alarm from behind galvanized me into an action swift enough to prevent the poor woman's head meeting Italy's finest marble. I had to carry her up the fifty-odd steps, and she wasn't exactly light. Wondering what to do with her as I staggered out into the blinding sunshine, I saw an angry-looking drunk tottering toward me, shirt torn open with one tail out, bow tie wrapped around his ear, looking as if he'd lived in his tuxedo for several months. One shoe was missing, which may have accounted for the tottering, though, since he didn't seem very drunk when he said: "That's *my wife.*"

"Good," I gasped, offering him three hundred pounds of sequin-wrapped flesh. "You take her."

"*What* have you . . . I . . . er . . ." He seemed lost for words.

"She fainted," I explained, wondering what he imagined had occurred.

"Oh, gosh! Yes, I suppose," he sputtered, hefting the burden himself, which had him tottering backward, until he gradually sank to the ground, wife on lap. "Yes. Thank you, sir!"

I thought he was handing me a tip, but it turned out to be his business card: George L. Fetoun, M.A. (Oxon.) M.D. (Harvard).

"I hope she's okay."

Dr. Fetoun produced a bottle of smelling salts — something I hadn't encountered outside a movie — and uncorked it under his wife's nose. The whiff of ammonia even from six feet away hit my sinuses like a cheese grater, so no wonder it had the wife immediately plugged back into life and flailing her arms in self-defense. One more bolt of ammonia hit me and, almost casually, I strolled over to the base of Big Egg and threw up half a pint of kebabs in a whiskey-bile sauce over its turquoise ceramic tiles.

The interior of my mouth now felt, smelt, and tasted as if I'd been gargling with a blend of paint stripper and vinegar. I couldn't decide which was worse, the stench or the burning. Where was some water? Looking around for the first time, I realized that the relative calm to which we probably owed our lives was a consequence of great self-control, not patient indifference. Men as well as women now lay splayed on the marble or cradled in someone's arms, being fanned with programs or handkerchiefs, and, judging by the faint aroma, resurrected via the aversion therapy of smelling salts. These were still a major commodity in the Arab world, clearly — perhaps fainting was still in vogue? — for dozens of people carried them, and evidently at all times.

Everyone's elegant clothes were so drenched in perspiration, wrenched apart, or torn from an hour in the scrum that we looked like survivors of a first-class cruise shipwreck mysteriously beamed down in the Land of Big Egg.

Dozens of soldiers suddenly appeared with jugs of water and plastic tumblers, which had those not served immediately clapping and yelping for attention.

"Ah, you! Paul-mister! You are okay?"

It was Omar, recently emerged from a shark-wrestling contest, by the look of him.

I gestured around, saying, "When you guys throw a party, man! — you throw a party."

"Power was cutting," he explained, edgily — as if it might be his fault.

"Oh. I thought I'd just blacked out after the tenth pint of Chivas."

"Pliss — no mention the Chivash."

"Whatever you say."

"You waiting-the here, yes?"

He bolted off, obviously with recently assigned tasks to perform.

I noticed Ahmed — actually I heard him first — helping a young woman across the marble. Her steps seemed unsteady and one arm was draped over his shoulder for support. Yet they were both laughing like seals.

"This good-frenn my, from the Can-adder," he announced. "Mista-Ball Obbers."

The woman was wearing an unusual dress made from black string with something like oil cloth beneath it. On her head was a tangled pile of satin rags in various hues, apparently pinned together by several real throwing darts — good ones, too, with feathered flights and steel-alloy shafts.

"Mister Bawl," she repeated, carefully assembling the syllables. "Obb-bersssssshhh!" The rest came through her nostrils in a series of equine bursts.

They were both drunk. Very drunk.

Ahmed tried to explain that Maria — for it was she — was an artist, an Iraqi artist.

"She's got everything she needs and she don't look back, right?"

"Schneeds? Lugbak?"

"Bog Zillan song he iss say!" Maria trilled, suddenly more alert.

I've never been anywhere they haven't heard of Bog Zillan.

"Yes, Ahmed: the answer's blowing in the wind and the times they are a-changing — but let's hope not too quickly to salvage your career, eh?"

"He Can-adder man-iss," Ahmed told Maria.

"That's right. And Canada Man suggests Maria could probably take you off in a taxi and show you Baghdad's best discos — so we'll know where they are. Right, Maria?" I tried to imbue this with meaning by covertly frowning at Ahmed and then exaggeratedly looking from left to right at officialdom.

She smirked back and surprised me to the core by saying, "A nod iss good ass wink to blind horse, yes?"

"Oh, indeed it is. You look after him and you've sold two paintings. Deal?"

"I only sculptur-ress."

"Fine. Two of those."

It was then that I recalled where I'd seen her: standing by three dripping five-foot plaster heads of Saddam that gave the President an appearance of having been deep-frozen. Small icicles hung from his nostrils, ears, even his eyelids. They'd certainly make fun gifts.

"Disco-dance, we-you, yes?" Ahmed asked, merrily, his feet a-tapping.

"Definitely. Now off you go, young people." I slipped Maria some money. "Go! Do your own thing in your own time, you hear?"

"Jerome Ting?"

Maria maneuvered him off as if she'd done this sort of thing before. I watched their erratic progress, until a cab finally whisked them away. No one seemed remotely interested, either — probably because most of them didn't look in any better shape than Ahmed.

Iraqi officials were beginning to regroup, I noticed, and spin doctors were obviously at work on the damage control for this PR Apocalypse. The band began to play once more, though far enough away to seem more like military muzack.

Then a brutally amplified voice announced: "We are please to inform that power is now back and delegates can please proceed back for Minister of Culture speech and accompanying cocktails party."

There was not exactly a rush to return downstairs to the Black Hole of Baghdad. In fact, no one budged, a few even backing away in alarm, many shaking their heads. Aides and assistants shot back and forth, ferrying their masters' voices on the matter. Before long, there was widespread panic among the Iraqi officials — and no generals were anywhere to be seen.

"Because of the unforeseen delays," another, suaver voice eventually boomed out, "we will be rescheduling this important event for·a later date. I am sorry to disappoint, but I know many of you have important meetings this evening and we would not wish for your tardiness. Our profound apology."

Delegates (presumably not wishing for their own tardiness) had already begun walking off long before this, and any important ones — the princes, the presidents — had vanished with the lighting. Security has its own agenda, after all, and in retrospect no one of any consequence had strayed far from the exit at any time during the party. Baghdad's power supply obviously did not inspire enormous confidence in Arab leaders. Or perhaps it was Saddam's power supply they mistrusted.

"Electricals *bull-sheet*!" announced Omar, heading into ten lanes of traffic while looking the other way — at me. "Power Baghdad *bull-sheet*!"

"Don't take it so hard. It's not your fault. Is it?"

"*My fawlz!* Why you saying is *my* fawlz?"

A thousand horns blared, brakes screeched, voices cursed at us. Omar either heard nothing or, long since used to it, ignored this critique of his motoring skills and ploughed on, threading his way through traffic and then, most terrifying of all, into five lanes of oncoming vehicles for two hundred yards, when he hung a hairpin left to join a ramp full of cars going his way — though not fast enough.

There were no seat belts, of course, so I'd clung to the visor and Omar's headrest for most of this suicide run, closing my eyes as a last feeble resort during the oncoming traffic bit. Now I'd finally had enough.

"Omar, you are a fucking diabolical driver! Did you know that?"

"You beeg bull-*sheet*-you!" he screamed. "Canada *bull*-sheet! You not country-own, you America state. Canada *bull-sheet* country!"

"I think Iraq's a big fucking pile of stinking bullshit! So there!" I sounded quite demented, but I couldn't stop. "Saddam Hussein's bullshit! Moustaches are bullshit! And you know *what*? The *biggest* heap of bullshit on earth is *you*, Omar! You! *You!You!*" I smashed the last three words out on his dashboard.

He swerved and twanged to a total stop. Now I'm dead for sure, I told myself, panting from fury's exertion. But Omar just slumped across the steering wheel, his body heaving and throbbing — presumably with mad rage. As he turned his head to peer sideways at me, however, I realized he was laughing like a maniac. Tears were even flowing. He started to beat the wheel, attempting to subdue the mirth long enough to say something. I couldn't imagine what it was going to be, and I'd started apologizing long before he finally spat it out, reminding him of the dates, our deep friendship, the strain of being stuck underground . . .

"You right-you saying," he eventually managed, amid a spray of saliva punctuation marks. "Iraq *bull-sheet*! Saddam-he *bullsheet*! Me-Omar, *me beeg, beeg, beeg bullsheet*." He looked up, mangled and sweaty. "You-me the good frenn, yes?"

I suddenly saw us both sitting there as if from outside. We were crumpled, sodden, frayed at the edges, and quite mad. The vision made me start laughing too, as I struggled to say: "It's *all* bullshit, Omar! *Everything*! Iraq, America, Canada, *me*, you: *bullshit!*"

Soon we were embracing, hugging, patting each other's shoulder and, in between shuddering fits of crazed laughter, yelling out *Bullshit! Bullshit!*

I fell asleep watching the news, which included a good hour's irrelevant stock footage of Saddam doing popular things at other times. There was footage of the Big Egg Party, yet this did not include any mention of a power cut — although it did include a full account of the speech not delivered by the Minister of Culture.

When I awoke, the note had already been slipped beneath my door. It read simply: "President Saddam Hussein has agreed to your interview. Please inquire with Information Ministry for your details."

My *interview*? What interview was this? Did he want to interview me? On his news program, maybe? Then I remembered scribbling a wish list of activities while in Iraq for the Foreign Ministry back in Cairo. It seemed a lifetime ago. "Interview Saddam Hussein" had also been fairly far down that list, as I recalled it. "Visit Babylon" had been number one. I wondered what I could ask him.

SUMMIT UP

The actual conference started the next day. Summits are a waste of time, as far as people like me are concerned. You don't get to attend the meetings themselves — the temptation to join in discussions would presumably be too great. You just get to hang around outside and wait for the official press releases or, if you've been doing it for years, for inside info from a delegate you've been blackmailing or bribing — who usually lies about the important stuff, anyway. If you're with the BBC or CNN or *Time* magazine, you can generally find a source who'll trade you some juicy tidbit on the understanding that you'll also serve as a vehicle for his nation's propaganda sooner or later. Closed-circuit televisions usually show the uninteresting parts of a conference live. The affairs seem to be divided up into fake discussions of issues previously discussed and agreed upon, and real discussions, in which some delegates will have previously discussed and agreed upon the issues in private and others will realize this and be pissed off. Since the only issue Arabs have ever agreed on is the destruction of Israel — and Egypt spoiled that by signing the separate Peace Accord engineered by Jimmy Carter in the late seventies — agreement of any kind was now generally more concerned with siding with your oldest, most powerful friends than it was with looking at issues objectively.

Back in Cairo, I'd asked Boutros-Ghali why it was that — Saudis excepted — Arabs had never managed to create a Washington lobby as formidable as the Israeli one.

"They wouldn't be able to organize it," he replied. "And even if they did, no one would be able to agree on a single course of action, so it would end up lobbying against its own interests."

THE ROAD TO BAGHDAD

It's often said that Israel was a European colony created by the British on Palestinian soil during the height of Arab nationalism and anti-colonialism. This is quite true. What's rarely said, however, is that Britain also created many of the Arab states — literally — by drawing somewhat arbitrary borders across the sands of what had been communal or semi-communal tribal areas. A glance at any map will show you just how arbitrary these really are: which other nations have dead straight lines as borders? And while almost no monarchy on earth can trace its bloodline back too far before running into problems — not to mention some deeply embarrassing antecedents — most can go a few centuries without much trouble. Arab monarchs, however, don't like to peer much beyond the twentieth century — if that far — because they find themselves at best tribal patriarchs (that is, committed polygamists with dozens of sons and countless daughters to prove their influence will survive and their tribe will grow in strength for at least another couple of generations) possessed of much livestock and many tents. The ruling al-Sabahs of Kuwait, though, find themselves shore pirates in the eighteenth century who assisted the Brits in stomping coastal Bedouin tribes and were rewarded with their teeny emirate and titles. Who knew then that it floated on a lake of oil worth hundreds of billions?

Boom!

That was the First World War, during which Germany revived a traditional alliance with the ailing Ottoman Empire — one that the Germans must still regret. When millions lay dead and the big guns were finally as silent as the generation they had wiped out, the map business boomed. Nothing east of France looked the same anymore.

War booty, like many things as the Modern Age dawned, was not as straightforward a business as it had once been. In the Middle East, a system of mandates was set up by the League of Nations under Article 22 of its Covenant. This had no precedent and was also a form of compromise. While the victors wished to retain former German colonies and the territories of the Ottoman Empire — which, in most cases, they had made considerable sacrifices to conquer — they had also made frequent pledges that their inhabitants would not be handed back to their former masters. There were, in addition, solemn promises that the annexation of territory had not been their aim in waging war. It wasn't their *sole* aim, true.

The mandates were not colonies but a form of trust in which the mandatory power administered the territory under the supervision of the League of Nations through a Permanent Mandates Commission. The League's supreme council defined the terms of the mandates and the boundaries of the territories. Although the United States was not a member of the League, as one of the former Allies it insisted that U.S. consent to the mandates was necessary. Thus all mandate proposals were submitted to Washington, which approved them on condition that "free and equal treatment in law and in fact was secured to the commerce of all nations."

It will come as no surprise to learn that many British and French statesmen viewed the distinction between mandates and colonies as no more than a convenient fiction:

> It is quite a mistake to suppose . . . that under the Covenant of the League or any other instrument, the gift of the mandate rests with the League of Nations. It does not do so. It rests with the Powers who have conquered the territories, which it then falls to them to distribute, and it was in these circumstances that the mandate for Palestine and Mesopotamia was conferred upon and accepted by us, and that the mandate for Syria was conferred upon and accepted by France.[9]

Iraq acquired a king, Feisal I, who, although a Hashemite imported for the job, turned out to be fairly successful. As the traditional defenders of Islam, Hashemites had acquired a kind of aristocratic status among the tribes that made their leaders shoe-ins for any pan-Arabic front-man post. Initially it had been proposed that Iraq become a part of the British Empire, but when the greedy, reactionary elements proposing this had been voted into silence, the country became one of the more successful products of the mandates. The only initial trouble came from Turkey, which insisted the northern Kurdish area around Mosul was Turkish territory, demanding it back.

In 1932, the British Mandate formally ended, and Iraq became independent, joining the League of Nations under British sponsorship. Not everyone in the country bought this smoke-and-mirrors act, though, convinced that Iraq was still under British hegemony. As evidence, the dissenters pointed to the British-owned Iraq Petroleum Company, which monopolized Iraq's oil resources. In August 1933, though, in an ominous sign of darker things to come, an army unit slaughtered three hundred Assyrian villagers in northern Iraq. Most Iraqis applauded this unprovoked massacre, unfortunately, and the soldiers went unpunished. Understandably, much of the Assyrian community decided to leave immediately for Syria. In creating its idea of what a Middle Eastern state should be, Britain paid little attention to the details, which — although they weren't visible on a map in London — involved millions of people who suddenly found themselves stranded as minorities by the stroke of a cartographer's pen. The same thing happened in India.

King Feisal I died suddenly that same year, to be succeeded by his son Ghazi. Handsome and popular, Ghazi was also reputed to be an Arab nationalist, yet in spite of these qualities he lacked his father's authority. Although he was able to make a start on developing the country's vast potential resources (after the first major oil field began generating substantial revenues in 1934), Ghazi found that the absence of Feisal made development of a viable political system more difficult. Even with the assistance of some able and devoted ministers and officials who had survived from the Ottoman period — including the exceptionally talented Nuri al-Said — parliamentary democracy failed to take root. No authentic political parties emerged, and elections were generally controlled by conservative personal and class interests. One bungling, reactionary, and authoritarian cabinet was succeeded in office by another that proved even worse. Politicians more like feudal barons didn't hesitate to organize tribal uprisings against the government of their rivals in office — and such uprisings could never be fully controlled. It was thus hardly surprising to find this quaintly barbaric style of politics increasingly opposed by an alliance of reformist middle-class intellectuals and young nationalist army officers inspired by the example of Kemal Ataturk, whose leadership and modernizations single-handedly transformed Turkey into a viable twentieth-century republic.

This alliance seized power in 1936 under the leadership of General Bakr Sidqi, although the movement ended ten months later, as it had begun — with assassination and a military coup. Its failure was largely because the reformist elements were soon set aside; the army was divided and most of the population was alienated from the new rulers. Yet, failure or not, the incident had momentous significance: it established a precedent for military coups in the Arab world. The Iraqi army had also gained a new self-assurance, and with it a taste for interference in political life.

This potentially lethal power was used quite wisely at first, to back a nominally civilian government led by Nuri al-Said, which ruled for the next twenty years, a period that saw Iraq steadily develop into the semblance of a modern state.

In 1945, after the culmination of what has properly been called Europe's thirty-year civil war, the global situation again drastically altered. The Middle East had been deeply involved in the Second World War — while Turkey had wisely remained neutral — and it was even more profoundly affected by the aftermath. The British retreated from their physical empire into an invisible one of global finance, leaving carefully orchestrated chaos behind them. A Muslim state of Pakistan in two halves a thousand miles apart was hardly equipped to survive, guaranteeing a series of insoluble problems for India. And a Jewish state in Palestine, backed by American muscle and money, similarly ensured trouble for the entire Middle East.

Neo-imperialism preferred chaos to order in the regions it regarded as vital to its interests: chaos is easier to control. Had the Americans not made such a clownish misjudgment in Iran, the area would still probably be much as it was intended to be. Had oil not been found anywhere between the Mediterranean and the Arabian Sea, of course, none of this would have happened. Similarly, when the subterranean lakes of fossil fuel are finally pumped dry, early in the third millennium, all of this will change beyond recognition once more.

Gamal Abdel Nasser's coup in 1952, and his subsequent quest for a United Arabia, set off a chain of events that in Egypt led to the Suez crisis and the "Tripartite Aggression" of 1956, a point which seems to mark the start of a new chapter in Arab history. Yet 1958 stands out as a key year for the Middle East generally, one that reveals the complex machinations, the checks and balances, the counter-checks and bluffs, of Anglo-American foreign policy in the region. In March of that year, King Saud was forced to hand over the reins of power to his brother Feisal after the Syrians revealed details of a plot by the Saudi monarch or one of his advisers to assassinate Nasser, thereby preventing the proposed union of Syria and Egypt. Feisal was widely viewed as less pro-Western and more pro-Egyptian than his brother. Then in May the deadly polarization of Lebanon between Lebanese and Arab nationalists — which the Suez crisis had intensified — escalated into a muted civil war. This simmered on throughout the summer, with Syria, now part of the United Arab Republic, aiding and encouraging the Arab nationalist rebellion in Lebanon against President Chamoun and his pro-Western government.

In Iraq, Nuri al-Said elected to help Chamoun, a decision that led to his downfall in July 1958. Masterly in politics, he was dangerously out of touch with popular opinion — especially among army officers. An Iraqi version of Egypt's Free Officers organization had been formed under Brigadier Abdel-Karim Qassem, choosing its moment to strike when the government had ordered troops stationed near Baghdad to move to Jordan — most probably with the aim of exerting pressure on Syria to terminate the union with Egypt. Qassem's forces faced minimal opposition, but, in contrast to Nasser's bloodless coup, Ghazi's son — now King Feisal II — his uncle the crown prince, and all but one member of the Hashemite royal family, along with Premier Nuri al-Said himself, were murdered. A new government soon declared itself, with Qassem as prime minister and minister of defense, and his army officers in the other key positions. The brand-new republic of Iraq swiftly announced its close alignment with Egypt. It seemed then as if Nasser and Nasserism had triumphed after all. With the fall of Iraq, the only effective remaining instrument of pro-Western policies had finally gone, or so it then seemed.

The United States reacted by landing ten thousand marines in Beirut at President Chamoun's request, while British troops were immediately flown into Jordan. Yet U.S. presence in Lebanon achieved curiously little. The Lebanese were encouraged to settle the crisis themselves, which resulted in General Fuad Chehab — the army commander who had maintained the neutrality of the armed forces in the political struggle — being constitutionally elected to succeed Chamoun. Lebanon then became more neutral and far less stridently pro-Western than under its previous leader, a situation that essentially gave the rebels most of what they wanted in the first place. The brief federation between the two Hashemite nations — Iraq and Jordan — had now also collapsed, and it seemed highly unlikely that a few British troops would be sufficient to keep young King Hussein on his throne much longer. But appearances were again deceptive.

In no time, the Syrians began to dislike the subordinate role they felt they'd been assigned to play with Egypt, and did not take to the state socialism imposed by Cairo on their traditionally dynamic and generally free economy. To compound matters, 1958 also saw the beginning of a disastrous three-year drought that hit Syrian agriculture — the country's economic mainstay — especially hard.

In Iraq, Qassem soon proved to be another sort of disaster for pan-Arabism. Before 1958 was over he had arrested and jailed his principal collaborator in the coup, Colonel 'Aref, who favored an immediate Iraqi-Egyptian union. Early the next year Qassem blamed an abortive Arab nationalist revolt in Mosul on Nasser, then he allowed the Iraqi Communists to strengthen their position at the expense of Arab nationalists — led by the Iraqi Ba'athists — and proceeded to maintain a precarious balancing act over the next four years by preventing either group from taking over the state. Nasser became convinced that Iraqi Communism posed a danger to the whole Arab world, which made Qassem, an unstable and inordinately vain man, develop a bitterly jealous and irrational hatred of the Egyptian leader.

Where Stalin had blown Soviet chances for extending the Communist sphere of influence into Iran and the Middle East by attempting to grab relatively unimportant central Asian Muslim states and meddle in Kurdish affairs, Nikita Khrushchev returned to Lenin's old policy of fostering strong nationalist leaders in the hope of getting Communism to infiltrate their countries more subtly. Nasser was naturally a prime target, but used his position ingeniously, manipulating Moscow to obtain cash, arms, and help with industrial development, while making sure its ideology flew back with every Aeroflot cargo plane. After abandoning Syria to its increasing divisions, which signaled the collapse of his United Arab Republic, however, Nasser became increasingly preoccupied with devising a form of Arab socialism and defining its ideology clearly in a lengthy charter.

This was met with a torrent of hostile Arab invective. The Saudis immediately denounced Egyptian socialism as atheistic; then the amazingly ancient and ailing Imam Ahmed of Yemen — who still inspired abject awe in his subjects — agreed with the Saudi assessment, causing the shadowy United Arab States of the United Arab Republic and Yemen to be dissolved. But the most violent abuse came from Syria, where a series of spectacularly unstable governments elected under the old constitution replaced each other in rapid succession. Various Syrian spokesmen accused Nasser and Egypt of inflicting a reign of terror on Syria, besides embezzling its state funds.

Yet Egypt's response when it came was louder and more effective than any of these criticisms — mainly because Cairo's propaganda machine was far more highly developed than that of any other Arab state. There could be no compromise between Arab socialism and "reaction": this was Nasser's theme. One of his favorite phrases stated that "unity of ranks is no substitute for unity of aims."

Despite the rhetoric, however, Egypt was still to some extent on the defensive. After a blazing row with the Syrians at an Arab League council meeting in Lebanon, Nasser abruptly announced that Egypt was withdrawing from the League itself. But in September 1962 an opportunity to regain the high ground seemingly presented itself. A group of pro-Egyptian officers in the Yemeni army revolted against Imam Badr, who had just succeeded his father as leader of the tiny country. The officers seized a few key towns and military installations, declaring a republic. But Badr had managed to escape, and the royalist cause was far from lost. His uncle, Amir Hassan, returned to Saudi Arabia from the United States and swiftly proceeded to rally Yemeni tribesmen against the new godless republic. Announcing assistance for the "revolutionaries," Nasser sent an Egyptian expeditionary force up the Red Sea to the Yemeni port of Hodeida. Thus ensued what is often referred to as "the Egyptian Vietnam" — guerrilla tribal warfare in the mountains for which the Egyptian army was heinously ill-prepared and totally untrained to fight.

The intervention met with slight opposition from Egyptians affected by it but was mostly a matter of indifference to the rest. Yet the fact of a Nasserist coup in Yemen raised Egypt's prestige in the rest of the Arab world when it most needed raising. By mounting the interventionary force to Yemen, Nasser also demonstrated to Israel that his was the only army in the Middle East about which it needed to lose sleep. And when key officer pilots from both Saudi Arabia and Jordan — whose air force commander was among them — defected to Cairo in October 1962, it demonstrated that the loyalty of the armed forces in the two Arab monarchies critical of Nasser was dubious at best.

Pan-Arabist emotion ran high once more, and was a potent factor behind a further coup in Iraq, on February 9, 1963. An army revolt, in which Ba'athist officers featured prominently, overthrew and killed General Qassem, installing Colonel 'Aref as president. He, of course, immediately declared his pro-Egyptian sympathies.

Between pressure from both Baghdad now and Cairo, Syria's flimsy government *du jour* could hardly be expected to hold out for very long. It managed precisely one month, then a military coup in Damascus wiped the slate clean of all the men who had been in power since the breakup of the Syrian-Egyptian union, and a new Revolutionary Command Council pledged itself to support "the new movement in Arab unity." Although this coup had not been led by the Ba'athists, as it had in Iraq, Ba'athists were, in fact, the only civilian organization — outside the old regime, of course — that was remotely capable of forming a government. Within a week, delegations from Iraq and Syria were in Cairo to discuss plans for the unity of the three countries who'd nearly been at war with each other a month and a half earlier.

Although this seemed like another glittering moment of triumph for Nasser, he suddenly decided that he couldn't get along with Iraqi Ba'athists — though God knows why — and that he had no confidence in Syrian Ba'athists. For their part, a handful of hopelessly idealistic members of the Ba'athist regimes in both Syria and Iraq had a genuine doctrinal disagreement with Egypt in their optimistic demands for democratic freedoms and collective leadership. However, most Ba'athists simply believed that Arab salvation could come through the Ba'ath Party alone, and to this end they were perfectly prepared to use methods that were every bit as ruthlessly totalitarian as anything in Egypt.

These tripartite unity talks were also not particularly helped by Nasser dominating them with his intimidating personality and his very long experience of total power. He even later made fun rather cruelly of Ba'athist founding ideologue Michel Aflaq's shyness, stutter, and inability to express himself clearly.

Although a vague form of agreement on a tripartite federation was actually reached on April 17, the union never materialized. Syrian Ba'athists spent May and June purging the army of non-Ba'athist officers and suppressing pro-Nasser demonstrations. After they were obliged to suppress an attempted pro-Nasser coup in July — and suppress it far from gently — Nasser blasted the Ba'ath openly for the first time, calling Syria's regime "secessionist, inhuman, and immoral." He then announced that Egyptian intelligence had uncovered an Iraqi-Syrian alliance against him.

This did little for Egypt's relations with Syria and Iraq, yet as these steadily deteriorated, Nasser derived some satisfaction from watching the Iraqi Ba'athists — who had already made themselves unpopular by their extreme violence and by renewing the fruitless, exhausting war with the Kurds that had debilitated Qassem's regime — divide into two factions, only to find themselves ousted by President 'Aref (whom they had tried to retain as a figurehead) and some senior non-Ba'athist officers. Nothing if not undyingly faithful to his slackwitted fantasies, 'Aref renewed the push for immediate union with Egypt yet again. By now, though, Nasser was caution personified. He suggested that the Iraqis first ensure their own national unity, which included solving that labyrinthine nightmare known as "the Kurdish problem" — then come back and see him.

By February 1966, with the civil war in Yemen still going nowhere slowly, the Syrian regime had begun to attempt patching up its differences with Egypt when it was overthrown by a radical wing of the Ba'ath. The new rulers loathed Nasser, but they truly despised the Arab kings, and they hated Israel with an all-consuming passion. While little King Hussein — still on that throne — was attempting to prevent Palestinian *fedayeen* from operating from his turf, Syria naturally gave them hearty encouragement and support. Accordingly, Israel's promises of very heavy retaliation were mainly directed at Syria. Nasser could hardly reject a Syrian plea for help under such circumstances; thus in November 1966 he signed a comprehensive Syrian-Egyptian defense pact. Not the most brilliant move of his career, since it left him with a commitment to Syria but not the power to control it.

A few days later, a mine exploded near Israel's Jordanian frontier, killing three Israeli soldiers. Although Syria was obviously the prime suspect behind any supplies for Palestinian sabotage attacks, Israel embarked on its traditional very heavy retaliation raid against a West Bank village. Yelling that their protection by the Jordanian army was pitifully inadequate, the West Bankers rose up in a revolt that was not that easy to quell. Nasser jumped at the opportunity to criticize Jordan's handling of the whole affair. But King Hussein had had about as much as he could take of Nasser by now, and he launched an uncharacteristically savage verbal attack on him that included the macho taunting accusation of hiding behind the protection of the UN Emergency Force (UNEF), which had by now made sure that all stayed quiet on the Egyptian-Israeli front since 1956. Casting aspersions on Arab manliness is like calling Israelis "Fascists."

By the following spring, as Israel's warnings to Syria grew increasingly dire, Nasser was being assured by his own intelligence, Damascus, and even the Soviets that an Israeli attack on Syria was imminent. Nasser requested the UN to withdraw its UNEF from Sinai (where, on Israel's insistence, it was only stationed on Egypt's side of the border). When this request was complied with, Nasser sent Egyptian troops into Sinai and announced the closure of the Straits of Tiran to Israeli shipping. The eyes of the Arab world were now upon him and his manliness. Even King Hussein, knowing no power on earth would let him hide from the inevitable war when it came, flew to Cairo on May 30 to sign a defense pact with Egypt. Presumably he also said sorry about his earlier outburst. Although this now gave Nasser defense agreements with both Syria and Jordan, the result amounted to little more than extra trouble, since there was no cooperation between the two countries and nothing remotely resembling an Arab joint command.

Arab states had whipped themselves into a frenzy of manly optimism, utterly convinced that Israel's final end was nigh. Even Nasser shed his habitual doubts about Arab military capabilities, developing inordinate faith in his own commander, the manly Field Marshall Amer. Most of all, though, he believed deep down that the United States would intervene to prevent Israel from attacking — thereby granting Egypt a manly tactical victory without the trouble of actually fighting. Nasser had even promised the Soviets that he would not attack first. Unlike its enemies, however, Israel did not keep an army that was primarily designed to sustain or change its government and put on impressive parades for public holidays. If nothing else, Nasser should have at least ceased being uncertain about the course of future events when the hawkish and very manly General Moshe Dayan joined the Israeli cabinet on June 1. Short of a public announcement that hostilities would commence on June 5, Israel couldn't have made its intentions any clearer.

On June 5, 1967, Israel destroyed most of the Egyptian air force before it was even airborne, attacking all seventeen of its military air-fields. The next day, Israeli forces whipped through Sinai, defeating the seven Egyptian divisions there and reaching the Suez Canal two days later. Some ten thousand Egyptian soldiers were killed or died of thirst during the struggle to retreat back across the canal.

For King Hussein, the Six Day War actually lasted two days. By the evening of June 7, having already lost the Old City of Jerusalem and the West Bank to Israeli occupying forces, Jordan happily accepted the UN Security Council's demand for an unmanly cease-fire. Egypt's Six Day War was also really only three days long: it accepted the unmanly cease-fire demand on June 8. Only Syria — which had confined itself to probing attacks — was left, no doubt feeling rather lonely, foolish, and unmanly as Israeli troops stormed up the Golan Heights and all but danced onto the Syrian plateau, occupying the key town of Quneitra. Syria accepted the cease-fire on June 10.

Nasser, one hardly need say, took this disaster rather badly. He had never really recovered from the shock of President John F. Kennedy's assassination, which had started the decline of U.S.-Egyptian relations — and thus helped Israel decide to strike. Nasser and Kennedy had liked one another; more importantly, Nasser trusted him and probably would have let himself be steered toward a peace accord with Israel under Kennedy's guidance. He didn't feel the same about the following admin-istration. But after June 10, 1967, it didn't matter. Egypt had no relationship whatsoever left with either Britain or the United States.

Nasser harbored no illusions about his share in the heavy responsibility for this unmitigated disaster, which was just as well — because no one else did either. With no reputation worth mentioning left to defend, during the evening of June 8 (Day 3 of the Six Day War), he announced on Cairo Radio that it was all his fault, he was no longer manly, unfit to lead poodles let alone a country, and that he would resign, handing over power to his vice president, Zakariya Mohieddin. While he was at it, he also fired unmanly Field Marshall Amer. Whether or not this was a calculated ploy seems impossible to determine, but Nasser was canny enough to intuit the public mood when he wanted to — and the public mood was an overwhelming cry of support for his manliness and the demand that he should remain in office.

He probably should have quit anyway, since little more than unmanly humiliation lay in store, and scarcely over three years later, on September 28, 1970, he was dead from exhaustion and a heart attack, aged 52. Even before this, though, his dream of Arab unity was being replaced by one of Islamic unity. Yet another phase in Middle East–West relationships had begun, setting the stage for a new breed of Arab leaders. To those who had found Nasser trying, what came next made him look like Old King Cole.

The 1967 war changed everything, including the reliance of Palestinian Arabs on Arab regular armies — led by Egypt — to liberate Palestine. Neither the Palestine Liberation Organization nor the Palestine Liberation Army had played any part in the Six Day War. The al-Fatah, the largest of the unofficial Palestinian guerrilla units, had, however, been carrying out sabotage attacks and bombings from bases in Lebanon. After 1967's disaster it chose one of its leaders as chief spokesman, and under the guidance of Yasser Arafat, ex-engineer and self-made millionaire, began to play a more prominent role on the world stage.

Yet the play everyone was now performing in appeared to be scripted almost solely by an American foreign policy obsessed with the theme of oil. After the assassination of Kennedy, and with the brief but notable exception of Jimmy Carter, those who governed the United States were never without close ties to the mighty global oil industry. Forced by anti-trust legislation to dismantle its monopolization of the U.S.-Saudi petroleum business, the Arab-American Oil Company (ARAMCO) merely sprouted different heads that may have been new companies with different names — Shell, Texaco, etc. — but were run by the same men who had once sat together on ARAMCO's board. They were not about to let control of nearly all the free world's oil slip from their grasp.

Although President Truman's eventual support for the founding of Israel — after much vacillation — delivered a savage blow to the U.S. oilmen's relationship with Saudi Arabia, they recovered quickly, finding distractions of various kinds to woo back Riyadh's princes, until political events made the House of Saud increasingly dependent on U.S. support and thus increasingly tied to the lifeline of U.S. oil interests. In return, Washington flattered and humored the Saudis, turning a blind eye to foibles like a human rights record and treatment of women that made Saudi Arabia a barbaric anachronism even by the generally modest standards deployed in these areas throughout the rest of the Arab world. From nightmarish liability, Israel soon transformed itself into an invaluable asset for the puppet masters of Middle Eastern oil politics in Washington. For the drama grew more complex as the players changed; and with complexity came the danger of straying from a plotline once so clear and yet now a twisting and turning labyrinth where one misread sign would lead straight into the Minotaur's jaws.

In 1968, after five years in the political wilderness, the Ba'athists recovered power in Iraq through — yes — a military coup. This time, however, they gradually succeeded in gaining a firm grip on the country, largely thanks to the tireless efforts of the civilian vice president of the Revolutionary Command Council, Saddam Hussein, widely viewed as a natural leader of unrelenting and ruthless determination who established absolute control over the proliferating internal security services and the military wing of the Ba'ath, emerging as undisputed strongman of the regime. President Bakr, the Ba'athist leader, had little power, providing a convenient front for Saddam to go about his business of eliminating enemies, both at home and abroad.

One of Saddam's first public gestures, revealing who really controlled Iraq, came in June 1972, when he took the bold step of nationalizing the Iraq Petroleum Company. IPC squealed in protest but they knew things had changed and eventually settled for fair compensation. The action broke a twelve-year impasse in Iraq's oil industry, which, like those of other Arab states and Iran, was still run by international corporations that controlled oil prices worldwide by dictating quotas and even shutting down production here or there if the need arose. The formation of OPEC — less effective and united than its PR presented it to be — and events like the closure of the Suez Canal or Syria's meddling with the oil pipelines running through it had begun to whittle away at Western control of the business — especially the British portion of it — but now it seemed in danger of being removed entirely. The threat of losing control over 90 percent of the world's oil production outside Communist countries called for drastic measures — and these would come in time. For now, though, assisted by the quadrupling of world prices in 1973–74, Iraq's oil revenues rose from $584 million in 1972 to $7.5 billion in 1974. The country's economic outlook was utterly transformed. Iraq was suddenly *a contender.*

A similar windfall came Libya's way, too, helping to make the name of Colonel Muammar Gaddafi, who had seized power from King Idris in 1969, another new force to be reckoned with. Even Arabs thought he was a riot.

Yet the Americans were still more obsessed with Communism and the Soviet menace than they were with studying new political realities. This obsession sabotaged their foreign policy everywhere, but in the Middle East led them to make two massive blunders.

The first was seeing in the rise of Islamist fundamentalism a useful bulwark against godless Communism. They pressured Nasser's successor and comrade in arms, Anwar Sadat, to ease up on the Muslim Brotherhood and encourage a religious revival. He'd imprisoned the Muslim Brotherhood's leaders after the 1952 coup, seeing them as a reactionary and potentially deadly menace. Now, against his better judgment, he ordered their release. Led further by the carrot of U.S. economic aid to his now impoverished nation, Sadat signed the separate peace accord with Israel, an action that made Egypt and particularly himself the target of both Arab political abuse and Muslim rage. In 1981, suspecting a coup, he imprisoned 1,500 Islamic radicals, including many divines. Shortly afterward, he was assassinated by Islamist extremist factions within the army. The Saudis, too, received U.S. wisdom on encouraging Islam to fight demon Communism; and they, too, would come to regret it.

So would the Americans responsible for it, as they witnessed the first glimpse of what they'd unleashed — courtesy of their second major blunder. Determined to avoid losing control of any more oil, U.S. support of Iran's corrupt Pahlavi regime — which was so extensive that the Shah amounted to little more than a U.S. quisling, with the CIA running the country — blinded them to the forces suddenly aligned with Ayatollah Khomeini. And even when the Shah fled, allowing Khomeini's triumphant return, Washington never imagined the result would be a sternly theocratic state — the first since the Dalai Lama left Tibet — resolutely opposed to all Western interference and positively hostile to Western interests. They had no idea how to cope with such an implacable enemy. This was when the unknown and as yet untried quantity, Saddam Hussein, first came in useful.

Iraq protected Kuwait — an American ally — from Iranian hostilities during the Iran-Iraq war, which flared up over rights to the strategic waterway shared by the two big countries. It lasted eight long years, ending inconclusively, and is often compared to the First World War in savagery, horror, and massive death count. When it was over, in 1988, Iraq's economy had taken a terrible beating and much of its oil industry's infrastructure was destroyed. By the time I arrived, two years later, prosperity was merely a facade to hide grim reality. The oil boom had bust long ago, and Iraqi revenues were reduced to a fractured reality along with everyone else's — except few countries had built such a massive house on foundations laid in sand. Saddam couldn't even pay the interest on foreign loans taken to pay off the interest on other foreign loans. He was being driven into a corner and increasingly saw no way out that did not entail drastic measures. No stranger to drastic measures — he'd once shot a general who disagreed with him during a council meeting rather than waste words — Saddam had never seen a corner before, let alone been driven into one, and he didn't like what he now saw. Yet, a master of ideological rhetoric and snake-oil dialectic, he knew that a thriving economy could easily be dismissed as materialistic, reactionary, and decadent in the face of Arab unity, imperialist aggression, the Ba'athist Struggle, or the "Zionist Entity." He could handle the Iraqis — it was everyone else that bothered him.

While not popular with other Arab leaders, and positively hated by Hafez Assad, the shrewd master diplomat and fellow Ba'athist who now ran Syria with an iron fist (and, bizarrely, had sided with Iran during the war, even cutting off Iraq's oil pipeline to the Mediterranean), Saddam still inspired many ordinary Arabs to revive pan-Arabist fantasies. His tough-guy stand on Israel, particularly after the ruthless Israeli air strike on Iraq's nuclear reactor, also won him the adoration of Palestinians, which in itself guaranteed additional popular approval. Furthermore, he seemed increasingly obsessed with strengthening his army and acquiring the kind of hi-tech weaponry he'd need in a confrontation with Israel — including development of a super-cannon capable of firing a nuclear "bullet" through Israel's almost impenetrable air defenses. Unfortunately, however, besides the current dire financial problems it faced, Iraq was also forced to deal with the same hostile states on three sides that it had been hampered by for most of its history. Kurds egged on by Turkey still threatened rebellion to the north, Ba'athist Syrians still posed a major military threat to the west, and fundamentalist Shia Muslim Persians now ruled by a theocracy had expansionist dreams to the east. Kerbala, a few hours south-east of Baghdad, with its shrine of Imam Hussein, the Prophet's grandson, remained Shia Islam's holiest site and thus, perversely, home to many of Iran's most revered clerics and holy men.

Although he could hardly admit it, Saddam must have been more painfully aware than most Arab leaders of the arbitrariness inherent in the cartographical process that had left him a country consisting of three irreconcilable factions: Kurds, the southern Shia Muslim Arabs, and a central Sunni majority expected to govern the querulous lot. He also quite clearly wondered at times just how unintentional that process had actually been. As the mechanisms of chaos left by parting imperialists like booby traps across their vanishing empires exploded into action, and as the invisible imperial rule of global finance continued with the work of pillaging developing nations to make sure they couldn't really develop much, it became easier to see that what had once seemed ad hoc measures were really stages in a carefully calculated plan to perpetuate Western hegemony indefinitely.

CRISIS MANAGEMENT

One of Iraq's most popular authors, according to the shelves of the Al Rashid's book and leather goods store, was Saddam Hussein. He was also one of the most popular subjects for other authors' books. Combined with his impact on the visual arts, including photography, this made him an incredibly popular guy indeed. Not many men I can think of have been this popular . . . while alive: only the late Pope John Paul II and Elvis come to mind. Maybe Sean Connery? The World's Biggest Bookstore in Toronto didn't carry any of Saddam's books, nor did the University of Toronto's Robarts Library. It seemed therefore an opportune moment to avail myself of some. I could get the author to sign them soon, too . . .

Looking along the shelves for a title that spoke to me, I prized out a volume called *One Trench or Two?* No subtitle; just "Saddam Hussein" in a simple, small, yet manly, typeface. It was a very slim volume: most poets manage more than forty-nine pages of large print. High-quality paper, though, and, I noted, printed in Switzerland. That couldn't have been any bargain. There *are* no bargains in Switzerland — even a hot dog costs $35. No one has anything printed or manufactured in any shape, form, or fashion in Switzerland, except the Swiss. Whoever costed out this job should have been aimed and fired. Let loose in the Ministry of War, he'd have the army firing bullets handcrafted at Cartier's by now, with Gucci bandoliers and Armani uniforms.

I looked for the price tag to confirm these suspicions, then had a helluva time turning its runic sum into dollars. Mainly because it amounted to just over three cents.

"Outrageous markup you've got on these books," I remarked to a woman tending the muscular wrought-iron cash register.

"Pardon me?"

There was something worryingly static about her face, as if some major system had crashed with no backup. Like Mohammed Ali in his bewildered twilight — except she was twenty-odd and probably hadn't been punched in the head mercilessly since she was five.

"What's your profit on an item like this? If it's not rude to ask."

"Tree sense."

"No, no — not, what does it cost? What does it cost you? See?"

"Off course I'm see. The book of President Saddam they coss us nussing."

"Nothing?"

"Off course."

"Ronald Reagan gets $35 for his book — although it is bigger. Ten times bigger."

"So Weegan should sell iss for tree dollar, yes?"

She was right.

"You must sell thousands a week at this price?" I suggested. "Even if people buy them as fuel they're a bargain. Do you have a bestseller list in Iraq?"

She thought I meant a list of the best cellars.

"I think maybe you are 'ere for the ween . . ."

"The ween?"

"Yes. You keep in cold floor the ween, isn't it?

"What exactly is ween?"

"Red ween, wheat ween . . . iss making from the grappesh." She drank an invisible toast.

"Right. Sorry. Wine. Made from grapes. Keep in cellars. No, I'm not in that business — although I'd like to be . . ."

I explained about bestseller lists. Iraq didn't have them. Probably for ideological reasons. But when we finally returned to Saddam's heavy sales figures, constant reprintings, the impossibility of keeping any stock, etc., she said: "No. No one buy them 'ere. You are first 'oo luke at one."

"In . . . what? A week? Month?"

"I haff 'ere four years, an' no personne are luking."

I found that hard to believe. Considering the quantity of them, someone must have been curious?

A cloning of Japanese businessmen walked by right then, and it suddenly seemed possible that the average hotel guest would not place much value on curiosity. Especially curiosity in a very foreign language.

"So why do you keep so many in stock if they don't sell and only cost a penny? You could get overpriced blockbusters, instead — books with legs, as they say. Like Robert Ludlum. Stephen King. Literary giants!"

"Books wiz legs?" she asked.

Her face had not done a single thing so far. It was on strike, or stricken. Now it suddenly tore in three and gaped, tongue flapping, eyeballs tumbling like dice. Frightened the hell out of me — until I realized she was just laughing — the first mortal to hear the joke that ends the world.

People passing obviously thought I'd made her cry. A couple of sheikhs rolled their eyes at me in sympathy: *women!* She kept jack-knifing with the spasms, too, then incorporating laughter with breathing until she sounded like a Victorian car horn. People in a boutique across the mall that sold nothing but handmade lace pointed and then looked as if they were vomiting into their hands. Obviously the bookseller was known for her frightening sense of humor.

It looked a bit painful, too, and I wondered if a doctor might be required. But suddenly she just stopped, ceased, switched it off. Her face recomposed itself into a zombie mask — albeit one with smudged mascara — and she went about tending her till as if nothing had happened.

"You want theese book?" she asked, a few seconds later.

"You okay?"

"Off course. I okay."

Off course was a good assessment.

"Wrap it up. What else do you recommend?"

"Nothing" would have been the quickest answer, but after much soul-searching and a phone call to some unknown adviser, she directed me to *The Revolution and Woman in Iraq*, an epic at fifty-four pages. I felt I ought to get an objective opinion, too, and finally came across *Saddam Hussein: A Biography* by Fuad Matar. The front sleeve elaborated: "A biographical and ideological account of his leadership style and crisis management. The 1990 Edition." I couldn't recall reading an ideological biography before, or a study of any leader's talents at "crisis management," so perhaps I'd learn something here?

The back sleeve reinforced this possibility, and sounded reassuringly objective as well:

Iraq, cradle of the greatest Arab civilization, is today one of the few countries being rapidly transformed from an underdeveloped backwater into a truly modern state. Endowed with the enormous riches of its land and its oil a real power, not subservient to the superpowers, is being born . . . . Socialism, Arabism, Islam, industrialization, nuclear energy, the Kurdish question, the liberation of women, relations with the great powers, with Europe, with the Third World, with Iran, with the Islamic world . . . on all these questions, even when they touch upon his personal life, the leader of Iraq has confided in the Lebanese writer Fuad Matar, who has devoted this book to the life and work of Saddam Hussein.

It made it sound as if he'd *dedicated* the book to Saddam — after all, one assumes a biography is devoted to its subject's life and work. Matar was further on described as "one of the top specialists in the Middle East." Among his previous works was a four-volume study of *The Fall of the Lebanese Empire* and *Where Is Nasser in Sadat's Republic?* What had the Lebanese Empire consisted of? I wondered. Some of the Syrian coastline? Or, considering there were four volumes, was it the Phoenician Empire Matar meant by this resonant title?

Saddam Hussein: A Biography set me back nearly forty cents, and had a great dust jacket showing the Saddam twins — one a laughing sheikh in gold-edged *abaya*, the other a confident, chin-tugging deep thinker in military uniform — sitting shoulder to shoulder against a backdrop of Group-of-Seven-style sand dunes. At nearly three hundred pages and fresh from the printer's it was a deal and then some.

I tried to get the bookseller's opinion, asking what she thought of Matar's book without making her feel trapped into releasing state secrets.

"It is bee-offry of Saddam his life."

"A good one?"

"There iss not other. This iss the oonly bee-offry for Saddam." .

The biography was printed in Great Britain, but I couldn't see a publisher, except A Highlight Production London U.K. It did have an ISBN number, though — if that means anything. Surely one of the top specialists on the Middle East wouldn't have to publish his own books, would he?

In the lobby I saw Ahmed, sitting next to Omar on a sofa in the waiting area. He looked rough. Very rough. It takes stamina to dance and drink and fornicate all night, then still be at the office by nine for a day's work. I'm not up to it anymore. It gave me up long ago. It looked as if it was about to walk out on Ahmed, too.

"Beeg troubles-him," Omar explained, when I'd cheerily asked what was up.

He patted Ahmed's shoulder consolingly, as the haggard Egyptian looked up and nodded ruefully to confirm this news.

Evidently Ahmed shouldn't have got yodeling drunk at the Big Egg party and disappeared with an Iraqi girl to spend the night making a conspicuous Berk of himself at various Baghdad nightspots, the last of which felt it necessary to request several local policemen to escort him from the premises after he'd refused to pay a whopping, intergalactic-size bar tab.

"Stealing-they the money of me," Ahmed explained. "Beeg theefs-this bringing-drink-table peoples . . ."

I asked where the maker of plaster Saddams was during all this and learned she'd left earlier. Ahmed couldn't be sure when or even where she'd left him. He'd met far better babes, anyway, he added. The night-club was jammed to the rafters with them — he'd take me there himself and prove it.

Omar interjected at this point, spending ten minutes attempting to explain without actually saying so that the club in question was a notorious clip joint for tourists, a virtual brothel stocked with virtual hookers working on commission — a virtual job, like tele-marketing. The virtual part was that the women implied they'd take you back to their rooms after more dancing and, particularly, more drinking. Even if you looked at the cocktail menu, you wouldn't notice the section in very small print listing obscure cocktails and "French-style" champagne at stupendously inflated prices. Or the reminder — probably all but obliterated by stains — that said all prices were in American dollars, which was also how they should be paid.

Ahmed was made for such a dive, and it was made for him, conceived especially with him in mind. He would have ordered beer or scotch — listed at prices that, were they in Iraqi dinars, would have seemed rock bottom: thirty to forty cents a pop, for Chivas Regal! He'd have assumed that, whatever the women ordered, it had to be even cheaper. More likely than not, the manager would send him the odd treble Chivas on the house. And no doubt, being a big shot from Cairo, he'd have ordered at least a bottle of champagne for the ladies. French champagne was two hundred dinars in stores — less than forty bucks — so, in a nightclub, it, too, seemed a bargain. Since he wasn't drinking it himself, he wouldn't have noticed that it was Seven-Up or Canada Dry served from a pre-opened (and probably rather worn-out looking) but genuine Moët & Chandon bottle.

The women knew when they'd made their night's commission, which was when they whispered in your ear that you might be more comfortable back at their place. By now, you thought you'd struck the motherlode — because it seemed as if all three, four, or five of them were suggesting that an obviously major stud like you could easily service them all together . . . and wouldn't you like that, darling? Then the bill came, and they could be certain there'd be one hell of a row when you found out what it really was. The manager had a couple of specialists for this situation, big guys who explained to customers that it wasn't very nice to buy all these girls so many drinks and then refuse to pay for them. They'd have to go to your embassy about this, and you'd have to go to jail until it was sorted out. If you tried to leave, they implied, it wouldn't be very good for your health. Why not just put it on your credit card and exit like a gentleman?

During all this, of course, the women would have vanished — as would your interest in them when confronted by the horror awaiting you if your embassy called your company, which would call your wife, who would want to know what on earth you were up to in a nightclub at 4:00 a.m. running up a $5,000 tab. What kind of nightclub was it, dear? No one can eat or drink that much in an evening. No, no, no — you'd pay all right, otherwise you'd *really* pay. On the other hand, if you just took the bill when it arrived and forked over a bundle of hundred dollar bills, with a massive tip, the women could be certain *they'd* hit the motherlode. By morning you'd either be very poor, or dead, or a Saudi prince who'd just blown yesterday's per diem.

The only thing that didn't make sense was Ahmed's vanishing wallet. The women wouldn't have taken it — they'd be dead meat — nor would the waiters, for similar reasons. The Iraqi artist wouldn't have been so dumb — we knew where to find her. Yet Ahmed insisted it had been stolen.

Until we were alone in the elevator.

"Not having-I the wol-ette, me. I identity the-card only. And little munnies."

"Didn't your Pappy warn you about places like that, Ahmed? Why would our artist take you there, anyway?" I suddenly wondered.

Ahmed's Pappy died when he was three, I learned. And Maria hadn't taken him there. She'd left him in their last disco after he'd molested her ("I was nice-her with . . . nice . . .," was the way he put it, but I could translate between the lines). A bouncer, by the sound of it, had kindly escorted him personally to what he still considered a fine establishment.

"This girls-there be-ewe-iffle, I not lie, Mista Ball. Ah-al-Lah! Soo be-ewe-tee-full." He re-ran and re-lived the scene for a few wistful seconds. "But this places too much ex-speng-siff, they. But you muss pay-you for such woomans . . ." He sighed, re-running memory again.

He hadn't left his wallet in the room, either, as I'd assumed. He didn't own a wallet. He just had his little plastic ID holder, with some government travel documents, and around twenty dollars in Iraqi money. It took me awhile — a couple of hours, in fact — to grasp that this was all the money he had brought with him. He saved it up especially for the trip. This was the first time he'd ever left Egypt — or home. He still lived with his mother, three younger sisters, brother, and an older sister who was married with three children. Just like Omar before Saddam City came into his life. By the time Ahmed had paid his share of the family expenses, he was left with about four dollars a month to spend on himself. It had taken him three years to save the money he'd blown in one misspent night.

His family hadn't always been poor, he wanted me to know. They'd lost their land during Nasser's reforms; and after his father died, penniless, things had gone from worse to diabolical. An uncle who'd been a *pasha* — a kind of fat-cat honorary nobleman — in King Farouk's day, and who still had some pull with the odd minister in Mubarak's regime, waved the wand of nepotism to wrangle Ahmed his job. It was a good job, but with a bureaucracy as titanic and stultified as Egypt's, promotions came slowly — if they came at all. You could start as a file clerk and, fifty years later, retire as a senior file clerk. It took more pull than the old *pasha*-uncle obviously commanded to climb up the ladder once you were on the first rung. Talent, drive, ambition, and character probably played a minor role, too — although Ahmed never mentioned whether or not they did.

He hadn't "blown" the money, either. When he announced that his wallet had been stolen (after discovering that his tab was $2,567), the waiter called the manager over, then the manager went to fetch two "financial advisers" (Ahmed admitted they did resemble ex-heavyweight boxers, but he insisted they were from the club's "Accountancy & Client Services" division). These "financial advisers" asked the women to leave. When they'd gone, the men were very friendly, suggesting Ahmed might have placed his wallet in another pocket by mistake, or stuffed it into his sock without realizing it. Why didn't they all check — just to make sure? By the sound of it, the check stopped just short of a rectal probe. Satisfied there was no wallet, the "financial advisers" then searched the washroom thoroughly, "even they examine inside tank-the water," then they all but tore apart the banquette Ahmed had occupied. Finally, they told him the police would have to be informed: he'd have to go with them to file a full report. Then he'd have to call his embassy and make arrangements for cash or a credit card to be rushed over to the club immediately.

Ahmed was weeping by now. We were in my room. I offered him some tissues, then poured him three miniatures of Chivas from the mini-bar. He needed it.

"So what happened? The Egyptian taxpayer footed the bill?"

"No. Having-me not any creddy cart. Me! They not giving-the for poor mans creddy cart in *Misr*." (*Misr* is an Arabic word for "Egypt." A lot of Egyptians are miserable, it's true — but there's no connection.)

Realizing the futility of his situation — he'd told the club manager he was Egypt's Minister of Trade & Industry, a close friend of the Egyptian Ambassador and of Saddam Hussein — Ahmed assured the "financial advisers" that a phone call would fix everything. He then called a friend also staying at the Al Rashid from a phone on the club's bar — where the music, and some Cairo slang, made it impossible to be overheard. The friend hadn't appreciated the 4:00 a.m. alarm call, but when he heard what the problem was immediately offered to help. The problem he heard, however, was that Ahmed had met a very charming young lady in what seemed to be an upstanding and reputable establishment (he'd probably said it was the Young Muslims' Birdspotting Association Tea Room). She'd invited him home to meet her parents, but the parents were out. She must have spiked his tea with something, because the next thing he knew these two big guys were there, holding a camera, and the girl was disheveled, clutching a bathrobe around her neck. He was no longer wearing any pants, either. The men said they'd photographed everything: him raping the girl, tearing off her clothes, tearing off his clothes. He was in big trouble. They'd give the pictures to the Iraqi authorities and the Egyptian Ambassador — after they'd beaten him into blood pudding. Unless he gave them $3,000.

Ahmed's friend didn't have $3,000, of course, not that Ahmed imagined he would. But he agreed that the international scandal following release of the photos, faked or not, was something that would shame all Egyptians — not to mention the undesirability of Ahmed being smashed to pulp. So the plan was this: the friend would rush over to the Egyptian Embassy, for which he had clearance authorizing legitimate access, and phone Ahmed as soon as he got there (at the number on the bar phone's dial, which he assumed was this den of blackmailers' line). Then Ahmed would get the "financial advisers" to drive him over to pick up the cash, leave them in the car as this friend, looking as ambassadorial as possible, greeted him at the door with an embrace. Once inside the embassy, Ahmed would rush out the back entrance to a cab the friend had already arranged, and they'd both return to the hotel. If the "advisers" started getting impatient and buzzed the embassy's intercom, no one would answer, most likely — and even if someone did, they wouldn't have a clue what the men were going on about: His Excellency was still at his private residence, and no one besides security staff was yet in the building.

There appeared to be a major flaw here, but I didn't want to interrupt Ahmed at this juncture, so I found him some Haig and a miniature of vodka — since he'd inhaled the first drink and it had done him a power of good — letting him continue.

Ahmed had spent a tortuous hour regaling the manager and his "financial advisers" with tales of the wide world beyond Iraq, where all doors were open to an Egyptian Minister of Trade & Commerce (as were all women) for whom, of course, cash was not even an issue, was replenished unquestioningly, like hotel soap.

None of the men had ever left Iraq in their lives, evidently (I'm not sure anyone has), and were eager to learn about places like Sweden, Las Vegas, and Hollywood. Maybe. It struck me that they might be grilling Ahmed cunningly, to see where he slipped up (perhaps they knew there weren't many ancient temples near Stockholm? And that belly dancers weren't a major attraction at the Hilton in Las Vegas? Ahmed certainly didn't).

But finally the friend called. Summoned to the phone, Ahmed had first to explain why whoever answered the friend's call had said, "Bar 007, can I help you?" By now the bar had closed; the music was no longer playing and the bartender, as well as the manager and "advisers" were all close enough to hear every word Ahmed said. He bluffed his way through it, though — "Salim, old chap, thanks so much. Yes. Yes. Oh yes. I'll pop right over" — the friend, fortunately, assuming he had a gun to his head.

Ahmed then left the club with his three pals, and they hopped into the manager's Mercedes, heading through the metallic pre-dawn to Egypt's stately embassy building. No sooner did they pull up, the entrance was flung open and the friend — looking fairly ambassadorial — greeted Ahmed, who jumped out, embraced, and accompanied the friend into the embassy . . . where a squad of very serious Iraqi Mukhabarat armed with Kalashnikovs were waiting in the wings. Checking that Ahmed was okay first, they then tore out the door firing into the air, surrounded the Mercedes, ordered the manager and the "financial advisers" to get out and kneel with their foreheads to the ground and hands behind their backs, handcuffed them, and kicked the shit out of them before dragging them away to a prison van that had pulled up along with five army vehicles and fifty-odd Republican Guardsmen.

The van then sped off, and everyone else dispersed, except two Mukhabarat agents who wanted Ahmed to assist them in writing their report. It was now that the friend asked if Ahmed had the film.

"I was going to mention that myself," I told him. "They wouldn't have given you the film without the cash, would they — not that there was any film — so how were you going to tell your pal not to worry that the photos would be handed to the authorities if you didn't have them?"

Ahmed hadn't considered this hole in his plot — mainly because he wasn't worried about photos. He wasn't really in *that* plot, but he was in a plight, a real one, too, so all he could think about was escaping from the three men. But he quickly came up with a feasible explanation for why he had the film: the hoods had kept his identity papers and diplomatic documents. They were going to give them back when he handed over the cash. The friend bought this, accepting that Iraqis wouldn't necessarily know how easily replaced such things were for Egyptians. But then he asked for the film, so he could destroy it immediately.

They got into an argument when Ahmed insisted he'd do that himself — which the friend took as a slight against his integrity. Ahmed suddenly realized himself that getting the Iraqi secret police in on the whole business wasn't such a good idea, was it? All this was a hushed exchange in the corner — or supposed to be — because at that point the Mukhabarat agent had intervened, reassuring both of them that no one minded how many tramps Ahmed raped in Baghdad. The bitches had it coming to them if they got involved with criminal elements. Ahmed protested his innocence: he hadn't raped anyone. It seemed no one believed him, nor did they care, though. The friend stormed off in a huff, and Ahmed spun his yarn to the agent, who then asked for the film himself. Ahmed tried to make it sound reasonable that he'd prefer the incriminating pictures didn't fall into the wrong hands. The agent understood his concern, but assured him that such a thing couldn't happen in Iraq. The film, however, was necessary as evidence when the men were tried for blackmail. Which would be happening in a couple of hours, since justice was swift here — an ideological thing again — the courts were never backed up, and punishments were usually meted out within twenty-four hours of any arrest. So hand over the film.

"Jeez, Ahmed! What the hell did you do?"

Now he began weeping again.

And he had then, too: he broke down and confessed the truth, begging, for his mother's sake, for Islam's sake, for Arab Unity's sake, to be forgiven. Yet, apparently, the agent wasn't at all bothered. He scribbled it all down, told Ahmed not to worry, extolled the virtues of Iraqi-Egyptian amity, then gave him a lift to the Al Rashid, adding on the way that the three men would be jailed for decades and the club dynamited — or at least closed down. No one would ever know Ahmed had been there.

It was the extolling Iraqi-Egyptian amity bit that bothered me. Since the peace deal between Sadat and Israel's Menachem Begin, there hadn't been much amity between Egypt and any Arab state. The last Arab Summit to be held in Baghdad had been announced in response to the separate peace accord, and was Saddam's second attempt to try on Nasser's shoes for size. There had been a previous Baghdad "non-aligned Summit" in 1978 after the Camp David agreements. The 1982 Summit did not take place, however — other Arab leaders weren't sure they wanted Saddam as their global rep, once they'd realized that was the real purpose of these summits. I didn't want to worry Ahmed with this, though.

"So what's the problem!" I yodeled. "You have the luck of the d—, the *Irish!* Here —," I handed him twenty dollars "— now you're back to square one. I can afford it. Hey, I'm the Canadian Minister of Trade & Commerce, didn't I tell you?"

But he wasn't laughing. He was still weeping. The problem, I finally gleaned, was that he seriously believed he'd landed three good men in terrible trouble and that Allah would never forgive him. He'd lied to his good friend, too, and now had no good friends. Nor did he deserve good friends. And what's more, he was being disciplined by his supervisor for bad behavior and irresponsibility at the Big Egg party.

Nothing I could say would convince him that, while their punishment might be somewhat overly severe by my standards, the three men from the club were not saints, and the place deserved to be shut down. And, anyway, they'd probably bribe their way out of it all. The local cops were clearly in their pocket, and they did have a lot to offer for their freedom. Drinks and babes on the house forever. That probably purchased quite a bit of freedom in Baghdad.

"I'll go and see if the club is still in business tonight," I offered. "Then, if it's open, will you believe me?"

He nodded dubiously, and after more consoling, I managed to propel him toward his room for a nap.

"You've had a busy night, and there's more to come."

"Not I-Ahmed," he groaned. "Never for me again-this. Now only Holy Koran and tea-drinkings."

"And a hair shirt. Sure."

That night I went to where he said the club was. The place was boarded up, with government documents pasted on the wood. Someone nearby confirmed that there had been a bar there, "a bad place, very bad — not for good Muslim place." It had been raided around lunchtime, everything inside, including people, carried out into a truck. I told Ahmed the place was open as usual, however, and that I'd seen the manager he'd mentioned. My advice was that he stay well away from the area. He seemed overjoyed, and only too happy to stay well away from that area.

SADDAM HUSSEIN: THE NECKTIE YEARS

At last I could get down to *Saddam Hussein: A Biography.* It proved to be quite a read, too — once I reached it. Fuad Matar had provided a Preface to his new addition, explaining why he'd chosen its title. His earlier choice had been *Saddam Hussein: The Man: The Cause: And The Future.* I admired all the colons. After this useful Preface there was then a lengthy Foreword, in which Matar enthused over his subject's handling of the recent Iran-Iraq bloodbath: "As he conducts the war, Saddam Hussein's nerves are made of steel; he is ready for victory, but equally ready to handle any setbacks as they come."

This was just as well, I thought, since "setbacks" were all that came. Evidently, Saddam went with the crew of the first tank to cross over onto Iranian soil on September 22, 1980. "Had his officers not insisted that he stay behind in order to lead operations, he would have remained fighting on the front throughout the war." Impressive, particularly since he'd had no military training. At Cairo University, in the early sixties, he was studying to be — and this will come as no surprise to many — a lawyer. It's fortunate that Fate had other plans. Imagine finding Saddam Hussein, Q.C., representing your spouse in the divorce settlement litigation. Although he's now Commander-in-Chief of the Iraqi Armed Forces, and he often wears army uniforms, he's never actually *been* a soldier.

Matar seemed intent on emphasizing Iraq's readiness for war — a boast repeated constantly by Iraq's propaganda machine in those days and one that was to backfire within the year.

> It is even said that there have been large-scale purchases of gold during the past five years in order to cover the Iraqi currency in the event of war. It is doubtful whether the numerous international studies on armaments have the correct figures regarding Iraq. Iraq has been buying massive quantities of arms over the past five years, but has kept a low profile and not put these arms on display.

This subterfuge was apparently so ingenious, the profile of these "massive quantities of arms" evidently lower than the horizon, because Matar went on to describe how the Iranians were fought with their own weapons, captured from them by Iraqi soldiers clearly unwilling to put their own "arms on display" at any cost.

Matar perceptively pointed out a number of firsts achieved by the war: it was the "first between two members of OPEC," the "first in which superpower intervention has been kept to a minimum," the "first in the region between a secular Arab national leadership and a religious leadership," and the "first war in which American arms are being defeated and Soviet and French arms are proving successful." He clearly felt obliged to add here that "the Brazilian arms purchased by Iraq are also proving effective." This was the first time I'd ever heard of a Brazilian arms industry. Weren't Iraqi soldiers fighting with American-made Iranian weapons a moment ago?

"It is important to note at this point," Matar concluded,

> that President Saddam Hussein has none of the complexes of a leader who doubts his rightful place in history . . . I can safely say that President Saddam is seeking to play a major role in world affairs. This role will bring about a very strong Iraq, no matter what the dangers.

After the Preface and Foreword to *Saddam Hussein: A Biography* came Matar's Introduction. This proved to be a potted history of the Ba'ath Party, showing how, although its doctrines, ideological positions, and political goals were faultless, it couldn't overthrow a blanket until Saddam Hussein and his "leadership qualities" came along. The coup of 1963, it was implied, suffered a revolution's equivalent of Sudden Infant Death Syndrome because "it was carried out when Saddam Hussein was not in Iraq."

By now I was nearly a quarter into the book, and, suspecting a Prologue, Prelude, Preclusion, and maybe even a Proem and Overture next, had to reassure myself that *Saddam Hussein: A Biography* was the main feature, rather than something censored into a paragraph of Appendix, followed by an Afterword, Postscript, and Epilogue. In fact, though, I was just about there, but I'd come across a whole section of photographs now that I hadn't even noticed in the store, including a few in which, although clearly out of doors, Saddam and almost everyone else in sight wore bathrobes and pyjamas (and if you're thinking Ba'athrobes?— so was I; but humor seems to be ideologically incorrect for Ba'athists). In one picture, eleven men — all but one of them in bathrobes — posed in two rows like a cricket team, three men squatting in front. Saddam, standing second from the right, looked like Clark Gable, with dark-checked pyjamas and a snazzy two-tone bathrobe with a monogrammed pocket and a silk belt with tassels. One man, in Roy Orbison shades, even had striped dark satin pyjamas with a white satin robe edged in gold on the collar and cuffs. The caption read: "Surrounded by his comrades, a souvenir photo before leaving prison. . . ." I then noticed the other photographs also showed him "inside the prison with his comrades." Prison looked more like a health spa.

There were photographs of Saddam's relatives, too — though not his father, who in a reversal of the normal tragedy died just before he was born. Saddam's mother looked like Anthony Quinn playing Mother Teresa; and his stepfather, who was also his mother's brother (an arrangement I'd like to have asked Saddam about, but forgot), resembled Eddie Murphy cast as Scott Fitzgerald with an astigmatism. The young Saddam seemed to be a different person in every photograph, until 1968 when the moustache — initially trimmed to look like Nasser's — came to stay, along with expensive-looking suits and silk ties, which alternated with an eclectic range of theme outfits over successive pages. He also once had a brother named Barzan (which is a quintessentially Kurdish name) who "shared with him the responsibility for carrying out delicate revolutionary tasks," and looked eerily like his stepfather.

It seemed important to Fuad Matar that the reader notice Saddam's theme outfits, since, somewhat unnecessarily, his captions always mentioned them: "His head wrapped in a keffiyeh, the Iraqi President visits Basra in 1979"; "Wearing his 'abaya' (Arab cloak) Saddam Hussein with his son during his official visit to Yugoslavia (in 1976)"; "Reading a paper and wearing Iraqi peasant dress"; and so on. This last picture, in fact, showed him wearing an immaculately tailored version of the three-piece mohair suit with long skirt and white keffiyeh that I would consider the uniform of the prosperous Arab merchant. But there seemed to be an overt attempt here to demonstrate that Saddam was an Arab — in case you suspected he was not. And I now suspect he isn't: he's a Turk. The reader's attention was also constantly directed to Saddam's affinity for manly activities: he could drive a car; he could drive a motor boat; he went hunting; he rode in tanks; he smoked cigars the size of telegraph poles; he could swim (something surprisingly few Arabs can do); and he was taller than every world leader ever photographed next to him. He towered a good three inches over Brezhnev and Yasser Arafat, for example, and only slightly less over Jordan's King Hussein. Now, I was personally very surprised to find out just how small King Hussein actually is. I'm not tall but I had to practically kneel to shake hands with him. And when I was interviewing Yasser Arafat, he had cause to remove his boots (in fact, he removed his pants too, since he was changing into the track suit he wore when he took naps), so I know he uses uplift insoles so drastic he must be walking on his toenails. This made Saddam around 5'6" or so. If such was the case — and I'd soon find out — Marshall Tito, according to one photograph, must have been just shy of four feet, and the Iraqi army obviously had a minimum height requirement half that of most armies, since many of the awestruck privates and corporals Saddam was pictured with came up to his waist.

Although the customary space was provided for photographs of Saddam standing with every small leader he'd ever met (and sitting with the rest) and for pictures that usefully illustrated the watershed moments of his rise and rise, an inordinate amount of room was devoted to family snapshots. There were four whole pages alone of Saddam swimming with his kids and horsing around on the beach in a tight little pair of colorful scants (he was in far better shape than me, I concede, but that's not saying much) and countless other shots of trips, picnics, reunions, hectic informal dinners, and all manner of family moments, concluding with the deeply touching: "Needle and thread in hand, President Saddam Hussein himself mends the sleeve of his eldest daughter Raghd's dress." Saddam Hussein: The Tailor of Baghdad.

Two things were absolutely certain from this lengthy photo-bio: one, Saddam's favorite wardrobe item had for many years been an ankle length, Prussian-collared black cape like Dracula's, and two, his taste in neckties had steadily deteriorated toward a nadir of such shrieking, polka-dotted, chevroned horror that I hoped he wouldn't be wearing one when I met him. He should have stuck with the bathrobe and pyjamas look — it suited him and would have made a strikingly original leadership image, every bit the match for Arafat's rigidly starched keffiyeh with hybrid guerrilla-goatherd outfit, or Colonel Gaddafi's pill-box hat, ski vest, Rive Gauche Bedouin cape, with Cossack pants and general dune-warrior ensemble (which is admittedly a hard act to follow).

Finally, I turned to Chapter 1 of *Saddam Hussein: A Biography*, which was called "A Rebel Against the Family: A Revolutionary Against the Regime" and was accompanied by a quotation: "I am the mother, I am the father," explained in parentheses as an "Iraqi saying, describing strength of purpose and ability." It sounded to me more like something God would say.

"Saddam Hussein was nearly eight years old when Michel Aflaq's Arab Ba'ath movement was evolving into a Party in Damascus," I read. Then the telephone warbled.

SADDAM HUSSEIN: THE PARTY YEARS

Omar. He was in the lobby.

"I know. I saw you there, remember?"

He was still there three hours later, waiting for me.

"To do what?"

"Go for Soom-it Gonfrensh place."

"Too boring, Omar. Just opening speeches today, anyway. Really boring. I'll go tomorrow, maybe . . ."

"No tomorrows — you are having Saddam meeting-with tomorrows."

"I am? I thought it would be after the conference was over."

"Yesh. No. It iss tomorrows for you meeting-Saddam with."

"Okay. Well . . ." I told him I'd better get on with my research.

"I am come for you-bringing Gonfrensh."

"Yeah, but I'm not going to the conference."

"I am drive for you . . ."

I gathered he'd been sent to take me to the conference and regarded the order as a sacred mission — one in which he'd now failed abysmally.

He wasn't sure how to deal with the situation, and I knew he'd just sit there waiting all day if I didn't go down.

We had coffee in the black granite bar. It felt like sitting in a huge Japanese laquer lunch box.

"I'll phone your supervisor," I suggested to Omar. "Where can I reach him?"

Omar prevaricated with a stream of incomprehensible protestations, until I was close to banging his head on the table with each syllable of the sentence I'd by now repeated thirty-odd times: "I - am - not - going - to - the - conference - to - day!"

Then he finally confessed that his supervisor was the incredibly fat man seated over in a corner dressed all in black, except for one of Saddam's old Op-Art era neckties. Omar nearly sank to his knees begging me not to go over.

The fat man in black was seated with three other men in pricey shimmering suits, who all looked as if they'd broken their share of bottles inside people's rectums before promotion took them away from dungeon duty. Since it's not polite in Arab countries to state your business before you've had coffee or tea and smoked several cigarettes, I took the proffered vacant chair, and introductions were made.

The supervisor was Major Tariq al-Jazzar. He knew exactly who I was, and the other men — another major and two colonels — shook my hand in turn, smiling and nodding their heads. Between all four of them there must have been a kilo of gold dental work. And there were definitely fifteen rings that could have come from the Liberace estate. One man wore three on each hand.

My surname seemed to be causing unusual problems, I realized.

"Bawl Rubbish?" a colonel queried.

"Ruv-verse," another man stated confidently.

"Bol Rubb-uss!" Major al-Jazzar announced.

"Ropperst?"

"Mister Bol is from Tornado," said the very fat Major, wiping at an amber jewel of coffee that had spilled to sparkle briefly precisely in the center of one of his necktie's many small white parallelograms — not one of its more numerous black trapezoid and oval forms. The Major kept dabbing at the spot with a napkin dipped in water: it *had* to be bothering him.

"Gan-adar."

"Granada?"

I kept nodding.

"Toranado is gapidall of Gannidder?"

"No, in fact, Ottawa's the capital, but only people in government live there. So it's small."

"Odd-uwwah?"

"Army must be there?" Major al-Jazzar surmised.

I said there were a few major army bases in the area.

"How many soldiers men?"

"Probably a million or more." I felt I should do my bit for national security: that would make Iraq think twice before picking on us.

"Billion?"

"Mill-yon-mill-yon!" al-Jazzar snapped.

"Only bresident and command council in Udder-wah?"

"Right."

Everyone nodded and began excitedly exchanging rattling Arabic comments. Clearly they thought this idea of a capital city reserved solely for government officials and the army a splendid one. I wondered if they had any clue what kind of government Canada had.

"Gann-adder bresident, he choose command council?"

I thought of explaining how alleged democracy worked, but since I'd never thought any modern Western democracy particularly democratic in practice, and since no matter what party, most politicians ended up corrupt scumbags (if they didn't start out that way), I couldn't be bothered.

"That's right. More or less. Our president has a few close advisers too."

"Army general?"

"Right. The army really makes all the decisions . . ."

"Bresident Granada chef of armies?"

"Of course. Yeah, the president is the army chef all right."

More approving comments were exchanged. Then someone asked if Canada was near Australia. No one seemed prepared to learn that it was above the United States — and *bigger*. A colonel peered into the roof of his skull, as if he had a map in there. They couldn't figure it out: *what was above America?* "Nord Bowl, Gann-ada?"

"Near. There's nothing at the actual North Pole — no land — it's just water. The South Pole's on a continent, though. With rivers and mountains. Except they're under a mile of ice so you can't see them."

All four were staring at me like four-year-olds being taught the Special Theory of Relativity. My little pocket diary contained a teeny one-page map of the world, so I folded it out in a pool of water on the table and proceeded with the geography lesson. First, of course, I had to establish where Iraq was.

Half an hour later little progress had been made. No one believed Britain was this speck in the North Sea. No one even believed it was an island to begin with. Some insisted Europe was Britain. The Soviet Union they had no problem with, though, making noises of deep satisfaction over the crimson blob. They obviously hadn't heard the bad news, yet. I'd had the diary since 1983 (evidently there were only two appointments, a party, and a TV program I'd forgot to watch that year) and the diary had had its map since 1982, presumably.

"The Evil Empire is looking more like a banana republic now."

I felt like adding that any day now the Czar would be back. The map had changed quite a bit in seven years. It was now on its way to looking more like it had back in 1914.

It occurred to me that their map would be something like Iraq as Africa, Britain and France as Europe, with the Soviet Union and Japan sharing Asia. China would be Korea. Canada would be Vancouver Island, the rest of North America all the way south of Mexico would be the United States, and Brazil would take up most of South America. Saddam owns an island off the coast of Brazil, and has major shareholdings in dozens of Brazilian companies. Brazil had clout in Iraq — where clout is all.

Since it was hard to prove that Canada wasn't America — you could barely see Hudson's Bay, let alone Ottawa, on my mini map — I gave up. I gave them the diary, too. It lay in its puddle while each of them waited to see who it now really belonged to. Major al-Jazzar suddenly scooped it up and slotted it through an inside jacket pocket. He wore a shoulder holster, I noticed. No one objected to his proprietorial move.

I tried now to edge around to the purpose of my visit, announcing that I had a meeting with their president the next day.

"Ellven-dirty," al-Jazzar agreed, casually. "I gumb take you heem."

"Great!"

"You like Bresident Saddam?" one of them inquired.

"Enormously."

"Wad-jew like off heem?"

"Leadership style . . . and I'd have to say crisis management. He's damn good at the crisis management stuff."

Nods.

"Iraq iss like Gann-adah?"

"Much nicer. More advanced."

They'd been told this before and knew it to be true.

"I am nod army major," al-Jazzar confided, raising his arms to display the acre of black mohair swathing his hippo of a body. "Zee! No ooni-vorme. " He laughed throatily.

The other three followed suit, amused to apoplexy by al-Jazzar's comic gifts, and raising their arms like mobster penguins.

"Day doo nod army colonels; he nod army major. We are see-grett pleas all."

"Mukhabarat," I said, knowledgeably.

"Mukhbrat, *lah!*" he scoffed. "Umm — we are Umm!"

The word sounded like a hesitation. The *Amn* were the Secret Police who watched the Mukhabarat, primarily — as I understood it, at least; they guarded the guardians. Although supposedly there was another unit of snoops who watched them, too. How does the song go: Most of us are guardians and the rest of us are guards? Well, that's how it would go in Baghdad, anyway.

"Great! What's that like then?"

Damn fine, seemed to be the answer. Spiffing!

I assumed the Summit warranted maximum snooping, so maybe they were taking a break from snooping on lesser snoops?

"We habb good live here Baghdad for Umm."

"I bet you do."

"Vare good live. Much pardies, whiskey, foods. You like pardy?"

"Who doesn't? We Westerners are party animals, didn't they tell you that?"

"Pardy am-mool? Iss drew? You like pardy, eh? Wizz whiskies, eh? And wizz —" al-Jazzar produced a curious thrumming noise and suddenly thrust his hips to and fro obscenely "— eh? You like diss pardy, eh?"

All four cackled, muttering, "Like *diss* pardy, eh?"

Being a guy, I was obliged to express my snickering, prurient glee at this reference to fornication. As I did, it suddenly dawned on me that these four guys weren't thinking about gals at all. They were thinking about guys — about guy-guy fornication. I didn't like the way they were now all looking at me either. Even back in the distant days when I was searching for my sexual persona (how'd you know if you haven't tried it?), I wouldn't have considered that being gang-banged by this crew of shifty sand pirates might have its hidden virtues and occult delights.

Later on I heard rumors of an island enclave in the Tigris near Baghdad's ritzier suburbs where a cabal of senior government and military personnel regularly staged Dionysian revels, wildly extravagant parties for young boys and older men, at which blind musicians were hired to be heard but not see what went on. And what went on evidently made even *The Meatrack, Mineshaft,* and *Fistpit* — or whatever those New York gay S&M dives were called — look like Miss Dainty's Bible Class. People died, in short, or rather, people were brutally murdered during acts of sadistic sex that truly earned their name. The reason this nasty scene survived with impunity (and I heard this from several sources over the following years) was that one of its regular guests occupied the Presidential Palace. And we think *Washington's* like the fall of the Roman Empire!

I'm glad I didn't know this at the time, however. I just pictured a smoky suburban villa furnished in Sicilian Baroque, a bowl of olives, some crackers, bottles of ersatz Chivas Regal, and a lot of grunting, sweaty men with cauldron-bellies in polka-dot boxer shorts, shirts, sock-suspenders, and patent leather loafers. *I just can't wait for party time, boys!*

I pretended to miss the innuendo and went on about the beauty of Iraqi women for a minute, noting the dismay cloud four faces. It wasn't even true: some countries have beautiful women, some beautiful men, rarely both — Canada's unique. This crew excepted, Iraqi men were staggeringly handsome on the whole, whereas Iraqi women . . . well, put it this way: Saddam's mother was a rare beauty. The male sexual aesthete in Iraq would have to be gay.

"So, is Omar in the Amn then?"

"Omar!" al-Jazzar exclaimed in disgust, as if recalling a venereal wart. "Omar he iss *driver*. No Umm!"

I wasn't going to be getting any state secrets out of this mob. But I finally explained Omar's plight, my priorities, and, after handing out some Canadian two-dollar bills — "for when you come to my country!" — managed to retreat on a cloud of billowing goodwill, eventually sending Omar home for the day, and getting back to *Saddam Hussein: A Biography*. Our coffees cost ten times more than the books I'd purchased earlier.

SADDAM HUSSEIN: THE QUESTING YEARS

Still "nearly eight years old," Saddam "had not yet had any formal education" since his "relatives" wanted him to become a farmer "like the rest of the family." However, the future Iraqi Minister of Defense, who was then his cousin Adnan Khairallah, "told him how he had learned to read, write and draw at school." They must have been very cut off, I thought, finding Fuad Matar soon noted that the family was then living in a place called Shawish. It wasn't shown on the ten-page map included in the Al Rashid's handsome free book, *Iraq: The Tourist's Paradise*, however. It isn't in *The Times Atlas of the World*, either — Shawinigan, Québec, is the closest the index gets to Shawish.

"Saddam Hussein decided to travel with his cousin to attend school in the village of Takrit. This was his first act of rebellion against his family." If Takrit — which is a small city today — was considered a "village" back in 1944, Shawish must have been one hut. Some relatives living in a place farther off caught the young Saddam sneaking away to school, however; but when they learned of his plan to get an education, they "gave him a pistol and sent him off in a car to Takrit." Clearly, the practice of packing a handgun in a seven-year-old child's lunchbox is a tradition of some antiquity. We shouldn't worry about its Western revival so much.

Saddam spent a year in Takrit, before traveling eighty miles south to Baghdad with his stepfather, Khairallah Talfah. The book didn't mention whether or not Khairallah's sister, Saddam's mother, accompanied them to Baghdad, where Saddam completed his primary education, "entered the secondary stage," and was twenty years old just over halfway down the first page. Eight lines later, Saddam had been thrown in jail for murder. It was like Oliver Twist, the plot of Saddam's life, but better paced. "He decided to become involved in political activity. This decision was reinforced because of an incident which occurred after the 1958 Revolution. An official in Takrit was murdered; the authorities accused Saddam of having killed him and threw him in jail. . . . In jail, Saddam Hussein met some of his comrades in the Ba'ath Party . . ." It seemed to be safer in jail than out, and, for a jail, not especially strict: ". . . they remained in prison until nightfall, when they were released to carry out their activities, returning to jail before sunrise." This probably explained why they spent all day in bathrobes and pyjamas.

It didn't explain whether or not he'd actually murdered the official in Takrit, though, or how he'd become so well-known that he "was eventually released as a result of national pressure." Halfway down page two, he was being asked "if he would be willing to assassinate Abdel-Karim Qassem. He accepted at once as he considered the assignment an honor." The assassination attempt sounded like a real cock-up, and a comedy of errors ensued. Saddam's role, it transpired, was to provide cover for the other gunmen, but he clearly panicked at the last moment, whipping out a machine gun and blasting away at Qassem's car himself. The leader's guards returned fire, killing or maiming several comrades. Saddam ended up with a severe leg wound, which he demanded a friend cut open to remove the bullets and sterilize with iodine. "He felt faint for a few moments, but then recovered." He was manly.

There followed a curious little hagiographical saga in which Saddam began to sound like Don Quixote or Nasruddin the Sufi. It took up five pages. Realizing he had to escape before the authorities found him, he "burnt some personal photographs" (just how "personal" were they?), put twenty-three dinars in his pocket, bought a horse for ten dinars, and rode off. Much detail was devoted to the terrible deprivations he endured: he missed lunch, got wet, and was once even so thirsty he had to buy a watermelon and share it with the horse. "Then he came across a house where a wedding feast was in progress . . ." — a biblical tone crept in — ". . . and he sat down, uninvited, to enjoy a meal of roast lamb. It was delicious." Indeed, it sounded so delicious that I suddenly had a craving for some myself, calling room service. Roast lamb seemed to be no problem for room service, either. They'd send it right up. A hamburger arrived an hour later.

Saddam was wearing a brilliant disguise throughout all this, too: he'd put on "old shoes." No one would ever recognize him now. A team of customs officials stopped him at one point, demanding to see his identity papers. How was he going to get out of this? "I don't carry identity papers," he replied. Okay, just asking, said the customs officials and drove off. The ingenious ploy worked! Saddam got hungry again and had a terrible time finding a decent restaurant, but when he finally did, the meal merited half a page it was so good. "And then he came to a river. It was night . . ." and the horse wasn't about to go swimming. There was nothing for it but to forge ahead alone. "With his clothes in a bundle upon his head, and his knife held between his teeth, Saddam began to swim across . . ." The water was quite cold. Like the Jordan, this river was "deep and wide," milk and honey on the other side. Tea and more roast lamb, actually, but not before another close call. Teeth chattering, Saddam heard dogs barking and walked toward "a farm house," intending to seek shelter. A woman opened the door and started screaming, "Thief! Thief!" This was "sure to attract attention." What could Saddam do? The woman's husband had by now appeared as well. "Do I look like a thief?" asked Iraq's future president. It was a gamble, but the husband said, No, you don't, now you mention it, and invited Saddam in for a meal. But it was a trap. When Saddam got up to leave, the husband "and other members of his tribe," who'd entered unannounced by Fuad Matar, said, "Where do you think you're going? You've just swum across the river in your clothes. This means something is very wrong and we are not going to let you go until we know what the truth of the matter is." How would he get out of this predicament? "What if I've committed a crime against one of the clans across the river?" Saddam asked them. "If they come here and kill me in your house, then my clan finds out I was killed among you — what good's it going to do you?" A stunning tactic, invoking the old Bedouin custom of hospitality to strangers. "Right," said the man. "That's true. May God protect us." Yet again Saddam had overcome impossible odds, and he went on his way. It was late and really cold.

Eventually, he came to an elementary school where — mystifyingly — his cousin Adnan, the future minister of defense, now "worked as a guard." Why would a rural elementary school in 1958 need a "guard"? I wondered. Obviously it didn't need him so badly, though, because "when Adnan saw Saddam he cried, then they both set off to the area of Ouja," where they had yet more "family and friends." Either Saddam had been moving in circles, or his family was gigantic.

From Ouja Saddam soon traveled with some comrades to Syria on a "secret journey . . . in accordance with the wishes of the Ba'ath." So secret was this journey that even forty years later we were not permitted to know its purpose, presumably for security reasons. But it, too, like Saddam's great escape, proved to be a hellish test of endurance, courage, and true grit. They started out with a jeep "but then had to continue with a donkey." Tight security prevented us knowing how many men were on that donkey. But this much is certain: "they did not stop to rest, and . . . lived through some difficult hours." They drank "water polluted with goat droppings" and were obliged to strain it. They had to sleep in a cave. Saddam had to walk for a while, too. And, as if this weren't bad enough, they only realized they were in Syria "after they had gone some way" into that country. I could sympathize with this, having once taken nearly the same route. Syria has an enormously long border, therefore signposts are not as numerous as one might wish, even these days.

Now they rested. They rested again in Boukamal, too, and even once more in Deir al-Zor. Well-rested, "Saddam Hussein spent the next six months in Syria."

Then he went to Cairo, on February 21, 1960, where he "enrolled at a school to prepare himself for the Law School at Cairo University." But he also "worked hard on strengthening the Ba'ath Party Command in Cairo." This caused him to suffer unspeakable indignities at the hands of Egyptian police: he was even "harassed . . . and had his rooms searched." Surely there was no other option but to leave? How could he endure such inhuman conditions? Again Saddam took an almost unbelievable gamble: he personally "informed one of the officials in the President's Office that he and his colleagues were not prepared to suffer such indignities . . . and the harassment stopped." No one else could have pulled off such an audacious stunt.

Being an ideological biography, I suppose, *Saddam Hussein: A Biography* did not trouble itself with trifles like whether or not Saddam actually got to Cairo University and received his law degree. It was suddenly 1963, and he returned to Baghdad after the next Ba'athist coup, to find that "lack of leadership . . . was a disease . . ." He was the cure, though. Soon he was buying arms and making bombs "from the explosives fishermen use." I'd seen fishermen in Tennessee stuff dynamite into balls of mud, lob them in, and then trawl the lake for blown-up fish, but I hadn't realized the practice was widespread. It's not very sporting.

But presumably this wasn't what landed Saddam back in jail, where he "read some books and, with what he'd learned, tried to raise the morale of Ba'athist comrades who'd been tortured." It didn't say which books he'd read. It didn't say he'd got married, either, but he must have, because he now had "a baby son, Adi, who was six months old." How Adi, at six months, managed to keep Saddam "well informed about what was happening outside the prison walls" was not at all clear.

Next he "had some files smuggled into jail." I thought he was going to catch up with his Ba'athist paperwork, but they weren't those sort of files. Like in old James Cagney movies, Saddam and his comrades sawed through the bars at night so the guards wouldn't hear. When the great escape was underway, Saddam, for unstated — or ideological — reasons chose to remain behind with a few other comrades. Maybe it was too late at night for them? Next, they were moved to another, clearly more secure prison, where "attempts were made to brainwash them." But "then things were relaxed a little . . ."

How would Saddam escape to lead the Revolution, though? The Ba'ath Party "was in disarray without his organizational skills . . ." Once more we saw the Saddam magic at work: "he convinced the prison guards that they were victims of tyranny just like him." Then he asked them to take him and several other prisoners to a restaurant, and "while the guards waited outside for them to finish their meal, Saddam and six comrades left by the back door." Amazing! Iraqi prisons seemed very unfamiliar with the principles behind incarceration, though. When prisoners ask to be taken to restaurants, the guards are supposed to laugh their heads off, aren't they?

But "escape from prison was essential this time. . . ." That, of course, makes a difference. If you don't really need to escape, it can be more problematic. "At three o'clock in the morning on 17 July 1968 Saddam Hussein, wearing a military uniform and his comrades led the tank assault on the Presidential Palace. . . . The long period of weakness was over; the second stage had begun." I assumed the second stage of weakness was far shorter than the first. The image of Saddam "wearing a military uniform and his comrades" was haunting, surreal, ideologically perfect.

A man named Saadoun Shaker — whom, I'd noticed in the photo section, often went hunting with Saddam — next recounted the events that followed, when Saddam purged the Party of undesirables: he even purged the people who'd helped him purge the previous people, because they were "hoping to take advantage of the fact." Ahmad Hassan al-Bakr was now made Prime Minister, President of the Republic, and also Commander-in-Chief of the Armed Forces. "Saddam Hussein chose to be Vice-President of the Revolution Command Council, without this being officially announced . . ." — for ideological reasons. It somehow sounded like a better job than the three others combined. "Saddam Hussein then surprised . . . Bakr by asking to remain out of power; he considered that he had fulfilled his role in bringing the Ba'ath Party to power." Bakr refused to accept this, however, and Saddam only finally decided to stay "after he had uncovered plots against Bakr. . . . He remained to play a special role; he was to remain a long time."

He sure was. He was also bothered by the fact that someone delightfully named Hardon Takriti would mysteriously "continue to try to broaden his influence." Since we hadn't met Hardon before now — and, indeed, he was never mentioned again — it was difficult to gauge the justification for Saddam's concern over Hardon's broadening influence. He didn't appear to be very influential. The name, however, betrayed his origins: it was like being called Hardon Torontonian.

The phrase "when he assumed complete responsibility," or variants on it, had cropped up a number of times since the Preface of *Saddam Hussein: A Biography*, yet I still wasn't sure what it referred to. Chapter 2 would fix this, though. It was titled "Two Leaders, One Command," and again began with a quotation:

It has never happened before, either in ancient history (including that of our nation since its dawn) or in modern times, that two leaders have been in power for eleven years within one command, without this resulting in a dangerous moral or practical imbalance

in leadership, and without their relationship ending in one of them driving the other out . . .
(Saddam Hussein in his first speech on 17 July 1979 after being handed overall responsibility by President Ahmad Hassan Bakr)

You could tell Saddam was a lawyer by training: all the caveats and its general ambiguity made this seemingly lofty statement impossible to refute. True, such a situation doesn't seem to have occurred for *eleven* years anywhere else; but in ancient Egypt alone it occurred a number of times for periods ranging from two to sixty-three years. In the Old Testament it even occurs a couple of times for quite lengthy periods, and British parliamentary monarchy is theoretically *based* on the principle. I'd have to raise this with Saddam.

Saddam, I noticed, didn't actually say in his speech that the situation ever did, could, or would happen in Iraq, just that it had "never happened before. . . ."

It has never, I doubt, happened before that a biography simply skipped eleven vital years in its subject's life, either. But perhaps ideological biographies are different, because *Saddam Hussein: A Biography* left Chapter 1 in 1968 and commenced Chapter 2 in 1979, with an account of what Ahmad Hassan Bakr did with his time:

He wakes up early in the morning and goes into his garden; he waters the plants and trims the rose bushes. When he tires, he rests awhile in the company of his grandchildren. He lives with his memories, which are for the most part tragic. His son was killed in a car accident when he was only twenty-three, at a time when Ahmad Hassan Bakr was still recovering from the shock of his wife's death. Then his son-in-law died, and Ahmad Hassan Bakr was left to care for his daughter and her children. Ahmad Hassan Bakr's tragic memories are not only personal. . . .

He suffered with the Ba'ath Party, too; he also had diabetes, for which he was "once treated in France." This was also why he couldn't travel abroad or repay official visits. "He restricted travel within Iraq to a minimum and went on tours only on the most important occasions. He is a sad and careworn man."

He has good reason to be, I thought. Funny, all those male heirs dying tragically like that. The usual reason cited for Bakr not making many trips during this period was that Saddam had put a gun to his head, told him to step down as president or else, and then put him under permanent house arrest. Even then there were rumors he was also being slowly poisoned. We were into a more accessibly historical realm of Saddam's life now, though — I'd read other books about the period from 1968 on — so it was good to learn what really happened, from a source that was clearly very authoritative. Who else would have known that Saddam had shared a watermelon with his horse?

The other, less reliable sources had filled the eleven years from 1968 with yarns about Saddam rising from Chief Torturer to eminence grise by wiping out anyone and everyone whom he felt remotely posed a threat to his claims on the presidency. It was comforting to learn that, in reality, nothing at all had happened — presumably from the ideological standpoint — worth mentioning during these years. There had been no coup, either. Indeed, the transfer of power was a truly heartrending story, with Bakr announcing that Saddam must take over the reins because he didn't want to become a pitiful spectacle of unmanly decrepitude like Brezhnev at the Soviet-American Summit: "hearing with difficulty, standing with difficulty, sitting with difficulty, even coming down the steps of the plane with difficulty" (surely this should have read *even sitting with difficulty?*). Saddam begged him to stay on for Iraq's sake, for the Party's sake, for the people's sake, for God's sake — but Bakr was adamant. Saddam denied he was worthy to take on such a role, but Bakr pleaded with him.

Urged now by the Regional and National Commands to step into the presidency, Saddam Hussein implored Bakr "to continue as head of state, but without bearing any of the exhausting responsibilities: he, Saddam Hussein, was willing to bear these himself." But Bakr wouldn't hear of such a thing: "he was not interested in the trappings of power." Thus it was that Saddam Hussein agreed "to assume complete responsibility." But only after a Revolution Command Council meeting over which he presided had unanimously voted for him to become the next president. In a stirring speech to the people, on July 17, 1979, he prophetically defined the course he would chart over the coming years:

Our duty is to strive for justice and to struggle against oppression. We will not accept that any comrade in our Party, or any member of the people, be humiliated. We will overcome tyranny in all its forms; we will safeguard justice when called on to do so. Power is not wielded for self-satisfaction; it is a burden we carry in order to translate principles into reality in the service of the people, safeguarding the nation and eradicating injustice.

There must be a place where you can rent these inauguration speeches.

Half the Revolution Command Council might have thought twice about voting for Saddam, if he'd told them they'd be dead within a week for "plotting against him." Indeed, plots against Saddam became the theme of the book from here on. They ranged from plots hatched by close friends and relatives, through plots hatched by countries with good people and bad leaders (Iran, Syria, Turkey, Egypt, etc.), to plots hatched by countries with bad people and bad leaders (Britain, the United States), and plots hatched by thoroughly Satanic entities (Israel). Neither Fuad Matar nor Saddam could even bring himself to write or utter the name Israel, referring to it only as the "Zionist entity." Like a space alien.

The rest of the book's eight chapters was an astounding morass of twaddle — ideological twaddle, of course — in which neither author nor subject appeared capable of telling the truth or addressing any issue directly. I wondered if Fuad Matar had brainwashed himself (or had assistance) to believe the tripe he wrote, then realized he couldn't have. Had he truly believed it, he wouldn't have required the arsenal of tautologies, euphemisms, gluey metaphors, and solipsisms that were his stock in trade. He wouldn't have needed to set Ahmad Hassan Bakr up as an animated billboard for doddering senility, watering his grand-children and playing with his petunias, if Bakr had harbored any intentions of stepping down. Nor would we have needed the telegram from tongue-tied Michel Aflaq congratulating Bakr on setting an example to the world's doddering dictators by retiring. Nor the two pages of Saddam as Mark Anthony coming not to bury Bakr but to urge him to stay in office.

At least we know why Saddam didn't tell the truth: he had ideological reasons. Anyone wishing to truly, fully, wholly grasp the reasons why Iraq's ideology could never agree with Iran's ideology, no matter if the stars fell from the sky and the earth was rent asunder, might wish to consult Fuad Matar's thirty-page disquisition on this fascinating topic in the chapter called "A Difficult Co-existence and a Certain War."

The style of Muslim Iraqi leadership, it must be said, was established back in the eighth century, just after Baghdad was founded. Even the historic, precedent-setting relationship between Saddam and Bakr is mirrored in the strange antagonism that invariably existed between sultans and caliphs.

It's worth quoting from the will of Caliph al-Mansūr, founder of Baghdad, to his son al-Mahdi, and delivered when he fell ill on his way to the Hijaz in the Islamic year 158 AH:

> Safeguard Muhammed and his message in his nation, then God will protect you and look after your interests.
>
> Ensure that the outposts are heavily manned, secure the borders and protect the roads and homes of the people; provide the people with the services that they need and ward off harm; always have money in store and make sure the treasury is full, for you know not what evil fate holds in store for you each day; recruit as many men and soldiers as you can.
>
> Never put off today's tasks until tomorrow, otherwise matters will accumulate and be lost; resolve each matter as it comes up, use your judgement and set your mind to it; have men awake at night so you may know what will happen during the day, and during the day so you may know what will happen at night.
>
> Take the initiative yourself; do not go beyond the bounds of morality. Think the best of people — yet think the worst of your appointed governors and secretaries; be always alert. Be wary of he who seeks your constant company, yet lend an ear to your people. Arbitrate in conflicts and appoint active deputies who will not be distracted.
>
> My son, do not sleep, beware of sleep. Your father has not slept since he inherited the caliphate; he never shut an eye but his heart was awake.
>
> This is my testament to you; may God protect you.[10]

Words to live by.

THE FIRST SADDAM

Major Tariq al-Jazzar was not the sort of person you want to see first thing in the morning. I had him knocking at my door just after 7:00 a.m. Through the spyhole's convex bubble, he resembled an inquisitive toad perched on a water-buffalo's bum.

"*Salaam aleikum.*"

"*Aleikum Wa'salaam*, Meesta Bol . . ."

The interview's time had been rearranged — probably for ideological reasons — and was to take place immediately.

"O, for Chr — I'll be right down."

Now, I admit, the previous evening, I had given the mini-bar a fearful rifling. But it was for Ahmed's sake — part celebration (the 007 Bar was allegedly still in business) and part consolation (his supervisor told him not to even think of promotion until the year 2020) — so we had to compare the contents of his mini-bar with those of mine, after we were down to the Campari with Bailey's Irish and grapefruit juice stage. And, once again reduced to that sorry predicament with his refrigerated thief, despite the angry thrashing we gave it — although, it must be said, establishing beyond all doubt and for posterity that the Al Rashid's mini-bars were, to the best of our knowledge, stocked identically — we felt it necessary, nay *imperative*, to summon up from Room Service a bottle of the five-star VSOP brandy from Turkmenistan advertised in a supplement to the regular menu only supplied to infidels or those who had proved themselves unquestionably to be deeply lapsed Muslims. I think Ahmed received his on checking in.

While the French cognac was $239.00 a bottle, the Turkmenistani brandy seemed a bargain at $5.95 for the same 750 ml. Ahmed and I, having sampled eight miniatures of the French cognac already, wagered that, poured from those same miniatures, Turkmenistan's unjustly uncelebrated product would prove all but indistinguishable from Remy Martin's grotesquely overpriced hooch.

We were very wrong about this.

Called something like Gnyud! — which evidently meant "bee's nectar" — it was supplied in a bottle that warranted the exclamation mark. There was something medicinal about it; there was also something wrong with it: under the ersatz lead wrapper around its top, we discovered not a cork, not a cap, but a plug made from some black, glass-like substance that appeared to have been sealed in under conditions of fierce heat, since part of it had melted around the rim of the bottle and was now fused to it.

"Iss vor sanidary reason," replied the Room Service waiter, when summoned back to deal with this stopper.

"We thought, besides explaining it, you might also be able to open it. . . . Might you?"

"Oben?"

"'Lah, fellow!" Ahmed had the hiccups — never a good sign. "Juss bloody-the . . . Hicket!"

"Pardonne, sir?"

"Jus' obe — Hicket!"

"Open it, is all he's really saying. 'Hicket' is a muscular spasm."

The waiter's mouth moved silently, trying various positions before saying, "Mowse-inna baff-um?"

"There's no mouse in the bathroom," I reassured him. "It's a very small, teeny-weeny, likkle —"

"'Lah! Good-sir, jus' ben-oh . . . oben i — Hicket!"

"—tapir."

"Huh? Tay beer? You like beer now?"

"Want a beer, Ahmed? No, I don't think so, but thanks for the offer. Any chance you can open the brandistan, though?"

"Oben?"

At this moment the television magically turned itself on. Many thousands of tanks were sweeping across the desert sands to a martial soundtrack.

The waiter was standing to attention, I observed, the brandy bottle held like a bizarre little rifle.

"Hicket."

"What is this, any idea?" I asked the waiter.

His eyes rolled down to tell mine to pay attention. Who should be standing on a dune, in military uniform, his arm a V-bracket of salute, his beret curved like some neat and slinky little creature upon his head, of course: Saddam Hussein! The tanks were firing now, their quivering barrels contracting and expanding, emitting tiny puffs of smoke. I couldn't see anyone firing back.

"What happened? The Iranians again?"

The waiter shook his head almost imperceptibly.

"The Is— Zionist entity?"

Nope.

"Turks? Syrians? Americans? Saudis? Martians?"

None of the above. It was just the nightly sign-off from your friendly local state-controlled information outlet.

"Hicket."

"You always stand to attention when . . . er . . . *he* comes on?"

"Yes, I am do," replied the waiter, at ease again.

"Oh. That's nice. Nice to have a routine, eh?"

"Ah, root een."

He then gave the bottle a mighty crack against the wall. Neither appeared to suffer much, but the stopper now rattled in the bottle's neck — in fact, it would have fallen out if upended. At least there was no mystery to the need for it to be welded in.

"Thanks. Want to join us? You're welcome to . . ."

The waiter looked from Ahmed to me and back, his face saying I'd rather slit my throat than put up with you two fiends for another minute.

"Hicket."

When we were alone once more, we made a funnel from the cover of *Iraq: The Tourist's Paradise* and carefully poured the brandy from Turkmenistan into four empty Remy Martin miniatures. Then we poured the miniatures into the fishbowl balloon glasses that came with the brandy. In color, it did not quite match the French cognac. It was paler, and with the grayish froth that began materializing on its surface, it looked exactly like urine.

"Remember, taste not color. Don't be put off by the color. That's cheating."

I knocked back the entire glassful. So did Ahmed. I heard him swallow when I did.

"Mmmm!"

The initial impression was of watery, mead-like honey, with a slight fizzing effect in it. However, this was immediately followed by a second column of something much like 180-proof, phenol-flavored paint-stripper, which roared around the mouth and plunged down the throat as if alight.

"Wahahaa-aaah-aah!"

We both dived at the mini-bar and ripped open bottles of juice — any juice — and gargled with their contents, beating the floor with our fists.

"Oh, man! Wh —"

Curiously, though, extinguished by the juice, the final effect was of fermented oatmeal that glowed in waves throbbing out from the stomach until you felt it in your fingertips and toes.

"Not-same this for Frenge bandi."

"No . . . more of a hydrogen warhead nose to it . . . bouquet of wet haystacks . . . some tanin . . . napalm."

"Bud-nod bad, um? Might wizz joos-mixing, then-or — Hicket."

The label showed a group of prosperous medieval serfs sitting with enormous ornate schooners in their hands on a semi-circular bench beneath a parody of a tree. On this tree was a hornet's nest larger than any two of the serfs, and from a hole in the nest came a swarm of hornets so dense they all but occluded the novel headwear these men clearly owned. The message? Drink enough Gnyud! and hornets won't bother you either, I assume. It was a Projuct of Tercmani Alkhool Colecttive, Bsg.

"What's Bsg?"

We finished the bottle at around 4:00 a.m.

It will thus be conceded that, three hours later, I was not irreproachably sober. Nor was I soothingly drunk. My skull had been replaced with a thick, very sensitive membrane that appeared to be playing squash with my heart. With every heavy sluggish beat, the membrane throbbed a second later — that's when I noticed that it had been coated on the interior, especially near the sides and forehead, with boiling tar. I was amazed I could stay inside this head.

The best thing for it would be to take a couple of aspirin, have a shower, and then pop over to interview the ex-Chief Torturer of Baghdad.

This had to be a bad dream, a very bad dream. And so it was. When

I awoke, the sun was shining, the phone was singing, and I felt — exactly as I had fifteen minutes earlier. Like shit.

"Meesta Bol? You muzz gumb down now."

"I'm just running out the door. Did they fix the elevators yet?"

"Elligators nod broblem."

"Oh . . . there was a minute ago . . . hold on."

I tipped out my toilet bag searching for an Anacin packet I'd seen there. When? Five years ago? And wasn't it another toilet bag? Thought was not possible, though . . . Thought not possible, not possible — don't even try . . . It became a maddening little mantra. Inside an envelope from the fourteenth century, or earlier, I found five blue pills, a bluish spansule, two tiny white pills, and one very large, somewhat eroded, grayish horse tablet. None looked familiar, but they could only be either antibiotics, airplane sedatives, or painkillers. I'd have known if anything interesting was there. Telling myself the mixture would almost certainly inter-react until it manufactured a near magical psycho-physical rejuvenator, energizer, analgesic, and super multi-vitamin, I threw them into my mouth and swallowed the lot with shower water.

Two minutes.

Hair. Teeth. Eye bleach. Aftershave.

Three minutes.

Clothes: no problem here. The disco banker's suit I'd had made for $35 in Cairo by the Russian ambassador's tailor. Or so he claimed. Apart from the flared pants I hadn't requested, it did look like something Brezhnev would have owned. In 1953. Flared pants were still cool in Baghdad, though. Saddam probably had a pair on right now.

Five minutes.

Notes: where were they? Ah, yes, scribbled on the back of the infidel's Room Service menu supplement.

Wifl Hm-ttlT: what had I meant by that?

I stubbed my toe on the bed's baseboard, then hopped back onto some small hard objects. Looking down, I discovered three intact miniatures: a gin and two vodkas. Good ones, too.

It's a very bad idea to believe that hair of the dog stuff: you wake up thirty years later in Emergency with people shaking their heads over you. But, on the other hand, it works — provided you just keep on drinking all day. Then all week. Thank God the government in its mercy taxes the stuff beyond reach, I was muttering, as I poured all three little bottles at once into a glass that, unwashed in living memory, could have served five old Croatians as a toothbrush holder and spitoon. Prune Nectar, little stir with forefinger, and down she goes. And up she comes again — or nearly. Only superhuman muscle control allowed me to halt its upward progress around mid-neck, then, breathing calmly, like a monk out gardening, coax it slowly back down until I felt it cascade into the lake of sulfur, bile, and undigested tarmac that hung where my stomach had once been.

Ten minutes.

The phone trilled.

"I've already left, so don't waste your current . . ."

Okay. Mirror: Hmm . . . It's Slobodan Draculic, Assistant Under-Secretary to the Deputy Minister of Serbian Nut, Bolt & Glue Industries. I could just waltz right on over to take up my post as Special Adviser on Democratic Ideology.

One thing about flared pants, I recalled, is that you're better off just spray-painting your legs if they're too short. If they're really short, though, say, just below the knee, it's a feature. These were just an inch too short, so they looked — like flared pants that were an inch too short. Like flared pants only a bagperson or an escaped lunatic would wear.

Twelve minutes.

Tape recorder. Batteries. Pen. Another pen. Pencil. Cigarettes.

Boy! That cocktail was doing some good, against all odds.

Twenty minutes.

I sat serenely on the bed smoking a second cigarette and staring at my "notes": GGsj — RevCon(1963)sy/hhjL/Plubb.

That was clear enough. Hadn't he known the '63 coup would occur? If not, why not? Seeing as he was such a big shot . . . Well, that would be rephrased.

A horse galloped across the outside of my door.

My how time flies. A worm of toothpaste squeezed across the tongue . . .

"You can't expect me to wake up at 7:00 a.m. and be ready to leave by — er, by 8:20, can you?"

"Djew zay djew gumb down," groaned Major al-Jazzar.

"So? They'll shoot you, not me, ha-hah!"

Just as you don't make jokes about having bombs in your baggage while going through an airport security check anymore (no one laughs, and you get a $50,000 fine), you don't make jokes about people getting shot in Iraq. People get shot for nothing there — the lucky ones, that is. If the planets are wrong that day you get a bottle broken up your ass instead — for nothing. If you can get shot for nothing, you can get shot for *anything*.

"Sorry. I didn't mean that. Really. I'll make them shoot me, too."

The Major, however, only found other people's potential torments funny — not his own.

"Idd okay," he pronounced. "We nod dlate."

"Well, why are we hurrying if we not late?"

"Draffig bad."

"Oh. Can't you just switch the siren on?"

"Zyronon?"

It sounded like a tranquilizer.

The back seat of al-Jazzar's Toyota Ideologue Sedan — or whatever his locomotive of a car was named — felt unnaturally springy. So did I. There was a strange, not unpleasant, sensation where my spine plugged into my brain. A bit like an Alka-Seltzer that was slowly dissolving there. I was quite perky. In fact, for someone who was about to demand a refund on the day an hour or so earlier, I was in supernaturally fine shape. For an overcast day, the sun was shining very brightly, too.

"Put the radio on, al . . . Jazzar's a cool name, isn't it? No, really. Not Iraqi, is it? Where'd you get it? I wouldn't mind picking up one for myself —"

Maybe I should shut up, I suddenly decided. Baghdad might break with all this good cheer in one happy little bundle. It looked quite cheerful already, though. Actually, it was quite an attractive city. Flowers, trees, cars — cheerful cars: lots of stickers and furry dangling dice. The people looked great, too. The women, oh man! The women looked fabulous!

It was then I recalled deciding that the women looked like shit, but the men looked fabulous. Maybe there were a totally different batch of people out today? Or maybe I was someone else. I felt much more like someone else, now I dwelt on it.

You'll never guess what, I could have been saying aloud. I took all these pills for a headache earlier on, and — you won't believe this — but one of them, the big grayish one, was, in fact, some Ecstasy I was given a year ago and assumed I'd lost. Harmless enough if you're flopping about a technodrome in Northern Ontario with five hundred other dope fiends, I suppose. But not precisely what you want to experiment with in Baghdad on your way to meet the Butcher, I mean, the Bakr, Bresident . . .

On LSD, you could probably bank on working out your karma in another life, by now. No calming technique I know would have helped on the back seat of the Secret Service sedan rolling inexorably toward the Presidential Palace, driven by three hundred pounds of serial-killing homosexual sadist. But on E, it was kinda fun.

I couldn't think of anyone on earth I'd rather be going to see than President Saddam Hussein, Leader of the Revolution Command Council, Commander-in-Chief of the Armed Forces, Director of State Torture Planning, handy with a needle and thread, too, and not a bad dancer. I was in heaven. So were the eight people we knew he'd killed personally, along with the 8,000-odd he'd killed impersonally, and then the 1.5 million or so he'd indirectly killed because he had ideological problems with Ayatollah Khomeini. Everyone had ideological problems with the Ayatollah Khomeini, but only Saddam Hussein, King of Crisis Management, Assumer of Complete Responsibility, The Bathrobe Ba'athist, had felt it worth 1.5 million lives and some $20 billion.

No one's all bad, I told myself — or someone did. You have to find the good in everyone, and just ignore the rest.

I hadn't realized that the radio was on, but it explained the blizzard of crackling static within which Tarzan was yodeling Gaelic laments.

"We gumb now Bresideschal Balace," moaned Major al-Jazzar.

Instantly, with a chilling and inexplicable certainty, I knew he would be dead from prostate cancer within the year. Don't ask me how. I haven't checked it out, but there's no doubt in my mind to this day.

I didn't feel high anymore, either — in the giddy sense. But I felt clear. Very clear.

At the gates I saw no signs of heavy military protection. But it was there. As soon as we pulled up soldiers appeared from nowhere, and in the landscaped grounds behind, there stirred many more.

"Owd car now, you," said al-Jazzar.

An officer, who was dressed like a million dollars of menace, asked for my papers, staring unblinkingly into my eyes. Gaddafi had guys like this around him, too; if you really wanted to make their day, you wore mirrored shades. They were trained to detect retinal movements that betrayed ill intentions. I wondered what mine betrayed.

Realizing he wouldn't want to see my "notes," I discovered I had no other "papers." What would Saddam have done in a situation like this?

"They're at the Al Rashid. The hotel likes to keep them in its safe. So they're safe. Are puns as popular with Arabic speakers as they are with, say, Italians?"

"Not really," the officer replied, thoughtfully. "Arabic lends itself far more to assonance and onomatopoeia. In classical Arabic you will find puns."

"Really? Terribly kind of you to point that out."

He saluted. So did I. The gates lurched open. I was clearly no threat to the state. Pity. I hopped back in and the car just cruised right on through. Then we stopped, as the gates were still locking electronically.

"Owd, you. Zerge, okay?"

"Sure."

I got out again, as two men felt every fold and crevice of my flesh and clothing. It was quite pleasant. And the gardens were overwhelmingly sumptuous, seething with green life, pulsing colored blotches, and lush, ferny grass. Yet they also looked artificial, and there was this odd sense of humming activity beneath the ground — as if this showroom layer of nature's life-enhancing talents were merely the deceptive roof for a warren of death-dealing androids. I was next gently groomed with a metal detector, tugged in a circle until I faced the Presidential Palace. Apart from the copper-green semi-dome of a UFO on its roof, the building could have been the Stalin Institute of Ideology & Machine tool-making, gussied up for a red-letter day. There was a theme of rectangles — three of them — then forty-odd windows, and a drive-in porch. All rectangles. On the roof, in front of the UFO dome, stood a spindly flagpole whose flag hung heavily limp as if soaked in grease.

Under the porch, I enjoyed another search just like the previous one. Then we were inside.

The sudden enclosure in dead concrete was tangible. I was no longer surrounded by life; instead, a deathly stillness hung everywhere. Major al-Jazzar did not come in: his status ended at the porch, and he seemed all at once a little, pathetic, confused man. A man who'd done many awful things, but in a dream. He was asleep, sound asleep. The men who beckoned and questioned and searched now were similarly like sleep-walkers. The farther you got into the labyrinth, the less life there was. These men enjoyed the privileges and perquisites of Roman courtiers — they could have more or less anything they wanted — but a pall of lassitude clung to their hearts, weighing them down. There was no life here. There wasn't much in Ancient Rome, either. And why would I expect to find life in the mission control from whence so much death was issued out?

And get a load of Saddam's tastes for interior decor! It made me want to dance a jig. He'd been in here now for eleven years — exactly the same period of time as he'd been out before assuming complete respon-sibility — and the joint had most definitely been remade in his image. He was a man of simple, straightforward tastes, ostensibly: as long as it was made of marble, or gold, or gilt. Lots of mirrors, though — but these seemed to serve an alternative, more pragmatic purpose. If the whole place could speak, it would only know one thing: I am President Saddam Hussein! King of Crisis Management! Look upon my works, ye mighty, and at least be impressed by the amount of money at my disposal . . . Elvis had better taste, but Graceland and the Baghdad Lair both had "Poor Boy Makes Good" writ large across their portals.

Besides being hidden watchposts, the mirrors served to confuse a stranger. You wouldn't find your way around this place easily if you didn't already know it. One corridor was entirely sealed off by a wall of plate glass and steel, with just one small door through it. On the far side were lab technicians in white coats and lead-shield aprons.

Jeez! I nearly laughed. After six metal detectors, I was now going to be X-rayed. The machine resembled an abandoned early prototype for the Stargate.

"You can walk through now," said an automaton. "Please pause on the yellow circle until I ask you to move on . . ."

"Those lead aprons never inspire confidence in the safety of these things, do they?" I asked. "You come with me, hmm?"

Polite laughter, then: "The lead apron inspires confidence in me: that's why I'm wearing it."

The item looked like his burden of guilt, too. His millstone.

If you try, you can feel X-rays. And I didn't need to try. It was like a billion microscopic threads of feathery dental floss raining through my cells. I'd be green and glowing when I walked out.

"Please to sit here," a Republican Guardsman requested.

We'd walked down a few short, stumpy corridors, left, right, left again, and then through towering gilded double doors leading into a tiny waiting room: four wingback chairs, a glass coffee table with magazines piled neatly in each of four corners. On the walls: some small watercolors of Arab life, and to the right of a towering single door, a six-foot portrait of Saddam as Lord of the Air. Military dress uniform, five hundred medals and ribbons, gilded silver scabbard, tassels, cap with an acroterion of what resembled molded cherubs on it, and behind, clouds — just clouds, and the high blue air, which is endless, and nowhere.

It was supposed to be daunting, one assumes, or at least impressive. Except it wasn't. It was the kind of thing some retired old queen of a choreographer would have hanging in his boudoir — and even he wouldn't take it that seriously. "Camp" was the word that sprang to mind.

I sat, as I've sat in countless waiting rooms before, waiting. We're all waiters. I felt I was waiting to see a dentist.

If there had been a clock, it would have been ticking. I had half a mind to walk out: I'm a busy man, I can't sit waiting while you're fiddling with the destiny of the Arab World. You're not the only one whose time isn't meaningless . . .

The inner door opened noiselessly, revealing a butler-like figure in white bolero jacket.

The dentist will see you now. "The President is waiting, follow me."

"Thanks." *Will it hurt?*

He was sitting behind the kind of gilt-shanked baroque desk that looks as if it will start cantering about the room whinnying at any moment.

It looked less like an office than an exhibit. The Baroque Room: You will notice the Gothic touches coming in during this period, but the overall effect is still one of appalling vulgarity and the most degraded parvenu ostentation . . .

If you want people to think you're working, pal, I thought, then put something on the desk. There was only the kind of telephone Mae West would have favored: big, white, lots of gold. He didn't look up as I was ushered in, but he had no particular reason to be looking down — unless he was as stoned as I now felt and found the swirling effect of his marble desktop far more intriguing than he'd previously ever realized it to be. There was a chair facing the desk, yet it seemed oddly small — probably because his was preternaturally large and also squatting on a slightly raised dais. Did lacking the odd few inches of airspace really drive men to these lengths?

When he looked up it was directly into my eyes, clearly calculated to be that way too, but the shock hit like a column of iced mercury pumped up the spine. He didn't blink, either. He didn't stand, and when I reached out my hand, paused a beat before extending a limp, dry, cool dead appendage. It could have been rubber.

I looked back at the eyes and realized what was most unnerving about them was that there was nobody behind them. Not the emptiness of peace you see in the yogi or rimpoche's eyes, this was the total absence of something most people possess in varying degrees on varying days. Life? No, it was much more than the deadness of the palace beyond. It was a missing part and a part as crucial as a head or limbs — probably the part we used to call the "soul."

It was not a pleasant experience, because you can't *not* have a soul. Like a black hole, his soul must have imploded under the weight of its own darkness and, though there, was invisible, gave out nothing, and viewed all in terms of mere utility.

I was of no use to him, it was clear.

"Please be seated," said a man I hadn't even noticed.

He'd been designed that way, too. His brown suit matched the mahogany paneling behind him, and his pallor was as gray as the air. I wondered if the T. S. Eliot spectacles were a recent European purchase, or an heirloom from some bookworm uncle. "Court Scribe" was his label.

"The President regrets to say that he can only give you twenty minutes of his time today. If you wish, we can try to schedule another appointment."

Saddam nodded, still staring, to confirm — what? Presumably, he had no idea.

"Thank you. Ask the President, please, what he would personally like to see achieved by this Summit."

The answer was a crock of shit. I felt like snapping my fingers in front of those dry, dead eyes and telling him to cut the crap — who did he think he was dealing with here? *The New York Times?* This was *Gandalf's Garden*, pal, and we don't print that tripe. We print other tripe. And sometimes, if we can't get it together, hey! we don't even bother to print the magazine at all.

I had the urge to start giggling, and my mind went utterly blank. I had to get out the menu supplement. I wonder if Saddam had ever tried Turkmenistan's finest brandy. He looked as if he'd tried everyone else's.

Hgl--link to MM/poli=f.

Now, what did *that* mean?

"I want to get some personality into this piece," I said, one scribe to another. "You know, some color . . ." Other than brown, that is. "Could you ask the President what —" I hadn't even noticed THE NECKTIE until now. It was a two-foot catastrophe of dominos repeated every three inches diagonally. I thought I'd burst into pulsating blobs of giggling ectoplasm, flop all over the floor and ceiling. "What he does with those few moments of truly free time he gets. If he ever gets them. You know, does he golf?"

"Cough?" inquired the Scribe.

"Not much of a hobby . . . er, no . . . what I mean is . . . books. What does he read? Does he read? Well, obviously he does read. But for pleasure . . ." I felt I'd asked how frequently he masturbated, judging by the response. "And movies? What about movies? Does he —"

"I enjoy verr mudge Godfader moofy," Saddam suddenly announced, in a sort of eminently reasonable voice.

"Marlon Brando, er . . . that one?"

"Yejd, Marclon Brundo. Verr fine agtor."

Maybe I should let Marlon know?

"That's your *favorite* film, is it?"

"Yejd, I wodge many time . . . widge vamily andt vrenn."

Only the one friend, is there? Yipes! I hoped I wasn't mumbling. How could he say *The Godfather* was his favorite film? How can I ask him if he identifies with the main characters?

"What is it that, er —" turns your crank? No. "Does it translate to your experience — I mean as an Arab — of the world. Or is it too American?"

The English wasn't that good: this needed a little scribal assistance.

"The President says he likes the action and the characters. And people are the same all over the world . . ."

"So true. I heard that the President's wife works as the vice principal of a school, and wh —"

"Prizipal," Saddam butted in, somewhat indignantly. "She wass promoded to prizipal on hair own merde —"

"Merit," the Scribe hastily added.

"Yejd. Bud now no longers vorking . . . too mudge rezpondabliss —"

"Responsibilities . . . Responsibility. She now has too many duties of state to be able to work."

You must miss that extra salary — it's tough, I know . . .

"Right."

Saddam muttered something, his voice like crumpling cellophane.

"The President would prefer it if you asked him about political matters only. His personal life is very precious to him."

So's mine.

"Does he . . . er, does he see himself as the second Nasser?"

Saddam jumped in angrily: "No! I am first Saddam!"

It was downhill from there on. I heard the same old grandiose generalities and barefaced lies that I'd been reading in Fuad Matar's book. It's really not worth talking to these people. They don't talk. They give talks. And they won't talk about the things it's impossible (for ideological reasons) to lie about: life, love, children, hopes, fears, mortality.

As far as I was concerned, Saddam could rot in his Arab paradise. I wasn't coming back — unless invited, of course. Outside, it felt clean again. The thing about E, though, is that it doesn't last very long. I could feel the Brandistan headscrew beginning to tighten again, and it seemed to be approaching the cocktail hour . . .

10:15 a.m! Surely not! I tapped my wristwatch, then listened for the beat of life.

"Izz gud wid Bresident Saddam?" asked Major al-Jazzar, humbly now, docile and little — at 300 pounds.

"You want the truth?"

"Yesje, trood."

"It was really fucking shitty."

"Hah! Vah king's jitty! Gud, hahah! Go Razjid hottel?"

"Drive on, James."

PART TWO

The Purgation
1991

Misrule, you see, has caused the world to be malevolent.
— DANTE, *Purgatorio*

"Defending democracy" . . . sounds fine; but to defend democracy
by military means, one must be militarily efficient, and one cannot
become militarily efficient without centralizing power, setting up a
tyranny, imposing some form of conscription or slavery to the state.
In other words the military defence of democracy in contemporary
circumstances entails the abolition of democracy even before war starts.
— ALDOUS HUXLEY, *Letters of Aldous Huxley* (1936)

To be men not destroyers.
— EZRA POUND, *Notes for Cantos* CXVII *et seq.*

THE EMIR'S TIMEX

Saddam wasn't very prime-time-newsworthy when I met him in May. His promotion from local nuisance to global Supervillain only occurred after August 1990. But this isn't why my interview with him seems somewhat insubstantial. In fact, I was considering reducing it to something like, "He said nothing worth recording . . .," or "I won't waste your time with his lies, bullshit, and waffle. . . ." I wish someone had done that with Hitler. But even George Orwell in his 1940 review of *Mein Kampf* wrote: "I should like to put it on record that I have never been able to dislike Hitler. One feels, as with Napoleon, that he is fighting against destiny, that he *can't* win, and yet that he somehow deserves to."[1] Much as I disapproved of Washington's demonization of Saddam, I wasn't about to take sides. Yet as I completed my book on Egypt back in the safety of Toronto I had the sense that something very wrong was about to go down over there in that part of the world where, mentally, I spent most of my days.

It was now January 19, 1991. Saddam had taken a leaf from Don Vito Corleone's book: the Kuwaitis, like the Tataglia family, were encroaching on his turf — *what's a guy gonna do?* He'd tried a meeting of the clans — several meetings, in fact — but the al-Sabahs were an arrogant bunch. They'd walked out of the last talk, Saddam claimed.

This had been held in Jeddah on August 1, 1990, between Izzat Ibrahim, then the Iraqi number two, and Prince Saad, Kuwait's prime minister, who had even optimistically announced the day before that he was "looking forward with open heart to the meeting with my brother Izzat Ibrahim, the leader of the Iraqi delegation. This is a passing crisis."[2]

He was right about the "crisis" part.

Like Don Corleone, Saddam also believed in the art of subtle persuasion. Of course, neither Prince Saad nor Sheikh Jaber, the emir of Kuwait, awoke to find himself staring into the glazed, doleful eyes of a $5 million racehorse, minus its body (and both men owned one), but there *were* 100,000 Iraqi troops encamped near the emirate's border and showing no signs of intending to leave. The emir demonstrated his confidence in Prince Saad's abilities and the imminent passing of this crisis by fleeing to the Saudi Arabian hill resort of Taif, along with the $2 billion he usually kept in Kuwait City banks for pocket money. The rest of the family's $100 billion stash was in a money bin far, far away.

I once met Sheikh Jaber. He sold me a glossy picture book about Kuwait, which I'd noticed on his desk and coveted, for $35, and claimed not to be able to "locate" any more U.S. currency to give me change for my $40. I said I'd take his wristwatch instead: it was a $20 Timex, a kid's watch. You don't amass $100 billion through self-indulgence and philanthropy, however. Like Scrooge McDuck, he went to enormous lengths to find five bucks in assorted international change rather than part with a ten-year-old Timex.

Now he was babbling on about preferring to see Iraq beaten and punished, even if it meant that Kuwait City was destroyed in the process: "We can build it again." He'd probably be even richer if pride weren't his Achilles' heel — but then so would quite a number of Arabs. When I'd asked him how he would characterize his nation's foreign policy (if it had one), he replied that the guiding principle behind "this sort of thing" was that Kuwait had as neighbors the three "nastiest countries on earth."

It was easy to understand why Sheikh Jaber had problems with Iraq and Iran, but what, you may well ask, had *Saudi Arabia* done to earn his scornful disapproval? In fact, it was something he viewed as equal in wickedness to any military invasion or threat to rape, pillage, and raze Kuwait City: once, at the start of a Gulf Co-operation Council conference, Saudi monarch King Fahd *had slept in late and kept him waiting*. The emir was an early riser.

I didn't want to give the impression that I thought he was strolling a one-way street toward the cuckoo lounge, so I told him — quite truthfully — that I'd once changed doctors after a similar outrage: this quack had a Mercedes and two mortgages to pay for, so he tended to overbook patients just in case a few no-shows set his five-year economic plan back a few minutes. Of course, my time wasn't as valuable as his, but I still saw no reason to be stuck for an hour reading *Today's Parent* in an overheated room that looked increasingly like a Crimean TB ward. However, I could tell that this sort of thing had never happened to Sheikh Jaber.

"Your *doctor?*" he kept saying, managing to make the word sound like *bumboy*.

The emir's time, of course, was worth even more than Dr. Katz's, and if King Fahd's snooze had relegated Saudi Arabia to pariah state, I wondered what Saddam's looting bender in Kuwait City was doing for Iraq in the eyes of Kuwaiti foreign policy. Sheikh Jaber had perhaps decreed that Iraqis would be treated badly by Kuwaitis at every possible opportunity for the next five thousand years.

They are tough buggers, too, the al-Sabahs. Don't ever hijack an airplane to or from Kuwait City: the government won't negotiate with you. It was this trait that first tipped me to the startling discovery that Sheikh Jaber and Margaret Thatcher were one and the same person: just sketch a shiny little goatee on Maggie, deck her out in biblical clothes, and — *va-voom!* — you've got your emir. Once during a hostage-taking incident in Kuwait, the hijackers, who'd begun by demanding $5 million cash, new pilots, gas, Chivas Regal, and so on, in exchange for a pregnant hostage, found themselves reduced to demanding a cheese sandwich in exchange for total surrender. This, too, was refused. They settled for a promise that they wouldn't be executed, and they weren't. They were sentenced to 170 years each in jail. When Terry Waite was trying to negotiate their release in exchange for some CIA agents in Beirut who claimed they were journalists, the Kuwaitis refused his request for a visa. What sort of person could refuse cuddly, noble Terry Waite a visa?

Answer: The sort of person who has $100 billion and doesn't particularly care what the Archbishop of Canterbury thinks of him.

Thus, most of my Arab friends thought invading Kuwait an excellent idea, and a number also felt that executing the al-Sabahs — all two thousand of them — would top off such an adventure perfectly. The phrase most often employed to describe Kuwaitis is best translated as *lazy containers of excrement*. They are not liked. But they don't care.

Kuwait is run on something much like the ancient Athenian model of democracy: that is, equal rights have to stop somewhere. And they do: with verifiably authentic Kuwaitis. Although the concept of work — "working *for* someone" — as a sin has not been enshrined in any constitution, as it has in Libya (where it is illegal for Libyans to work), Kuwaitis nonetheless believe in this concept fervently, piously adhering to its austere strictures in their daily lives. Most Libyans, of course, have a private business and an office, where they can sit all morning sipping tea or coffee, smoking cigarettes, and reading the newspaper without fear of interruption. The business of Libya is not business, it's drinking tea or coffee. The business of Kuwait is not business, either. It's changing money. (Because they're cash rich, paid in U.S. dollars for their oil, they must remain vigilant of currency shifts, since these can result in enormous losses in profits.) Having an office for a company whose business is drinking tea or coffee is considered wasteful in the emirate, largely because rents in Kuwait City are among the highest on earth, and indeed it contains, per capita, the highest concentration of wealth on the planet. Whereas there are poor Saudis, there are no poor Kuwaitis (it may be illegal). Of course, it's all relative: there are al-Sabahs who are barely worth $20 million — and their marriage prospects within the upper middle class are negligible, limited to hunchbacks and 400-pounders. But even if you've only got a pitiful $20 million, you're not about to do your own laundry or wash up or file paper or answer the phone, are you?

This is where other Arabs and non-Arab Muslims come in. The pyramid of Kuwaiti society is more or less like this: Kuwaitis sit in custom-built private Lear Jets half a mile above the apex; Palestinians run all the successful businesses and would own them, too, were it not illegal — they must have a Kuwaiti partner — then middle management is handled by Egyptians, Syrians, and the like; Pakistanis and Muslim Indians, forming the pyramid's base, collect garbage and polish the marble; and finally, below ground level, Philippinas cook, clean, do dishes, get raped by the males of the house, and look after the kids. They seem to get beaten up a fair bit, too. I'm not suggesting they don't mind being raped, but the only complaints you regularly hear about involve getting beaten up. Sometimes they get raped *then* beaten up. (This isn't in their job description.) A son will rape them, then beat them up to show them that the raping business was clearly their fault: if they hadn't been there, he wouldn't have wanted to rape them, so *obviously* it was their fault (the courts look favorably upon this defense). A virile father will do this, too. But the Philippinas get beaten up quite frequently by the women of the house, the harem, as well, for being such sluts that no male is safe from their evil allurements. For their part, the Philippinas would probably complain to the authorities a bit more often if the authorities didn't respond by throwing them in jail and deporting them back to the slums of Manila.

I read of a case recently where the authorities simply had the girl whipped, then taken back to her employers, who beat her up for neglecting her duties and trying to cause trouble. She complained about this beating, too, and was publicly whipped again, then returned to her employers, whose patience had clearly been strained to its limits by her shocking behavior. So they killed her and left her body out in the desert for jackals to eat.

All in all, this is pretty faithful to the original Greek model for democracy, in which, for example, slaves obviously couldn't be given a vote without wrecking the whole concept of slavery. Likewise, women . . .

An Egyptian friend of mine once worked as a file clerk in Kuwait. Before this, he'd been indifferent to the subject of Kuwaitis whenever it arose. After, however, if the subject came up, he would say about the worst thing you can say: that no words described his loathing.

"I live in air-conditioned box," he told me, describing his life in Kuwait City. "I drive to work in air-conditioned box. I work in air-conditioned box. I come home to air-conditioned box. A rat he live better."

"Oh? What rat was this?" I thought maybe a Syrian had the penthouse, or something.

"No. Not a rat — *any* rat they living better."

What irked him — and Arabs generally — most was the lack of camaraderie between Kuwaitis and others. Just because someone is richer, in, say, Egypt, doesn't mean you treat him any differently or he treats you any differently. You hang out together at the mosque five times a day, where all are equal in the eyes of Allah, so it's a little hard to keep interrupting and resuming an abusive or obsequious relationship five times a day. Deep in the bloodstream of most Arabs, whether they live in high-rises or tents, flow the old nomadic tribal ways, where all property is communal, and any stranger in need is your brother. So, how come the Kuwaitis don't share what they've got with their brothers?

The looting of Kuwait was thus viewed more as an enforced sharing of the wealth, the way income tax can be seen as obligatory philanthropy. As for murdering the al-Sabahs, if the emir was anything to go by, that was the *only* way the concept of sharing would be driven home.

Of course, Saddam didn't view himself as Robin Hood: he viewed himself as The Godfather. And his idea of sharing, or rather his ideology of sharing — as rudimentary as the al-Sabahs' in its way — was that he got to keep their money instead of them. But, admittedly, he also had big problems, *very big* problems, and could unquestionably make better use of the money than Sheikh Jaber, who, besides wanting as much of it as possible, had no actual *use* for the stuff at all.

The end of the war with Iran saw widespread discontent among Iraq's masses, who were now even grumbling openly about their leader, which was not only ideologically incorrect, but also illegal. Demobilized soldiers returned from the killing sands to find that Egyptian immigrants now had their jobs — something many of the Egyptian immigrants soon regretted bitterly, or were *made* to regret. There was even a nongovernmental crime wave (probably centered around the 007 Bar). I also learned from a fairly well-placed source that close associates of Saddam had been offered the privilege of viewing videos shot during the actual executions of their professional colleagues, the thieving and equally diabolical Ceauşescus of Romania. The message these associates derived from their viewing experience was that, in the event of a similar revolution by Iraqis, The Leader wouldn't be the only one to have the wrath of his public explained to him very tangibly and at great length before he died. The amateur proctologists and the party animals on their island in the Tigris were fairly certain that they wouldn't be overlooked when the fun began. They also knew that the preservation of their lifestyle wouldn't make a particularly good rallying point for the country. *Something* had to, though.

Kuwait was ideal in this respect. The al-Sabahs, guilty of the same crime as Iraq's hierarchy — living too well — were already despised, for a start. Also, Kuwait's greedy overproduction had been depressing global oil prices for some time now, something which the *Saddam Times* ceaselessly identified as the root of all current evils; Sheikh Jaber, even when asked nicely, had declined to write off the stupendous debts owed by Iraq; the ancient dispute over territory made an excellent pretext for hostilities and would garner massive populist support; and, finally, none of the other Arab countries (except Syria, which always objected to anything Saddam did) would lift a finger to help. Indeed, Saudi Arabia and the other peninsula states even suppressed news of the invasion for several days, not so much to think about a response, but to wait for someone else to show them what to think about a response.

Arabs love to negotiate, and Saddam knew that if he controlled all of Kuwait he could easily make a settlement for the bits he really wanted, install a puppet Kuwaiti government, and still have plenty of money to keep everyone happy in both countries. After all, it *was* one of the richest places on earth that he'd invaded. The only sand-fly in the unguent was America. Saddam later even confessed that the Americans' lightning response had forced him to alter his post-invasion strategy. "Kuwait is now ours," he told Turkish Prime Minister Bulent Ecevit, "but we might have refrained from taking such a decision if U.S. troops were not massed in the region with the threat of invading us." Had these troops not been there, Iraq "would have attempted to develop the status of the temporary revolutionary administration" established in Kuwait after the invasion. Saddam, who had clearly believed the United States was bluffing — negotiation not retaliation would end the crisis — admitted his forces were simply not strong enough to take on the Americans: "We would not have been able to ask our people and the armed forces to fight to the last drop of blood if we had not said that Kuwait was now part of Iraq. We would not have been able to prepare our people for the possibility of war."

What Saddam didn't say, though, was that his "provisional government" wouldn't stand up to much scrutiny as a legitimate body: no one could find any Kuwaitis willing to join it.

SADDAM AND BUSH NEED COUPLES COUNSELLING!

— U.S. anti-Gulf War bumper sticker

THE SCAPEGOAT AND THE GIANT
WITH NO OPINION

What on earth, you may well ask, made Saddam think that the United States was bluffing? Well, herein lies a tale.

On April 12, 1990, a bipartisan U.S. delegation visited the president of Iraq, primarily to lodge complaints about his country doing things that only verifiably authentic friends of America could do with impunity: develop chemical, biological, and nuclear weapons. Plus he should quit making the Israelis nervous. According to the Iraqi account of the meeting, however — and there's no reason to disbelieve it — much of this yack session concerned the role of the Western media.

"Democracy is a difficult thing," Senator Alan Simpson usefully explained to Saddam. "I think the troubles you have are with the Western press, not with the American government. The press is full of itself . . . they take themselves for wise politicians, geniuses. All journalists."[3] I've been wanting to tell Senator Simpson what a wise and brilliant comment I thought this was, but he doesn't return calls. No wonder Saddam wasn't that thrilled to see me a month later, though.

Much of this delegation consisted of senators from the mid-West grain states, who were particularly worried about the threatened imposition of sanctions, since Iraq imported most of its grain from the people who put them in office.

Curiously enough, an account of this powwow between Saddam and the senators had still not been written into the congressional record six months after it took place. But since, among his many talents, Saddam runs a publishing company, and he's always thinking ahead, the room was bugged in the interests of literature. Appearing under the eerily prophetic title "The Confrontation," a transcript of the meeting was soon available to Iraq's reading public.

It wasn't just the room that was bugged, either — Saddam was bugged, too. But what bugged him was a Voice of America broadcast on February 15. As he complained to Senators Bob Dole, James McClure, Simpson, and Howard Mitzenbaum, this outrageous broadcast had compared his regime with the fallen Communist tyrannies of eastern Europe. Like Romania. "The success of dictatorial rule and tyranny," the voice on the Voice of America had said, "requires the existence of a large secret police force, while the success of democracy requires abolishment of such a force." The Voice didn't say where the CIA and FBI undercover or covert ops people fitted into this — although, to be fair, the Voice didn't claim that America's democracy was successful, either. Instead, it went into great detail about thousands of Romanian citizens only too happy to shed their blood in violent conflict with "well-trained security forces armed to the teeth" in order to be rid of the Ceaușescu kleptocracy. The Voice then listed other states where secret police could be found: predictably, China, North Korea, Iran, Syria, Libya, Cuba, and Albania. Bad places, places that America couldn't be friends with — unlike Edens of liberty such as Saudi Arabia, whose record as one of the worst human-rights violators on the planet was clearly yet another product of a wise-ass media too full of itself to recognize the reports of watchdog organizations for what they really were: goddamn-pinko propaganda. The Voice concluded with a sort of Lofty Ideals Moment: "We believe that the 1990s should belong not to the dictators and secret police, but to the people." The sentence sounded oddly incomplete, though, as if it should have been ". . . to the people who put them there," or perhaps ". . . the people who are really in charge of the planet."

Saddam can be forgiven for assuming that the broadcast represented the U.S. government's views, considering its source, and this was his main beef with the senators, that "a vast campaign has been launched against us in America and in the countries of Europe." But "Decent" Bob Dole had concrete proof that this couldn't be so: "It doesn't come from President Bush. He told us yesterday he was against all that."

Then where does *all that* come from? Who does the Voice of America really work for? Russia? Obviously, this gaping leak in his explanation bothered Dole, too, for he later felt obliged to recall what had *really* happened: ". . . a person who was not authorized to speak in the name of the government, a commentator of the Voice of America — which does represent the government — has been removed." Presumably, Saddam thought that "removed" meant *removed*. But let's get this straight: if the voice wasn't the Voice, was Senator Dole then reassuring Saddam no one in Washington believed for a moment that he was a tyrant like Ceaușescu or that Iraq possessed "a large secret police force"?

Saddam had heard enough about Ceauşescu by now.

This wasn't the first time he'd complained about the Voice's comments, either. He'd had his foreign minister, Tareq Aziz, haul in April Glaspie, Baghdad's U.S. Ambassador, to receive a formal protest against what was then termed "a flagrant interference in the internal affairs of Iraq."

In a following cable to the State Department, Ambassador Glaspie wrote that Iraq's regime regarded the voice's broadcast on the Voice as government-sanctioned "mudslinging with the intent to incite revolution." The Romania analogy especially had been "deeply damaging."[4] She then added something guaranteed to cause pandemonium back in Washington, even in 1990 when the rotting edifice of the Soviet Union looked about as threatening as Lenin's embalmed corpse: "The Soviet embassy is also busy here ensuring that news of the editorial has been spread throughout Baghdad."

Those *damn* Commies! Still trying to foment revolution among the downtrodden masses even when few masses were more downtrodden than their own!

Glaspie later dashed off a letter to Aziz, stating that "it is absolutely not United States policy to question the legitimacy of the government of Iraq nor to interfere in any way in the domestic concerns of the Iraqi people and government. My government regrets that the wording of the editorial left it open to incorrect interpretation."[5] *How wonderfully this was phrased!* Clearly the Voice's concluding statement *ought* to have been: "We believe that the 1990s should belong to people like dictators and the secret police." To make sure that the Voice's editorials would never again risk triggering the Apocalypse by wrongly accusing Iraq, China, North Korea, Iran, Syria, Libya, Cuba, and Albania of being tyrannies run by secret police, the U.S. Information Agency was informed that, in order to safeguard the integrity of its Information, all Voice editorials must henceforth obtain written clearance from the State Department before they could be broadcast.

Appeased by all this, presumably, and now growling at Kuwait, Saddam himself next hauled in Ambassador Glaspie. It was 1:00 p.m. on July 25. I got a transcript of this meeting from the same source who told me about the Romanian videos, and for a while thought that I alone possessed answers to the most vexing questions that the Gulf War raised. But it seems that Saddam wanted the world to know whose fault it really was that he screwed up so badly, because the transcript was being leaked all over the place. The State Department must have been horrified, and they tried to minimize the significance of the conversation, suggesting also that the Iraqi version might be incomplete. But no one has ever challenged the transcript's authenticity.

The meeting must have taken place in the same office as mine had, and I initially wondered if Ambassador Glaspie had also taken the sensible precaution of getting high on psychotropic chemicals before being subjected to Saddam's twaddle, forgetting, of course, that she wasn't a wise-ass journalist and that he probably viewed her as of some use to him. But he didn't tell her how much he liked *The Godfather*. Instead, he told her in very plain terms that he'd just about had it with the al-Sabahs and might have to get medieval with them very soon. He advised the United States not to get involved, although this proved unnecessary, for Glaspie next reassured him that "we have no opinion on Arab-Arab conflicts, like your border disagreement with Kuwait."

Since we know Saddam was once on the CIA payroll, we can reasonably speculate that he was once doing something that the men in black wanted done in the region. With the CIA involved, this "something" was probably in the checks and balances department — and what needed the most checking and balancing in Washington's view was Iran.

Historically, all of Iraq's squabbles with Iran have ostensibly been over control of the Shatt al-Arab Waterway, and Ayatollah Khomeini was nothing if not a traditionalist. In the grip of post-revolutionary fervor, Iran was making expansionist gestures in that region. But, as always, Iraq had more to lose — it would be landlocked — than Iran had to gain. Khomeini, however, wanted to thumb his nose at the United States by gaining control of the region's oil flow. It was an ideological thing. Yet it is highly likely that Kuwait would have been annexed during such an Iranian expansion — Khomeini disapproved of the greedy al-Sabahs as much as most Arabs did, and he wanted to punish them for their unIslamic behavior as much as he wanted to rip off their oil.

There is little reason to doubt that Saddam was led to believe his war with Iran had U.S. blessing and thus U.S. gratitude. But when it was over, he saw remarkably little gratitude coming his way.

Saddam conceded to Ambassador Glaspie that the United States was free to choose its own friends in the region, of course, adding, "but you know you are not the ones who protected your friends [the Kuwaitis] during the war with Iran. I assure you, had the Iranians overrun the region, American troops would not have stopped them, except by the use of nuclear weapons."

We know Saddam was perfectly aware that this may have been true in 1980, but that it definitely wasn't true in 1990. "SADDAM WARNS ARABS," yelled a headline in the *Egyptian Gazette* back in January that year, going on to say more quietly that what Saddam was warning Arabs about were the dangers presented by an end to the Cold War. In short, these dangers were that America no longer had to worry about a nuclear confrontation with the Evil Empire every time it felt like meddling in Middle Eastern affairs.

However, Saddam didn't want America to get the impression that a conventional war would be much more fun either, telling Glaspie: "Yours is a society which cannot accept ten thousand dead in one battle . . . we know that you can harm us although we do not threaten you." He went on to refute this last statement somewhat ludicrously in his very next sentence: "But we can harm you. Everyone can cause harm according to their ability and their size." This must be a Ba'athist version of the Marxist credo, *To each his need from each his power.* Saddam continued with grim predictions, adding: "We cannot come all the way to you in the United States but individual Arabs may reach you.

"You can come to Iraq with aircraft and missiles but do not push us to the point where we cease to care. And when we feel that you want to injure our pride and take away the Iraqis' chance of a high standard of living, then we will cease to care and death will be the choice for us. Then we would not care if you fired one hundred missiles for each missile we fired. Because without pride, life would have no value." He was exaggerating Iraq's capacity in the missile to missiles ratio, as things turned out.

Sheikh Jaber, percolating in Taif by now, would have agreed entirely with the pride stuff, though — but it would have been Saddam's life that had no value to the emir, not his own. He knew exactly the value of his own life: $100 billion.

Saddam must have felt he'd made his point by now, and he didn't want to scare the Ambassador — she was only a *woman*, after all — so he went on to assure her that Iraq did not place the United States among its many enemies, and that he and his fellow Arabs would work out a solution to the Kuwait problem, sooner or later. "We don't want war because we know what war means," he told Glaspie. Then, lest this sounded unmanly, he yet again cautioned: "But do not push us to consider war as the only solution to live proudly and to provide our people with a good living. We know that the United States has nuclear weapons but we are determined either to live as proud men or we will die."

Pride may well be the root of all evil.

Next Saddam wanted Glaspie to relay a message to President Bush, telling her to say it had come to Saddam's attention that certain elements with links to both the U.S. State Department and the CIA were engaged in plots to persuade the more conservative Gulf states to cut off Iraq's economic aid — although he knew that President Bush and the secretary of state, James Baker, couldn't possibly be involved with anything so wicked. "Iraq came out of the war burdened with $40 billion debts —," the figure had doubled since I'd last heard it, "— excluding the aid given by Arab states, some of which consider that too to be a debt, although they knew — and you knew too — that without Iraq they would not have had these sums and the future of the region would have been entirely different."

Then Saddam returned once more to his obsession that the Western media were out to tarnish his image. "The United States thought that the situation in Iraq was like Poland, Romania, or Czechoslovakia. We were disturbed by this campaign but we were not disturbed too much because we had hoped that, in a few months, those who are decision-makers in America would have a chance to find the facts and see whether this media campaign had had any effect on the lives of Iraqis."

Who knows what *this* meant?

Glaspie clearly did not want Saddam to feel bad about *anything*, however, pointing out that the Bush administration had recently rejected any idea of trade sanctions against Iraq, and reminding him that the mettlesome editorial had already been apologized for. "I am pleased," she announced, beginning to sound like Senator Alan Simpson, "that you add your voice to the diplomats who stand up to the media. If the American president had control of the media, his job would be much easier."

According to John R. MacArthur, George Bush was, in fact, *about* to make the president's job much easier.[6]

Glaspie further assured Saddam that President Bush, far from seeking antagonism, wanted "better and deeper" relations with Iraq and to see an Iraqi contribution to peace and prosperity in the Middle East. "President Bush is an intelligent man," she speculated. "He is not going to declare an economic war against Iraq." Only a very stupid man would do such a thing, one assumes.

Whether frightened for her own safety or suddenly overwhelmed by an awe of Saddam's tremendous achievements and manly vibes, it's not clear, but for whatever reason Ambassador Glaspie suddenly felt the need to voice her personal admiration for his "extraordinary efforts" to turn Iraq into the most advanced nation on earth, or at least rebuild the place into something a notch above most Arab states. "I know you need funds," she added, maternally. I thought she was about to offer him a personal loan.

Evidently remembering who she was again, she once more affirmed that the United States had no opinion on the Kuwait border issue. "I was in the American embassy in Kuwait during the late sixties," she then confided. "The instruction we had during this period was that we should express no opinion on this issue and that the issue is not associated with America. James Baker has directed our official spokesman to emphasize this instruction."

All the same, said Glaspie, she had been instructed "in the spirit of friendship" to determine Iraq's intentions. Saddam understood, saying it was only "natural and proper" that the United States should be concerned when such a treasured thing as peace was at issue. "But what we ask," he added humbly, "is not to express your concern in a way that would make an aggressor believe that he is getting support for his aggression."

To translate this for Ambassador Glaspie — who must have betrayed her confusion over who exactly this "aggressor" was — Saddam went on to say that he meant, of course, Kuwait, whose lowering of the world oil price was seen as an act of aggression, threatening the livelihoods of millions of Iraqis, "harming even the milk our children drink and the pension of the widow who lost a husband during the war and the pensions of the orphans who lost their parents."

Wiping away a tear, I wondered who the orphans who *hadn't* lost their parents might be.

Saddam grumbled on about the treacherous, lying, dissembling, two-faced Kuwaitis, whose word was not their bond, whose agreements were invariably broken. Still, despite all this, Iraq's leader thought peace was not unattainable. In fact, Saddam suddenly announced, he had agreed with Egypt's president, Hosni Mubarak, that there would be a high-level meeting in Saudi Arabia between Iraq and Kuwait: "He just telephoned me a short while ago to say the Kuwaitis have agreed to that suggestion."

Glaspie was ecstatic, crying out, "This is good news. Congratulations!"

It must have been a sickening spectacle, since Saddam felt compelled to terminate it immediately, once more warning that "if we are unable to find a solution, then it will be natural that Iraq will not accept death."

I hoped Glaspie would query this — *I thought you just told President Bush that everyone in Iraq would willingly accept death?* — but she just told Saddam that she'd been considering postponing an upcoming trip to Washington on account of the toe-curling Kuwait situation, but, heartened by this great chat they'd been having, she would now go on July 30 and make a point of speaking to President Bush as soon as possible. About what, she didn't say. But she did leave the following Monday. The following Thursday Iraq invaded Kuwait.

And following the leaking of this transcript the shit hit the fan. Indeed, there was a period where it looked as if someone in Washington was considering Glaspie as an ideal candidate for Person To Blame. After all, it does appear that she wasn't taking Saddam's dark hints here seriously enough. This was precisely one of the accusations leveled at her. Someone also even suggested that her Arabic was so poor she could barely understand what Saddam was saying at all — as if she'd reported to Bush that Iraq planned to open a Disneyworld franchise near the border, hoping to make a mint out of the Kuwaiti tourist trade. The troops were merely there to help build it. It has proved curiously difficult — impossible, in fact — to ascertain whether she made a report at all, let alone get hold of it.

In Glaspie's defense, I would like to point out that her Arabic is impeccable and that she received the posting to Baghdad because she was more qualified than anyone else willing to take the thankless job. After all, you don't make yourself available for ambassadorial positions to end up in a dump like Baghdad, or anywhere there's likely to be trouble. Trouble means work, and ambassadorships shouldn't: they should mean fabulous accommodations, twenty-four-hour limo services, cocktail and dinner parties, and plenty of uninterrupted time to write books. You don't want the president or prime minister on the phone every ten minutes nagging you to death, do you? And you don't want your evening's entertainment limited to a couple of Bruce Lee movies currently enjoying the scratched and bleached twenty-fifth year of their first run. Afterwards: A nice chewy kebab and your fifty-third glass of mint tea. No, it's Paris, Rome, London, or nothing, I'm afraid.

April Glaspie doesn't need me to defend her, however; she did the job herself in a *New York Times* interview. "Obviously," she said, when asked if she'd failed to read the writing on Saddam's wall, "I didn't think and nobody else did, that the Iraqis were going to take all of Kuwait. Every Kuwaiti and Saudi, every analyst in the Western world was wrong too."[7]

Except Hermann F. Eilts. Glaspie forgot to add this — I hope — since one would think she had access to the expertise of a former U.S. ambassador to both Saudi Arabia and Egypt. Near the close of the Iran-Iraq war, Eilts wrote this:

> Should Iraq win, or should the war end with the Iraqi military machine still reasonably intact, Kuwaitis fear that they might again be pressured by their stronger neighbor for total subservience or territorial concessions. At a minimum, the protracted negotiations prior to the Iran-Iraq war over Iraq's demand for the Kuwaiti islands of Warbah and Bubiyan would doubtless have to be resolved quickly in Iraq's favor. Kuwait obviously hopes that by providing financial and other support for Iraq, it is buying the latter's goodwill. But goodwill is an effervescent commodity in Gulf politics, as it is in international politics anywhere and as the Kuwaitis well know.[8]

Much as I'd prefer to think of goodwill fizzing high-spiritedly around the globe, it seems to do far more melting away. Fizzy or fading, either way, Eilts seems to have better supply lines for information than the U.S. State Department. *The New York Times* didn't get into it, though, and Glaspie, regarding the abysmal performance of "every analyst in the Western world," next confessed, "that does not excuse me."

I disagreed with her: it seemed a pretty good excuse, as excuses go. But she did conclude by adding that "people who now claim that all was clear were not heard from at the time." Glaspie herself also hasn't been heard from in quite a while now. She hasn't been *heard of,* either.

The vital clue to this whole business lies in her comments to the *Times.* Glaspie says that no one thought "the Iraqis were going to take *all* of Kuwait." So they presumably thought that Saddam might just take *part* of Kuwait? This implies that the United States would have been prepared to accept a little rearrangement of the map as long as it only involved the disputed islands and the border area.

But let's look at the whole Glaspie-Saddam conversation again. Saddam is quite forthright about the likely stomping Kuwait will soon get, and Glaspie is downright vague about everything except the fact that the United States has no opinion on inter-Arab feuds. Three times Saddam tells her things aren't looking very good for the al-Sabahs, and three times Glaspie assures him that Washington doesn't give a damn about anything Arabs do to each other. He tries everything he can think of, short of asking Glaspie outright, to ascertain whether or not he's going to find himself facing Uncle Sam when he rips Sheikh Jaber's face off. But the only answer he gets — even after threatening the American Ambassador with terrorist attacks on her home turf — is that the United States just doesn't have an opinion. *We're as dumb as we look,* she might as well have said.

Is she misreading him, or misleading him? It's a tough call, but I'd say the odds are that we're dealing with the latter. Saddam is no Gandhi, after all, and when he says he might have to invade Kuwait, you can be fairly certain that he's actually saying that he will *definitely* be invading Kuwait unless given reasons not to. *Gee, I dunno, we have no opinion —* this does not seem much like a reason to refrain from nose-picking, let alone imperialist expansion. To a man like Saddam, it was the green light he'd been asking for all along. This explains why he seemed so unreasonably confident up to the incursion and then so shocked, stunned, and baffled after, when Baghdad seemed likely to become yet again a pile of smoldering rubble.

But why would the United States, in effect, hoodwink Saddam into invading Kuwait? If it were in order for the U.S. military to have an excuse to reduce the Iraqi army to a more manageable size, why wasn't the incursion stopped way before Saddam's troops reached Kuwait City? And if this too were deliberate, why would the United States want Kuwait City reduced to rubble? The answers do not blow in anything like the wind, or even the surprising strength and skill of Iraq's army — the only surprising thing about this was apparently its pitiful weakness and radiantly inept strategies.

Yet there is a kind of "unified field theory" that explains everything, or so I was told by a man who worked in the Bush administration. Bush, this man said, was getting very pissed off with the Kuwaitis, who had been creating havoc in the European money markets ever since they discovered that simply by moving their money from one currency into another they could drastically alter the exchange rates themselves. For example, $20 billion in Swiss francs shifted into German deutschmarks caused the franc to fall and the mark to gain in value. Knowing this, you could thus buy another $20 billion worth of Swiss francs on margin at rock-bottom levels — which with 5 percent leverage gave you $400 billion in francs — then change the deutschmarks back to francs in one block, sell off the leveraged currency, then repeat the whole process over and over again, moving into pounds or yen if you felt like a change of scenery. All it took were a few phone calls and you made a few hundred million every time. Legally. The only reason the al-Sabahs were able to do this, of course, was that they had too much money.

The Europeans had complained to the Kuwaitis and been ignored; then they'd complained to Bush, who complained to the al-Sabahs — and was also ignored. They are an arrogant bunch, as I've noted. And, besides, it was fun — better than gambling, because you couldn't lose. The relationship between Kuwait and America could be described thus: Kuwait was a banking system in search of a country, and the United States was a country in search of a banking system. Clearly, it would take some heavy unforeseen expenses to have any impact on people with $100 billion and counting at the ready. Unforeseen expenses caused by unforeseen actions, like demolishing Kuwait City and setting fire to every oil well in the emirate.

The beauty of this as a scheme was that not only did it stop the al-Sabahs from having too much money, it did it by siphoning their cash into U.S. pockets. Who was going to rebuild Kuwait City? Not the Kuwaitis, that much was certain. After saving the country from becoming a province of Iraq, the Americans would deserve, at the very least, all the contracts they wanted. And the whole world knows that only Texans understand how to put out oil fires. So, the Iraqis got to lose their menace, the Kuwaitis got to lose their money, and the Americans got both *kudos* as global cop, plus the money. The perfect crime!

But the beauty didn't end there. The Americans got to bill the Saudis for their entire war — a global security force doesn't come cheap, either — and they also got to establish a permanent military base in Dhahran, where by coincidence they had built the world's largest airfield just after the Second World War.

The late great Saudi patriarch, King Ibn Saud, had once enjoyed propelling himself up and down its vast runways in the wheelchair that had been a gift from Franklin Delano Roosevelt — one ailing old bugger to another — during the meeting scheduled to break the news about this great new idea the West had come up with for Palestine's future.

The Summit *à deux* had taken place upon the U.S. Navy's destroyer, *Quincey*, in the Great Bitter Lakes area of the Suez Canal. The old dune monarch had to be talked out of bringing a herd of sheep, a barge of vegetables, and several hundred retainers on board, eventually settling for a few dozen retainers and just enough sheep to feed himself and his entourage (custom required him to feed everyone else too, and it wasn't easy to tell him that this was unnecessary). Even then he had his tent erected on the deck to sleep in, and the crew had to regularly swab a poop deck awash with poop, gore, blood, and sheep entrails before the captain saw it and went berserk. Roosevelt, a dedicated smoker, even had to wheel himself into the ship's elevator every time he needed a burn, because Ibn Saud's religious principles didn't permit him to be around smokers (at another meeting, Churchill had rudely informed Ibn Saud that his own religious principles did not permit him to go more than ten minutes without a slug of cognac and never at all without a huge tobacco turd stuck in his face).

When Roosevelt explained what had been going on in Europe for the past five years, the old king seemed suitably shocked. Then he said that when such a terrible thing as the genocide of European Jewry occurred among his people — which was evidently quite often — the victims always received the choicest property of those who had wronged them. "Give the Jews Germany," he suggested. Roosevelt told him the Jews didn't want Germany, they wanted Is —, Palestine. Well, replied Ibn Saud, they couldn't have it. What had the Palestinians done to deserve such a punishment? Besides, he added, Palestine was already taking far more than its quota of Jewish refugees. It shouldn't take any more of those, let alone be expected to vanish. Roosevelt claimed to have learned more during these conversations than he had from the "combined memos of [his] entire staff."[9] He ended up promising the Saudi patriarch something he shouldn't have promised him: that nothing would be done without prior consultation with all Arab leaders. Roosevelt was dead three months later, unfortunately, and his successor, Harry Truman — after a vacillation that made Hamlet look like General Patton — was ultimately more concerned about the Jewish vote than the approval of desert nomads, despite anguished pleas by the oil brigade.

After the creation of Israel *ex nihilo*, it was these anguished pleas that caused a frenzy of placation down Riyadh way. To his dying day, Ibn Saud couldn't understand how a country with any dignity could ignore the solemn promise of its leader. He believed the earth was flat too, though.

Among many puzzling gestures of palliation, the Dhahran airfield mystified people who saw it most: why was it so big, for example? And why was it on the edge of the world's largest deposits of Arab D-grade, the champagne of oils? Was somebody planning to ship out oil by air one day?

General Norman Schwarzkopf, landing for the first time on the giant airfield, probably knew the answer to these questions already. His dad had led the CIA-backed coup in Iran that stomped an inchoate democracy — and an attempted oil industry nationalization — and re-established the thieving Pahlavis on the Peacock Throne. Schwarzkopfs have a long history of Middle Eastern meddling. I like to think Daddy S. had once shown Junior S. the airfield when it was still under construction, saying *Son, one day all this will be yours . . .*

Yes, indeed, there are plenty of persuasive reasons for thinking that the Gulf War was not necessarily yet another U.S. foreign policy cock-up. The most persuasive of all, however, is the presence of George Bush himself in the Oval Office.

No man in American history has held so many positions of such power for as long as George Bush quietly managed to do over some twenty years: four as president, eight as the only vice president who has ever held significant portfolios (terrorism, narcotics — two activities that also, coincidentally, and perhaps ironically, experienced boom growth during those eight years), a lengthy spell as CIA director, and so on. Not bad for the son of humble Texas oil barons. At least Richard Nixon had to claw his way up from the orangutans, like Saddam. All three men, coincidentally, were lawyers by training, too. And *Hussein v al-Jaber* was Bush's masterpiece. It's said he refers to it himself, however, as the *Revenge of Vietnam*.

As he's prone to do, Norman Mailer wrote something very astute about George Bush for a profile in *Vanity Fair*. Echoing April Glaspie, he noted that Bush was ". . . a very intelligent man, but he'd have trouble passing a first-year course in philosophy." Mailer saw through the *wimp* facade, too. For George Bush is like one of those malevolent characters in William S. Burroughs' novels: anonymous, cold-blooded, taciturn, inert, and deadly. Perfect qualities, of course, for crisis management.

VISIT IRAQ BEFORE IRAQ VISITS YOU
— Graffiti outside a tourist office in Bahrain

A VIENNESE WALTZ

Sometimes we do things without realizing fully quite why we're doing them. I just needed to be a witness — that was all I could explain to myself — and fortunately, or unfortunately, my editor at *Saturday Night* magazine, Anne Collins, seemed to understand. With very little certainty of gaining more than prodigious expenses, she okayed a commission to head for the Middle East and write about . . . whatever there *was* to write about. I would have gone anyway, though. The torment of watching this "crisis" on CNN was making me crazy — and *that* was making everyone around me crazy. Although they dutifully told me I was crazy to go, I probably would have been crazier to stay. As soon as I'd left, however, I was convinced they were right and I was wrong. And crazy.

Crisis had turned to war, of course, and the entire Middle East was suddenly an area of darkness, turmoil, and terror. A place no airline would fly to. Even Royal Jordanian — which had no choice *but* to fly there — didn't want to fly there. Its elegant black and gold jet was in airplane quarantine out on a stretch of tarmac so remote it took a coach trip from New York's JFK main terminal to reach the dilapidated and probably disused check-in facility serving it. A confused and unruly lineup created the eerie impression that one was already in Jordan. Not expecting too many American tourists, I still didn't expect to be the *only* non-Arab, the only passenger whose suitcase was smaller than an upright piano, the only passenger who was not carrying three ghetto blasters, one microwave oven, two Chevrolet drive-shafts, a four-foot polyester Donald Duck, and a pair of matching baroque plastic floor lamps with tasseled shades.

I then realized that these passengers were probably not a package tour bound for sunny Jordan — *Escape Winter!* — they were probably being deported. As Iraq's sole ally, Jordan was the enemy now, too, theoretically. I bet *that* news had them quaking in the Pentagon war room. Multicultural societies have got to stop deporting and imprisoning their own citizens every time there's war — either that or stop having wars. As a bumper sticker I'd seen earlier had proclaimed: "If war is the answer, then it's a stupid fucking question."

These Jordanians seemed a little too cheerful for people whose lives had just been abruptly uprooted, however. I asked the dapper, immaculately groomed fellow beside me what this exodus was about.

"Deported? No, no, no. We are returning to witness the collapse of Zionism and the triumph of Palestinian rights."

"You're Palestinian?"

"No, sir. I am Jordanian. But finally the Palestinians will be gone from Jordan, and peace will return."

"I see. You think that Saddam will bring about Israel's collapse?"

He nodded, utterly confident, saying at length: "Saddam has vowed it."

There was probably little that Saddam hadn't vowed by now. I wondered if he'd vowed not to call America's bluff ever again. Were his nerves still like steel? Maybe that was the problem: nerves should be made of more fragile material if they're to be much use.

This war brought out the worst in Americans, too, I noticed. The demonization of Saddam (from hero to zero) had lasted five and a half months — to psyche the population up for war between the sons of light and the sons of darkness. Once this was under way, though, fear had to be replaced by a malicious loathing concealed within locker-room, bully-boy humor: the devil had been evicted from hell and now he was going to get his butt kicked.* We passengers — who had evidently not been able to Love America and were thus now obliged to Leave It — weren't treated very nicely, either. In fact, we were treated like a herd of potentially dangerous sheep.

"Wahya goin' t'Jordan, sir?"

"Vacation."

He looked me straight in the eyes.

"Y'ree-lies thaysa wahr-on?"

"That's why I got such a great deal from my travel agent . . ."

"Th' stayit deportment *has* ish-ewd traal 'vize-ree."

"Issued a what?"

"Traala-vize-ree."

"A travel advisory?" Where had his v gone?

"S'rite, sir."

"Aren't they for weather?"

"Yew trine t'be ferny wimmy, sir?"

The final indignity was being hit up for an extra hundred bucks — for war insurance. A Royal Jordanian official assured me, however, this was standard procedure in the event of war.

Descending into swirling mist onto the Vienna tarmac, and taxiing to a slow stop, where visibility was suddenly and mysteriously improved, our plane revealed itself to be ringed by troops and armored vehicles. Peering out through drizzle and scratches on my porthole, I hoped this *was* Vienna. But it looked too orderly to be anywhere farther east. Down near the plane's motor staircase, a man with a black raincoat and beard, as well as a lifetime's experience in being sinisterly authoritative, spoke fluent static through a walkie-talkie. He seemed to be coordinating the activities of several men who were toting complex electronic gadgets. No one looked like airport personnel.

---

* Sad*dam* (with the stress on the second syllable) translates somewhat literally to "learned one." On the other hand, *Sad*dam (with the stress on the first syllable and a nasal "a" as George Bush used) translates to "shoe-shine boy." Bush was as conscious of this as he was of the way his singular pronunciation sounded to non-Arabic speakers: *Sodom Hussein* — and it was invariably *Sodom Hussein, the dictator* (as if Bush's listeners would have otherwise assumed he meant some other Saddam Hussein).

I always feel like a terrorist after the eastbound transatlantic flight, and I usually look like one, too. As the doors sighed open and I stood to retrieve hand luggage before the inevitable stampede began, I looked back down the curved corridor of our flying train to find myself but one of many terrorists. Most Arab men can grow a beard overnight, but now that the neckties had been loosened and the keffiyehs that had served as blankets or cushions were employed as scarves, the overall effect was something like the *Abu Nidal & Friends: 1991 World Tour.*

We were ushered past a gauntlet of Uzi-toting soldiers, who looked visibly tense as we wove unsteadily thirty yards through the freezing spray of dawn mist to our new plane. Viennese faces stared from the breath-frosted glass of windows in the terminal. People were talking excitedly and pointing at us. Everyone assumed an Iraqi death squad had been plucked out of the iron gray vapors, and was now bound for the Big House. I suddenly wished I were in the warm, chocolate-flavored air of the terminal with them. Maybe a family would adopt me, carry me home to their Alpine lodge, clothe me in lederhosen, and feed me schnitzels with coffee cake for all the days of my life. I suddenly didn't want to be going into the Land of Death today. I felt as sick — literally *nauseated* — of war as an old and wounded soldier. I presume nothing would have stopped me from staying in Vienna, but then I felt as if on a bridge across worlds, gazing back upon a fading dream as the living nightmare began.

We weren't just leaving the safe familiarity of the West, either, we were also leaving the FAA safety features of Royal Jordanian's finest jumbo jet for — what? One of those jets you never see anymore, that was *what*: its oil-streaked turbine engine tubes bolted to the tail fins, its body dulled by a finely pitted sheen of corrosion, and various of its non-vital structural parts blatantly missing. The *Caravelle*, was it? Taken out of service in 1963? For a reason like — safety? The tail fins didn't look to me like the best place for jet-turbine engines to be placed. Everyone had to board it by the rear, where a ramp staircase hung from its rump in an unseemly fashion, and *the passengers climbed in two-by-two, hurrah! hurrah!* Eager to see if the old heap flew . . .

It was open seating — neither arrangement nor numbers corresponded with those on our old boarding passes. I was as outraged as Sheikh Jaber would have been. Then I was alarmed: they'd put us in a plane they not only didn't *mind* losing but also a plane that they positively *wanted* to lose. And after we'd collectively purchased some $20,000 in "war insurance" for a flight supposedly all the way to Amman in the previous vehicle. What if this were a scam? What if King Hussein, via Royal Jordanian, had a deal going with Saddam to collect fat insurance checks on airplanes downed by the Iraqi air force? Twenty thousand dollars for the three hours we'd be airborne bought a lot of coverage, I'll bet — war or no war. It wasn't even a Royal Jordanian plane.

Jordan boasts another airline, though, *Alia*, named after a wife of King Hussein. Amman's airport is the Queen Alia International Airport, too. Queen Alia died in an aircraft crash. Prince Hassan, King Hussein's scholarly brother, had told me this, and he didn't see why I found it obscenely inappropriate.

"You wouldn't name a rifle club after John F. Kennedy, would you?"

"Why not? We have one named after Ziggy." Ziggy is King Hussein's nickname.

"Yeah, but he wasn't assassinated by a lone gunman."

"He nearly was," Hassan protested. "They always miss, though."

"Besides, *everything's* named after him . . ."

"Except the airport."

I'm glad my brother isn't king: I couldn't handle it.

I heard the ramp creaking then shuddering, then it closed with an awful finality. Our new flight attendants looked as soiled and weary as we did. No one cared whether hand luggage was secured in the overhead compartments or stowed safely beneath our seats. Some of the overhead compartments wouldn't close or were actually hanging off their hinges, anyway, so hand luggage dangled from seat backs, overflowed in the muddy aisle, and was heaped, stacked, piled, and dumped everywhere but on passengers' heads. It's the only time I've ever wanted the crew mime artists to instruct me in the use of seat belts, safety procedures, and life vests. But none appeared — probably because most seat belts were, like mine, vestigial stumps of tired steel, or because no procedures would summon any kind of safety to aid this rotting hulk. And one hated to think what kind of shape the life vests were in, if they existed at all beneath these frayed, lumpy seats.

The fools even started singing patriotic songs the moment their ship — after a wait of several hours that no one ever thought of explaining to us — had whined, roared, and rattled its way back up and out into the endless expanse of blue. I was evidently the only one not overjoyed to be Jordan bound. Soon we had the darkening skies to ourselves: the belt from here on, all the way to Iran, was marked "War Zone" on a colored *USA Today* map. The traffic of earth's upper air had all been rerouted, and there were rumors that finding a flight out was now next to impossible. The absence of a cocktails trolley began to irk me more than the absence of the pilot's reassuring voice, the absence of any in-flight catering, and, indeed, the absence of any flight attendants. Where had *they* gone?

WAR IS MENSTRUATION ENVY

— *U.S. feminist anti-Gulf War bumper sticker*

ROOM AT THE INN

Amman looked very dark — *especially* dark — as we descended in a deafening howl of rattling iron and then crunched in a series of shattering bounces onto the runway. This achievement was celebrated by many spirited rounds of thunderous applause and Cherokee-war dance ululations from the women.

A bleak, forlorn appearance to the baggage claim and immigration area made it seem as if the whole place had been unused for years, abandoned. Fully expecting rigorous and enthusiastic body searches during hours of savage interrogation, I was surprised to find a lone uniformed man who looked as if he'd stepped out of a Second World War Royal Air Force movie. He politely asked me to unzip my bag, then, as if merely establishing that the zip worked, asked me to zip it up again.

"Have a nice day," he said.

The night outside was bitterly cold, and there were no stars. The only lights on in Jordan seemed to be the ones illuminating the path of my yellow Mercedes cab as it creaked off down a huge, deserted modern highway. Then even these were switched off.

Few sights are eerier than a city under blackout and curfew. You can *feel* its shadowy bulk of buildings and humans, but when you don't see any people at all, anywhere, you soon begin to doubt your feelings, suspecting the worst has happened: the population has vanished. Or perished. As we turned off and hissed through increasingly more opulent suburbs, however, I began to see the odd mobile anti-aircraft installation and its crew positioned in darkened driveways or alleys. Some of these installations had a wall of sandbags erected around them, and all were heavily camouflaged with mottled tarpaulins and even actual branches from evergreen trees with dull drooping needles hanging from them.

The soldiers would look around anxiously on hearing our sleek engine and would usually raise their Second World War sten-guns, clicking off the safety catches and staring intently at both driver and passenger. My driver made reassuring gestures, flashing his lights and waving at them. We were pulled over only once, and even then we were waved on again almost immediately when the soldiers saw that I was not the kind of passenger they needed to worry about.

The Amman Sheraton was having a quiet night too.

"Have you come to our country for the whore, sir?"

"If there's only one, I'll leave her to you guys, okay?"

"You are a journalist, I think?"

"Yes, I'm with *Saturday Night,* do you get that here?"

"You may try in the shop over there, sir. But foreign papers are late this week."

"Oh. Well, perhaps you haven't heard, but there's a war on."

"Yes, sir. We are hoping this whore will pass soon."

Jordanian businessmen tended to talk about the war the way the British discuss weather.

"I will give you best suite with press discount, sir. Okay?"

"Press discount?"

"Fifty percent for you, if you stay one week."

"Eighty percent, and I'll stay one month?"

"Seventy-five?"

"Ninety, plus lots of free fruit."

"I give eighty percent and, of course, for you fruit is free, yes?"

"You take Visa?"

"We accept only American dollars cash now, sir."

Obviously, Jordan's relationship with international banking had taken a turn for the worse. "Cash, hmmn? Big problem for me. I tell you what: I'll pay you dollars, but pegged to Jordanian dinars at today's exchange rate. Okay? And you'll have to make it ninety percent off . . ."

He had to ask the manager.

An empty lobby doesn't indicate a hotel's current occupancy rate anything like the availability of its manager does. The Amman Sheraton's manager was at my side within thirty seconds.

"You are most welcome, sir. We are always happy to see foreign journalists here — *always*." He took me aside, conspiratorially. "You have U.S. hundred-dollar bill?"

"Is the pope a Christian?"

He had to think about this for a moment. "Ah! Give it to me now and there will be no other charge for you, okay? And I will put you in the Presidential Suite."

"The Presidential? Which presidents have stayed there?"

"*Henri* Kissinger has stayed there. And *Shems* Baker."

"So it's really just a Secretarial Suite."

"There is staff bedroom too, of *course*. You can bring your journalist friends, and I will provide all cocktails free of charge."

"Done!"

"And you may use my secretary for your needs."

"You okayed this with her?"

"It is better for you while we redecorate the Press Center."

Now, I may not be as intelligent as George Bush, but even I could read between these lines. The only business in town these days was from foreign journalists, and they were staying where they always stayed: The Intercontinental. The Press Center there had clearly been long established; the one at the Sheraton wasn't being redecorated — it was being constructed. The manager figured I'd make a good bird dog for the journalistic trade if he gave me enough incentive to have my colleagues back to my place for drinks. And he sure did. The Presidential Suite normally cost $1,200 per night; I'd suggest that, at less than $15, as things turned out, it was a bargain. I slipped him the money furtively, since he must have just comped the room. A 99 percent discount would be hard to explain to his superiors — if he ever saw *them* again.

"This must be fun," I told the bellhop. "Being at war with America?"

"American people are our good friends," he replied.

"Not anymore."

"King Hussein his *wife* American — King Hussein good friend to the President Rhea Gaan."

"I guess Reagan forgot to tell Bush that."

"But Ish-Ray-El they drop atoms bomb on Amman city."

"No wonder it's so quiet."

What Israel *had* promised its neighbor was that, should one Scud missile pass over Jordan on its way from Iraq to Tel Aviv, then the Israeli Air Force would regard it as a hostile act in need of massive retaliatory action. The little king must have been nervous out in his little five-star palace there: Saddam was hardly the kind of person he could ask not to fly his missiles over Jordanian airspace. And the Scud isn't exactly the kind of missile whose flight path is that predictable to begin with.

"This Presh-dental Suet, sir. It is okay?"

"A little poky, but I'll manage. Where's the mini-bar?"

"Not minnie," he said, leading me around to the room's private cocktail lounge, where six stools perched around a teak bar stocked with liter bottles of liquor.

"I suppose it will have to do. Here."

He took the outrageous tip and backed out, bowing.

The room would do. It would *have* to: there were no others on that floor.

A letter on my mogul's desk from the manager himself informed guests that "Air Raid Shelter is in the Discotheque." Which was conveniently located on the lower ground floor. Nearby, a card wedged into a kind of menu holder announced that appearing at the Sheraton's Disco all week was: "Basil Akimbo McPherson: Calypso King from Barbaros." The poor bastard should get another agent, I told myself.

The lobby store's most recent newspaper was some Cypriot rag dated January 17. Its headline will probably be carved on the editor's tombstone. While the rest of the world's press that day shrieked out things like "America Attacks!" Cyprus awoke to "Saddam Backs Down over Kuwait." A "source in Baghdad," I read, "today confirmed reports that President Saddam Hussein had reached yesterday a bi-lateral agreement with Kuwait and the United States, ending the six-month-old crisis . . ."

"I didn't realize this," I told the storekeeper.

"No, no!" he said, snatching the paper from my hands. "This wrong. They is warrings now!"

"Are you sure?"

"Yes, friend. Sure. But this all for foreign newspaper I am have. Look! You take *Times of Jordan* . . ." He pointed out that the *Times* was aware of the war.

I made a deal to swap him the bale of Western magazines and newspapers I'd brought in for twice their cover price value in his merchandise.

"At wholesale," I added. "I haven't even read them. You'll make a pile when I tell foreigners you've got the latest issue of *Time*. People *love* that magazine."

He had a fine collection of Saddam Hussein lapel buttons and Palestinian flag pins. He also had a copy of Faud Matar's classic: *Saddam Hussein: A Biography*, upon which his markup was nearly 2,000 percent over what I'd paid for it in Baghdad the previous May. An entire shelf contained nothing but copies of *By Way of Deception* by ex-Mossad agent Victor Ostrovsky and journalist Claire Hoy. The book contained enough information — including charts, graphs, blueprints, intelligence manuals, and even the Mossad's own report on the Danish Security Service — for anyone with the resources to start their own rival Mossad. None of the information in it was true, the Israeli government had claimed — which is presumably why they tried to prevent its publication with court injunctions all over the world. The offices of its original Canadian publisher were mysteriously broken into around the same time. The book had taken courage to write and even more courage to publish, yet most of all it showed how powerful the written word could still be. From contacts in the Mossad itself, and from people in both the SAS and Britain's MI 6, I'd heard that Ostrovsky's book had forced a total restructuring of the organization. "It did more damage than if Mossad HQ had taken a direct hit by a nuclear warhead," was the way an Israeli had phrased it. Like the Mukhabarat and the CIA, the Mossad is an organization that operates as a law unto itself. I had a lot of time for *By Way of Deception*. It also occurred to me that the book might make a nice gift for the right person.

"How come you have so many copies of this?"

"Big seller-this," replied the storekeeper. "Vare got. *Bay go Deception*, you know this?"

"They made a movie of it, right? With Veronica Lake and . . . oh, what *was* his name? Victor Mature?"

"We not see here this movie yet. You bring wideo?"

"I can send one."

I asked him to reserve ten copies of the book for me, then said I'd go fetch his bale of print media.

I found the bellhop before he went off to meet with his investment advisers about my tip's potential. It wasn't easy getting him to believe that I wanted all the newspapers and magazines now heaped on a sofa to be pressed by housekeeping like clothes, then folded so they looked as good as new.

Meet the press was next on the agenda. A tire-squealing five-minute cab ride whisked me through driving sleet to the Intercontinental, which stood nearly opposite what had been until quite recently the American Embassy, but was now empty, protected by Jordanian artillery from — presumably — squatters. A wit had hung a sign on the door knocker that read: "Gone fishing, back soon."

The hotel lobby bore much evidence of its current clientele's low-rent caliber: for example, a prominently placed notice board was festooned with notices scrawled on business cards, bar bills, or toilet paper — most of them facetious. "Will the bit of crumpet with RAI come up to my room at 2 a.m. any day of the week — Rupert Murdoch wants to make her an offer." RAI is the main Italian TV station. Rupert Murdoch — a.k.a. "The Dirty Digger" — is an Australian who now owns much of the world's media. I doubted if he also reported for them from war zones, however.

The Intercontinental's Al Hanah Pub & Wine Bar was a simulated British boozer — complete in every detail down to the Pakistani bartenders. One only had to open the door to know that this was where the world's press were monitoring vigilantly the young Gulf War — and had been since it was just a little crisis the previous August. This was the Land of Mighty Expense Accounts. The place was packed to capacity, wreathed in smoke, and no one was drinking wine. Here were the household names of foreign reporting from Melbourne to Manchester, from San Francisco to Hong Kong, from Tokyo to Turin, from Harare to

Stockholm. Those who weren't here were over in Dhahran letting the U.S. military dictate their copy. Everyone was now gathered around a monster TV for the 10:00 p.m. news in English. Journalists prefer not to learn foreign languages, for ideological reasons.

I got talking to a couple of Australian reporters who'd arrived from Baghdad the day before. Their cab had cost them $3,000.

"I said to the guy, 'how about $2,000' and he said 'how about you stay in Baghdad?'"

The pair roared with laughter, spraying Amstel over my shirt. But something was pissing them off. As CNN's Peter Arnett — now the only Western journalist left in Iraq — appeared on the TV screen, one said: "It's a farken scandal what those CNN bastards got away with there."

It was widely believed, evidently, that Ted Turner had made some kind of deal with the Iraqi government before the war started — bought the TV rights to it, for example.

"It makes me bloody puke," Oz One said angrily. "The minute the farken air raid starts, everyone is ordered at gunpoint dan to the pissen shelter — except farken CNN. That's ow come they got exglusive coverage. It farken stinks, mate. And now there's farken shite-face Arnett like farken Saddam's Lord Hee-Haw."

Peter Arnett had a tough decision to make, and he made the right one, I think. But why was he the one to stay? It was Bernard Shaw's voice we heard over the phone as Desert Storm blew in without warning. Bernard hasn't left Washington since. Yet Arnett hasn't been on CNN much since, either — and he wasn't on it much before. Yet he was one of the numerous journalists covering Vietnam to make himself particularly hated in the Pentagon by revealing exactly how unjust and barbaric America's little war really was. Now he was sitting in the Al Rashid Hotel, which, everyone felt, would thus not be targeted by U.S. attacks. Personally, I thought that with Bush in the White House, it might become a prime target merely *on account of* Arnett's presence, and I feared for Pete. They don't make 'em like him anymore. In fact, they don't make 'em at all.

The Al Hanah contained a fair cross-section of today's media, I suppose: inexperienced journalists with no knowledge of Middle Eastern politics or Arab history, and old "Middle East hands," bored and alcoholic, feeling they'd seen it all before — which they had. The press relies increasingly on news agencies for most stories concerning Arab countries, and most major networks and newspapers have their Middle East Bureaus in Israel. Normally this works out well enough; now, however, reporters for the bureaus found themselves stuck in Israel, and big media operations were panicked. The Saudis — no doubt on the advice of their military advisers — were not issuing visas, and most of those in the Dhahran press corps were handpicked the way White House reporters are: because they're known to be docile, malleable, and receptive to the president and government in general.

From Israel, we were soon hearing items like "Sex in gasmasks" or "How the U.S. Military's Patriot Missile experts adore Israeli girls." From Dhahran, of course, we heard only what the military censor wanted us to — although the better option would have been for all media to clear out in protest. From the crew gathered nightly in the Al Hanah, we heard rumor, hearsay, tripe, twaddle, and miles of pure waffle. They were ever-anxious to meet their daily deadlines with *something* (even if it meant virtually creating a story or serving as a conduit for all manner of propaganda) because otherwise those mighty expense accounts might come under scrutiny.

Keith Traynor was reporting for a British fascist tabloid with offices on Fleet Street. Apart from a break at Christmas, he'd been in Amman since early September 1990. "Ah was fucken undescroybable," he decided, about to describe a Jordanian beauty contest he'd recently covered. "Ere, *Abu!* Gittus 'nuver coupla pints-ah Double Die-mund, woojah." Barely less loudly, he added for my benefit, "Fucken Pakky cunt knows nutten 'bout poor-rinn beer, do 'e?"

"Have you tried to get into Iraq?" I asked him later.

"*Fuck* 'at! I was back 'n forff fer most-ah time, wunn-eye? Ba-chew *carn* gi-ah dee-cent pint or mee-yewl anywhere in fucken *Bag*-dad, can-ya? So fuck 'at, know-ah *mean*? An' ya get-ya soccer on *Jor*-dun teevy, doan-cha?"

He reckoned he'd run up a $35,000 tab so far, regarding it as a perk for such dangerous work.

"Keef!" yelled another South London accent across the bar — this time the nasal twangs of a woman.

"Oh *fuck*! Maw-*reen* . . ." Keith groaned. "Sah fucken bint wiv ITN, a royt fucken pain she is. An' a fucken li'lle prick-tease, in case ya wundrin."

She looked more like a Liverpool barmaid, in black leather miniskirt, cleavage-viewer blouse, and hair dyed with ink.

"Oo yew-wiv, 'en?" Maureen asked me, one arm coiled around her waist to support the elbow of her cigarette wrist.

"*Auckland Gleaner.*"

"Awk Land — where-zat, 'en?"

I told her, and she mused for several minutes over what a marvel it was that New Zealand could support a newspaper able to send someone all this way. I could just as well have said I was with *The Venusian Post.*

Someone I knew from *The Independent* finally rescued me from Keef and Maw-reen. Over a burger, he filled me in on the situation in Amman, which was fairly simple to sum up as "the place you get exiled to when you start to enjoy hell. The worst punishment is boredom, and here we're so bored we'll write a story about your jacket."

"It doesn't do media."

"Well, *there's* a great angle to begin with: 'Writer's jacket speaks out on Gulf War — world exclusive.'"

At 2:00 a.m. there were some fifteen hacks and hackettes in the Sheraton's Presidential Suite, conspicuously *not* being impressed by its opulence.

After I'd said to someone comparing his mini-bar with my cocktail lounge, "Son, back where I come from *that IS* a mini-bar," I noticed no one even asked who I was working for. They assumed it was me.

At 3:30 I received the call from London I'd been waiting for, from an Arabist who'd spent several years attached to the British Embassy in Amman. To avoid being overheard, we were obliged to speak in a mixture of pig Latin and obscure references, which someone in the room evidently identified as Beirut Arabic.

"You were in Beirut for a long time?" he asked.

"Not really. Just a week."

"Then where did you learn to speak Arabic like that?"

"Notting Hill Gate."

"Oh."

When I awoke, the Presidential Suite looked as if several teams of crack-addled burglars had been to work in it, three of whom were now asleep on the sofas. One was Oz Two, I realized.

"Ah farken Jeezer!" he moaned. "Me 'ead 'urts! Gottenny az-prinn, pal?"

Since one whole bag of my luggage consisted of nothing but medicines given me by an Egyptian pharmacist for the aid of civilian Iraqis, I did indeed have, not Aspirin, but something that would certainly fix a headache all the same. Or any ache.

"Take all four of these, cobber, and I guarantee your headache will vanish." I handed him four Percodan.

"Ah, fanks, mate. Yer-ra gent."

That, I thought, should produce some interesting copy for the *Melbourne Marsupial* or whatever it was for which he reported.

DESERT SHIELD IS NOT A FEMININE PRODUCT

— *U.S. feminist anti-Gulf War bumper sticker*

SANTA CLAWS

Sheikh Assad Bayoud al-Tamimi is spiritual leader to a number of terrorist cells, including the extremely nasty Islamic Jihad. I went to visit him in his heavily fortified spiritual retreat in central Amman. A young man masked with a keffiyeh, wearing an assortment of paramilitary outfits, and clutching a Kalashnikov that he wasn't taking very good care of, opened the four-inch-thick steel door after scrutinizing my passport through a grille.

"Don't worry, it's valid."

"Afumboogel-hah!"

"Didn't catch what you said, but this always works for me: *Sabah al-kher. Sigara? Dekhkhant?*"

"*Naa'm,*" he confessed (he did smoke, he did want a cigarette — and, yes, the Arabic for "yes" does sound as if it means "no"). "*Aahlen. Ma'alboro? Tetekel-laami el-'aarabi?*" he wanted to know now.

"No, I don't speak a word, pal. But I do have Marlboros." I pulled out a pack to prove it. "Shall I ram the whole packet up your ass with my boot, or do you prefer smoking them the traditional way?"

"*Ah! Ma'alboro. Shokran 'zeelen.*"

"And you don't speak the *Inglizi*, we now know. I might just give you one *Ma'alboro sigara* — *sigara mucho got* — though not the whole pack that I've misled you to expect. *Ismi* Bol Rupperse all the way from *Kanadi* just to see *Sheikh Tamimi* — hey! that rhymes." I smiled a smile of guileless amity.

"*Ah! Kanadi* — *Kanadi* ver gut, yesh?"

"Yes, indeed, Canada's ver gutter than you can imagine, O Freedom-fighting-one. Let me in, and I'll write a letter of recommendation to our immigration board for you — although when they hear you've blown up buses for Sheikh Tamimi they'll probably be begging you to get on the next plane . . ."

"*It-faad'el.*"

Come in. Music to my ears. He started the lengthy process of unlocking this most manly of doors.

It's essential to keep on babbling at such times, because, firstly, it prevents them being able to think at all (let alone think they won't let you in) and, secondly, it gives the impression that you have many, many good reasons for being let in.

Thus, finally I was shown into a musty, unpleasantly cold room cluttered with books and furnished with old, fat politburo sofas and chairs. The decomposing hallway we had to walk through to reach this room was piled high with the tattered evidence of political subversion: demo placards crudely emblazoned with "Death to Amerika" slogans or clumsy representations of George Bush dressed as Uncle Sam and being variously hanged, burned, stabbed, and beheaded by countless cartoon Arafats, Saddams, and a broad variety of other noble Islamic warriors.

"I just love your Palestinian sense of humor."

"Ah! Faleshtine, uh? Ver gut Faleshtine, yesh?"

"*Aiwa!* Absolutamente. Now take your cigarette, tell the boss I'm here, bring me some mint tea, and cut out your revolutionary bollocks. Scuttle off, *m'ism haazi bil 'aarabi?*"

"*Aan'la aaf-'em.*"

"I know you don't understand — that's why I'm saying it. And tell Sheikh Tamimi that his Gee-Hat murdered a very good friend of mine and I've come to register a formal complaint, so he should get his fat butt down here toot sweet. *Minfadlak.*"

He smiled back, and said thank you as I lit his Marlboro. Then he asked me if I wanted tea, going to no doubt have someone else make it.

On a coffee table that may once have been used for a rostrum by Spanish table dancers, there were several issues of *Islamic Jihad* — the magazine, not the bloodbath. The art direction was truly appalling, but there were some great cartoons, the best of which showed George Bush on all fours, with his pants crumpled around his knees, while Saddam Hussein enthusiastically sodomized him, and he gave a gleeful-looking Yasser Arafat some very deep throat. I kid you not. Of course, you couldn't actually see any private parts, but you didn't need to. Given my poor Arabic and the magazine's poor printing, I *think* that the caption read something like *Now, O George Bush, it is your turn to discover what it feels like.* I mailed George a copy from the Sheraton, but he never wrote to thank me or even to say it had arrived.

On the surface, Tamimi is a nasty piece of work, and underneath he's a nasty piece of work, too. His political and religious views can really be best summed up by looking at his recent bestselling book — not the contents, just the title: *The Destruction of Israel Is a Koranic Commandment.*

In April 1990, Tamimi had issued a fatwah authorizing suicide in the course of attacks against Israel and promising a place in paradise for those who were killed in this manner. In November, the Sheikh called for attacks against the United States for its deployment of soldiers in the Gulf. Now the wicked old bastard had virtually declared war on the whole world — except for the areas of it that supported him — announcing this macro-jihad with a poster and handbill campaign around town. One of his handbills had even been among the Presidential Suite's official hotel junk mail:

In the Name of Allah, the Most Compassionate and Merciful
ANNOUNCEMENT OF JIHAD

The most venerable Sheikh Asaad Bayoud al-Tamimi of
al-Aksa Mosque (Jerusalem) lets it be known to all Believers
that the hour has come when Wicked shall depart to wrath
of Allah. The Sheikh has decreed fatwa against all infidel
supporters of Great Shaitan Amerika and the Zioniste occupyers

of Palestini lands. All martyrs are now certain of place in
the Paradise. For details phone 56845.

So I'd phoned.

There was a lot in the way of "details" that I wanted to know about
the latest and most terrible of all jihads, and I was getting mighty impa-
tient when a scholarly looking man came to announce that the Sheikh
was ready to see me now.

Supposed to be sixty, Sheikh Assad Bayoud al-Tamini looked more like
ninety and could have been Santa Claus's wicked twin brother: the cumu-
lus cloud of snow-white beard frothing over black robes, and a *posture*
that was malevolent in itself. He was perched uncomfortably on the edge
of a large, decidedly bad-natured armchair in a stark, characterless room
enlivened solely by the two images hung on its walls. One was a gigantic
but disastrously faded photograph of Jerusalem's al-Aksa Mosque —
symbol of Israeli-American oppression of Islam and site of Tamimi's spiritual sinecure — and the other a smaller, newer shrink-wrapped pic of the
Sheikh himself enjoying a friendly chat with Saddam Hussein. Both men
sat in the kind of gilded, rococo thrones that were a dime a dozen in
Baghdad's Presidential Palace. Saddam wore a fetching white suit.

The Sheikh peered disapprovingly at me through spectacles shaped
like small TV screens. In the same sort of medieval academic robe
worn by leaders of Iran, he looked somewhat unreal surrounded by
prodigiously armed paramilitary minions and older, scholarly men in
threadbare sweaters, thrift-store overcoats, oily scarves, and frighten-
ingly mildewed boots. It was so cold in this room we could see our
breath. Someone indicated an armchair I could use, and an ancient
man with teeth like burnt matchsticks and one baleful eye instantly
poured me a shot glass of hot tea that tasted more like boiled entrails
flavored with mint.

I never know how to start these sort of meetings off. So I picked up a
copy of *The Destruction of Israel Is a Koranic Commandment*, which was
conveniently lying on my side table, and held it up, pointing to
the title.

"When I first saw this, Sheikh Tamimi, it made me want to scribble
'*no it's not*' underneath in magic marker. Now, you must hear that a lot,
right? So what's your reply? To those people who say that? . . . Where

does . . ." I trailed off mid-sentence.

Tamimi was staring at me like Hannibal Lector. It was an accomplished stare, long and unblinking.

Finally, after much muttering with a hobo scholar, the Sheikh said, "Holy Koran calls for deshstrooshun of Iss-ray-el."

"No, it doesn't. Where does it say *that*?"

There was again prolonged muttering.

"It is in Holy Koran," Tamimi eventually replied. Nice try.

"No, it's not. *Show* me."

A scrabbling ensued, the Sheikh and his disciples having trouble finding a Koran, it seemed. At length one was produced and Tamimi spent some fifteen minutes rummaging through it, looking perplexed at times, and once even turning to check the cover — making sure it wasn't the Amman telephone directory he'd been poring over, perhaps? Finally, he grunted with satisfaction, gave me the evil eye again, and began to read:

And We gave (clear) warning
To the Children of Israel
In the Book, that twice
Would they do mischief
On the earth and be elated
With mighty arrogance
(And twice would they be punished)![10]

The Sheikh looked up smugly.

"Could I see that?"

Someone passed me the weighty tome, which fortunately had English and Arabic side by side. Fortunately, too, Tamimi, like the rest of his kind, no matter which faith they cloak themselves in, was just abusing scripture.

"This whole passage is about the two destructions of Jerusalem," I complained. "Nebuchadrezzar's and then the Romans in AD 70. It's quite clear." I wondered how the Islamic calendar dealt with pre-Hegira dates — you see AH but there's no BM or BH — as I tried to read footnotes in type about a thirtieth of an inch high. This was laughable. "Look *here!*" I yodeled. "The footnotes say the same thing, for

Chrissakes! Then over the page you've got three different suras saying that judgment and punishment are Allah's alone — and *they* come in the hereafter. So your title is wrong, isn't it?"

"You are not unnerstand Iss-laam," Tamimi grumbled darkly.

"With all respect, your . . . er, sheikhness, I think *you're* the one who doesn't understand Islam. Anyone who thinks their religion wants them to kill themselves or others had better look at it more closely — or get another one. Another religion, I mean . . ."

This was not the most sensible thing to say. Horrified whisperings erupted all round the icy room, sounding like gas leaks or intercom static.

"Are you Moose-leem?" asked the Sheikh, sounding like the very soul of tolerance now — unnervingly.

What difference would that make?

To change the subject, I asked Tamimi about his latest proclamation, wondering if we in Canada could soon expect death squads and random bombings from his shadow warriors.

"There iss Moose-leems ebbrywheres," the Sheikh replied, waving his delicate, withered hands like a conductor ending a symphony.

He gave this vague statement some thought, then, obviously feeling he could be more specific, added, "Loog what is happen-ned to the Meyer Kahane . . ."

Kahane and his Jewish Defence League had been Brooklyn's answer to Tamimi and his Islamic Jihad, until Kahane was gunned down recently in New York. Had the Sheikh's boys been behind this job?

Tamimi smiled knowingly, looking around at his motley staff, some of whom also began smiling knowingly. A man with one arm offered the Sheikh some segments of orange while, presumably oblivious to Celestine coincidence, Tamimi continued: "The arm off Iss-laam iss ver long. Eet can reaching to ebbry corner off woal world and pluck out hiss enemy. Any berson whoo kill the Jew he iss my vollower."

I asked if the Sheikh felt any kinship with Nazism.

"The Hitt-lerse," he replied with a deeply self-satisfied smile, "wass goot frenn to Grand Mufti off Jerusalem. Eben diss, grade Sherman liter wass think to emm-brass off the Iss-laam. You haff know this?"

In fact, I did. I often wondered if that would have made him Grand Mufti of Berlin. I also knew that Hitler's favorite movie was *King Kong* and that Saddam's was *The Godfather*. I wondered what Tamimi's favorite movie might be.

Since everyone seemed to be in such good spirits now, I saw no harm in asking. Nor did the Sheikh, evidently, but the answer took much muttered thought.

Finally he replied, "I am like *Brish Obber Reev-kvai* too mush. Also *Dah-Pardi*, veeth Petta-slersh. I wash on wideo theese flims."

Initially, I assumed he was into Hindi movies. It was awhile before I realized that the spiritual head of Islamic Jihad's favorite films were, in fact, *Bridge over the River Kwai* and *The Party*, starring Peter Sellers — Tamimi's favorite actor, by far.

"Peter Sellers was Jewish," I pointed out.

"Too mush clebber ag-tor, Slersh Petta."

My toes were growing numb from the cold, and I was getting fed up with this bloodthirsty old cleric, so I asked him if he, too, thought Saddam capable of liberating Palestine.

"Saddam Hussein iss thee ess-ward — iss ride vording, ah! — iss sward off Al-lah," confirmed Tamimi. "Whoo can wizz-stand thee sward of God?"

America sounded like a good answer.

I was happy to find he had an appointment, because it was beginning to feel like a very long morning.

A little boy of four or five watched me from a nearby doorway as I extracted myself from Tamini's bunker. Like many Palestinians, this boy had reddish curly hair with a freckled-egg complexion. I walked over and asked him his name. It was Hussein. Trying not to be the enemy, the ugly American, I asked him a few trivial questions, then what he wanted to be when he grew up.

"I want to go Jihad," he said, smiling broadly, "and be the martyr for God."

I wanted to be a pirate when I was four.

Here was the real gulf in the Gulf, though: minds, hearts, and souls that simply cannot understand one another . . .

DENIAL IS NOT A RIVER IN EGYPT, IT FLOWS THROUGH THE HEART OF AMERICA

— U.S. bumper sticker

APOCALYPSO

When the Israelis threaten you with heavy retaliation, they aren't joking. It's a city for an eye and a town for a tooth: but the idea is essentially prophylactic. If you don't want someone to bother you, there's no point sending them Valentines — just ice them, blow them away, *terminate* them with extreme prejudice. When the Scuds started falling on Tel Aviv, I thought *Oh shit! Here we go* . . . A glance at the map will show you the problems involved in firing missiles at Israel from Iraq without them passing over any other countries on the way. Everyone was in little doubt that, sooner or later, Amman would once again be illuminated at night. A little too brightly.

To familiarize myself with air-raid procedures, I suggested to the Amman Sheraton's manager that a cocktail party in the Discotheque/ Bomb Shelter would be a popular idea with the world's media. Knowing how desperate they were for stories, it was bound to be well-attended.

And so it was. Some three hundred people — at least half of them Jordanians — packed into the place and swarmed all over the canapés and Lebanese Cabernet Sauvignon. A local DJ arrived with orange crates full of vinyl records. He set up, plugged in, and turned on . . . John Denver!

"What else you got here?"

"Theese the Shon Den-verre!"

"Listen," I said. "Whoever it was told you that people *like* John Denver was lying, okay? Because *no one* likes John Denver. John Denver makes people want to puke. Also, John Denver is not disco, 'kay? John Denver is not anything, in fact. He's uncategorizable. Lots of people are shit, but you can't say that John Denver's *shit* — you have to say something like *What is that John Denver shit?* Am I making any sense?"

"Theese my golleshun off the re-gords," the DJ told me, pointing at his orange crates. "I am have ebbry moo-jick me. You see for you zelve."

"Thanks."

Man, he had some howlers down there! He had fire-hydrant moisteners like I've never seen. These were *escapees*: surely no one had released them? *Gianni Spaldini & His Hot Five Play the Monkees Greatest Hits* . . . *Amorosa: Rocky Kulukundis Plays Music for Lovers* . . . *Bobby Vee's Velvet Collection* . . . *Acker Bilk: Stranger on the Shore* . . . *Twisting All Summer: The Tremelos* . . . *Mrs. Mills' Party Favourites* . . .

Then I hit a rich vein of reggae. Who knew that Andy Williams had done a reggae album? Just *one*, though, fortunately.

"Who was responsibile for the removal of John Denver?" boomed a deep, rich, sonorous Island voice.

"Me. Hoo yoo?"

I didn't expect to find myself face to face with Uncle Tom: tattered straw hat, checked shirt with the sleeves ripped out, worn, baggy old jeans that ended in frayed tassels an inch above the ankle and were held up by a rope belt.

"Bazeel McPherson," said Basil McPherson.

We shook hands and I gave him my name.

"Fond of John Denver, are you? No wonder you had to flee Barbados."

"Fond!" The word shuddered through the air like a Cruise missile. "No black man is *fond* of John Denver. I *despise* John Denver with a deep and abiding feelin' of ab-so-lute horror. And I was coming to shake the hand that — I sincerely trust — did some permanent damage to that most hideous of songs when plucking the needle from its grave in the groove."

"That's a relief. When are you on? If you're on?"

"You think *these* are my street clothes, sir?"

"Yeah. What's with that . . . er . . . costume, anyway? Is it traditional Calypso singing garb or what?"

"It is the folk dress of the freed slave right across the impoverished rural south of our great land, sir." He sounded like someone practicing for the annual Martin Luther King Pseudo-Biblical Rhetoric Award.

"Great *island*, surely?"

"Hummh?"

"You said *great land*, see? And, being from Barbados, you probably meant *great island*. Right?"

He beckoned me closer. He must have been 6'4" at least — *he'd* never get a photo op with Saddam. To him it was presumably a whisper, to me it was a rumble: "I am from New Or-*leenze*, sir! Not Barbados. But the situation here being what it is — a naked shame and an humiliation to a man like me — I thought it prudent to ah-*edit* my origins, as it were. You with me, sir?"

"Yup. So what do you sing, then? Cajun stuff? Zydeco?"

"No, sir! I am the King of Cajun Calypso. I personally repatriated the Calypso from the slave islands to from whence it came: Louisi-*anna*, sir!

That is where it was born. And it was not then a music for white tourist imperialism. No sunny skies and rum cocktails in my songbook, sir! I am a *Blues Man*, sir! The Blues are in my blood . . . And so is the Calypso. Thus, sir, what I sing is what Blind Lemon, Mississippi John, or the *Wolf* — or any of those fine, great souls — would have sung had they been by Caribbean shores instead of in that God-forsaken Delta!"

"Oh."

"This is Bazeel Akimbo McPherson's own Truth, sir."

"I'm sure it is. How does it go down with the audiences here?"

"So far, I have played two nights. The first night one person came. The second night four persons came. I see, however, that word-of-mouth has done what no amount of advertising or self-promotion could ever do. Look at all these *people*! This is proof that music cuts across all borders and boundaries. I shall not disappoint them, sir! I shall be dee-vine-leeeee innnn-*spired* tonight!"

"I can't wait. Wow, look at that."

The RAI TV crew had set up their camera and were testing lights, revealing two other crews on either side of them from . . . Serbia and East Timor, maybe?

"You're gonna be a star, Basil. You're gonna be on the evening news around the world, pal."

"*Damn!*" Basil's face lit up, his eyes gazed into a future fecund with fame and glory. "You are right, sir! I will sing them my *masterpiece*."

"What's your, um, your masterpiece?"

"You, sir, will remember this moment all the days of your life! For this was the moment you were first made aware of *BAM's Apocalypso!*"

"Bamze?"

"BAM — Bee, Ay, Em: Bazeel Akimbo McPherson. BAM is going to be the name of my orchestra, you see?"

"Got it. And, man, I love that *Apocalypso*. Wish I'd thought of it."

"No one but I could ever have thought of this!"

"Of course not. I didn't mean it like that. I meant it as praise. You know?"

Now a good eight feet tall, Basil Akimbo McPherson, future mega-star, strode proudly through hordes of fans to prepare his masterpiece for its unveiling.

"Are you Ruzzian Intelligenze?" asked a man with a clipboard and moustache.

"No, Canadian Apathy. Sorry."

He shouted something to a colleague who also had a clipboard and moustache. Then I heard the colleague shout my way:

"Canadian attache? Yah, dat's fine. You vill give inder-few? Vee are Tay-Vay Beograd, yah?"

"A fine city! Much excellent concrete," I yelled back. "No do inter-views. Canada Law say no interview with Serb peoples. Sorry!"

"Vie no Serbinderfew?" the nearer man asked darkly.

"Don't know. Secret. Usually means we're about to invade a country or declare war, though . . ."

"Hey, *Slobod!*" he screamed after his colleague, running back across the disco.

That should give the Serbs a break from Gulf War news, I thought.

When you provide free alcohol to a hundred-odd journalists from all over the world, you're in for trouble. There weren't any fights yet, but a couple of very loud arguments could be heard.

RAI must have sent their fashion reporter — and she must have been the object of that notice in the Intercontinental — for a young woman dressed for a night on the Via Veneto had swept into the disco with a look on her face that said *Oh Dio! Not another B party!* She was taking it out on the crew until an extravagantly bearded fellow arrived to distract her with a scroll of telexes. As I wandered out into the lobby, I could hear her whining in Italian about the canapés, the drinks, the people, her shoes, him, them, it . . .

The only kind of human more unbearable than a major TV star is a minor TV star. It was probably no mistake she'd been sent to cover Armageddon.

The manager greeted me with gasping joy. He couldn't thank me enough. I had brought honor to his house. I would eat and drink free there into the sunset of my years. How I must have worked to invite so many fine foreign journalists!

I'd merely mentioned it to a couple of lounge lizards at the Al Hanah and let human cupidity do the rest.

The bookstore man was equally overjoyed. He'd made a killing with my bale of print, and he wanted more. Maybe I should charter one of Alia's flying scrap heaps and make a bulk purchase of day-old news-papers and magazines in Vienna? Forget the war; become rich; buy some camels? Life was so full of possibilities!

When I returned to the disco, Basil was setting up on a kind of little podium, Slobod from TV Beograd was at the pushing stage of a major fistfight with one of RAI's crew, Keith Traynor was just standing up and feeling whether or not his bleeding nose was broken, having picked a fight with the wrong guy — a seven-foot Viking — and X from one of London's independent papers was doing the Funky Chicken with a funky chick and in a manner so funky lewd that one photograph of it would have Lady X polling her coven on who was considered to be the Ghengis Khan of British divorce law.

After a James-Earl-Jones-Does-the-Gettysburg-Address kind of introduction, during which Basil Akimbo McPherson left the world in no doubt that it was staring at the face of genius, he said: "The Archangel Gabriel whispered this song into my ear a little while ago. It's dedicated to all of you, to FREEDOM, and to my black brothers in the U.S. Army over there across the desert sands in Saudi Arabia. Leave the white man's army, my brothers, DESERT this desert! I say, LEAVE! Mutiny! For the ship of freedom must sail on! The title is . . . A-POC-CAL-LYPSO!"

"Bravo!" someone yelled. "Fuck America!"

"Fuck you!" a voice yelled back.

"Fuck the Shorge Boosh!"

"QUIET!" boomed Basil. "For I bring the message of Angels!"

He then commenced a kind of Bo Diddley effect with his glittering guitar: much echo, one chord. Having clearly established a rhythm not unlike the Calypso, he began to sing:

Old George Bush he is a very little man,
Always trying to do the very worst he can,
And it's never less than very pitiful to see
Skinny little white men try to prove their virility.
By starting the Persian Gulf Apocalypso
Persian Gulf Apocalypso
It's always 'Honey, read my lips — oh!
Baby, let me dock my marines and ships-oh!
For the Persian Gulf Apocalypso . . .'

The next verse of *Apocalypso* was so stupefyingly infantile that Basil was lucky no one paid him any attention. The Archangel Gabriel's literary gifts had clearly been expended on the Koran: this late period was worse than Wordsworth's.

With the bookstore man's help — obtained with the promise of fresh newsprint by the ton — I banished the more pugnacious guests to the weird tavern upstairs, then collected "a donation" for the party from all men and any women with purses. From at least 150 people, I ended up with a total of $63.76 in U.S. funds, 11 Swiss francs, 15 deutschmarks, thousands of Italian lire, nine Australian dollars, and about twelve ounces of coins in unidentifiable currencies.

My finances had taken a sudden turn for the worse, and, after realizing I'd left Planet Credit, I knew I'd be landing on Planet Big Trouble unless I found the Money Meteor very, very soon. Before settling down to watch an exceptionally horrific Nazi movie — which, for some reason, the Israeli TV channel showed every night — I booked a call to my editor back at *Saturday Night* magazine in Toronto.

READ MY LABIA: NO MORE WAR

— U.S. feminist anti-Gulf War bumper sticker

JOHN FRASER'S CHASSIDIC SONG

A rosy-fingered dawn cracked over the rain-lacquered streets of Amman, its reflections setting fire to ten thousand windows on the stacked white cubes of the city. Israeli TV, from Jerusalem, had some curious ideas about what the viewing public expected from its early morning programming. A little after 6:00 a.m., this member of the viewing public found himself obliged to watch the "Chassidic Song Festival" — dozens of young men and women who'd escaped from a sixties' Reno lounge act singing "Hava Negila" and other ageless classics. The previous morning it had been similar or perhaps the same people, but this time wearing white gloves and — don't ask *me* why — Hawaiian garlands, while engaged in what appeared to be a sixty-minute version of *The 20-Minute Workout*.

I was getting a little sick by now of listening to journalists drunkenly complaining that there wasn't enough fighting going on outside their hotels, or that there was too much fighting going on inside them. I hadn't come here for *this*. But I wasn't going anywhere until some distant wheels started turning — and they hadn't yet. I'd called down five times now to see if the hotel operator remembered me. He did, but he still couldn't get a line to Canada.

Just as I was beginning to think that, if I gave it time, Chassidic music could grow on me, the phone screamed and yelped for attention. I cradled the poor little thing on my shoulder and cooed it to sleep.

"Paul?"

"Who's *this*?"

I wasn't expecting a man's voice.

"John Fraser in Toronto."

"O shi—"

"What? Speak up. It's a bad line."

Now, John was the editor of *Saturday Night* magazine, but he wasn't *my* editor. Anne Collins was my editor, and I worshipped the ground she floated over. John, however, wished me harm, great and dire harm. He never said so — he never *spoke* to me — but I *knew* so. By mistake, I'd given one of his books a bad review (who knew then that he'd be editor of *Saturday Night*?). I came to realize that it must have been a temporary lapse of critical judgment, for was not the book in question excellent in every way? Indeed it was. But they don't let you retract reviews. So he wished me harm. And if I were in his place, I would have wished me harm, too. Revenge is one of life's great unsung pleasures, and I sensed that its ineffable sweetness had just been stirred into John Fraser's soul by some foul quirk of fate.

"I was calling Anne, actually. Nice of *you* to call, of course. Really nice. Wonderful to hear your voice. How *are* you?"

"What do you want? I've got to get home to dinner." *Home to dinner* . . . I wondered if I'd ever be saying those words again.

"Money."

"You'll have to talk to Anne."

"Where is she?"

"Home sick. A cold."

"*You'll* have to help me, then. Can you wire $10,000 to Amex in Amman?"

"No."

"I'm fucked without it. There's no way out of here, and I've just encountered some heavy expenses."

"No doubt."

"It's going to be a great story, John."

"Anne will be pleased."

"Listen, just wire the money, okay? We'll sort it out later."

"Impossible."

"Not for *you* . . . Ask Conrad — he can afford it. Can't he?" Conrad Black owns *Saturday Night* magazine and much else — including the *Daily Telegraph* and the *Jerusalem Post*.

"Listen. If it were up to me, I'd leave you there without a cent. But, for some unfathomable reason, Anne's very worried about you. I like Anne a lot, and I don't want her to worry . . ."

"So?"

"I'll tell her you called and that you're fine, and everything's fine. Okay?"

"You miserable Welsh bastard — I knew this would happen sooner or later."

"But I bet you didn't dream you'd be *there* when it happened, though, did you?"

I threw the phone on the floor and kicked it. Then retrieved it. "I'm Welsh too, you know. We should demonstrate a little patriotic brotherly love, don't you think?"

"It's not a Welsh trait. We Welsh are miserable, back-stabbing bastards. You said so yourself. Or were you going to say what you said in that review? Which was, let me think, yes: Fraser is quite clearly —"

"Stop it!" I howled. "I didn't mean *that*. I had flu that day. My sciatic nerve was pinched. Someone smashed into my car. My wife left me. My dog died. Debt collectors had besieged my apartment. The Mafia were trying to kill me. The devil appeared in a vision and made me do it . . ."

"I am rather enjoying this, after all."

"I'm not. I'm not having any fun, John. None at all."

"It's getting late. Listen, I tell you what: I'll call Anne and tell her exactly what you told me."

"About the book?"

"Yes. No, silly — about the unforeseen expenses, the $10,000, the American Express office in Aden —"

"*Amman!* Not Aden. Please don't fuck me up, John. I don't need it right now."

"Be sure to tell me when you *do* need it then, okay?"

"It's so lonely and desolate here that I keep . . . I — John? *John!*"

He'd hung up. Instead of being angry, though, I missed him. A familiar voice — even a fairly unfamiliar familiar voice — means a lot at certain times. Like Chassidic music, maybe John could grow on me — if I gave him time. And if he gave me time to have that time, of course.

I met Prince Hassan for coffee. He's a nice guy — for an Arab prince — and we knew each other on a scholarly basis. He had no idea that I wrote anything but academic treatises that were 95 percent footnotes, or at least I assume he had no idea. Otherwise he wouldn't have dropped so much gossip on me. Quite a character, that brother of his, *quite* a character . . .

Today, however, Hassan looked and acted sick.

"There are many problems, many worries," was the explanation.

No, I didn't say: *Like what? Like your brother getting mixed up with Baghdad's Butcher, you mean? Like being at war with America, you mean? Or do you mean like the fact that Israel's about to wipe Jordan off the map?*

You have to be discreet with these characters. Besides, what worried him most was "the refugee problem" and rumors that American bombing raids had demolished several ancient sites of major importance, including one of the many buildings scattered between here and Europe that are called "Oldest Christian Church in the World." Hassan's account, however, made this place sound as if it were odds-on favorite to be the real thing. He took more than just a keen interest in old stuff — old stuff was his very life. Which is why there are more and better preserved ancient sites in Jordan than anyone who's never been there realizes. Petra is just the tip of the buried pyramid. I'd once accused Hassan of fabricating them all, but he's such a serious fellow that he was about to show me the state accounts to prove the state couldn't afford to build a public washroom let alone a facsimile Roman town.

"I hope we meet under better circumstances next time," said the prince, as I prepared to leave.

"A next time in itself will be better circumstances."

"True. *Maa'as-salaama.*"

"*Nahaarik sa'id.*" Have a nice day.

KICK BUTT, THEN WHAT?

— *U.S. anti-Gulf War bumper sticker*

THE RAINS DOWN IN AFRICA

I decided to see what there was to Prince Hassan's worries about a "refugee problem," and shared an old wreck of a Mercedes cab with the *Toronto Star*'s Paul Watson out to the Iraqi border. Watson is a connoisseur of wars and human catastrophes: he loves them, he can't get enough of them. He's the only person with one hand ever to win a Pulitzer Prize for Photography, too. You don't have to be Sherlock Holmes to realize this means he must use a small automatic camera — and he does. One of the Sheraton's waiters asked me about Watson's missing hand: where had it gone? I said he'd been born like that (his mother had watched too many episodes of *The Fugitive* when she was pregnant). The waiter absorbed this puzzling information, then confided that Watson must have been a thief who'd escaped punishment in his previous life. I didn't tell Watson this, of course. Muslims aren't even supposed to believe in reincarnation, anyway — although things get a little confusing after you die, so who knows?

We'd acquired a government minder for this trip into forbidden zones — Abdul, he was called, a fat, laconic, mean-looking son-of-a-bitch, with a big black overcoat and a perpetual *I-know-things-you-people-never-even-dream-of* expression on his swarthy moon of a face. He'd organized the cab, and it was a piece of shit — a piece that he probably had an interest in, too. The heater didn't work, and one of its many crunchy encounters with solid steel or rock had left the rear door with an inch-wide buckle through which a jet of subzero air streamed in at about waist level for the next ten hours. Abdul started disliking me the moment I started disliking him — which was when I inquired why he'd selected the worst heap in all of Amman for a long trip in the dead of winter.

"Not damages," he protested. "This is the air vent for you good fresh air. This Mercedes car, no sheet piece."

"Sod off, Abdul. If you'd have said it was because you were making some baksheesh from the deal I'd have a lot more respect for you. If you'd have *asked* us if we wanted a piece of shit for a hundred rials or something a bit less like a motorized meat safe for one-fifty, we'd have happily —"

"— told you to fuck off," Watson suggested.

"Exactly."

Now we were heading through that part of Jordan inserted like a plug between Syria and Saudi Arabia. It's known as "Winston Churchill's hiccup," this bizarre boundary, having evidently been sketched out by the much-overrated British prime minister, pop historian, and drunken bore after a particularly well-lubricated lunch.

Out past the stacked canyons of Amman, the sole road to Ruwaishid (the border town) is also the main highway to Baghdad. It heads straight through the "hiccup" between low hills into some of the bleakest, most desolate landscape I've ever clapped eyes upon. A wasteland of black, football-sized rocks, it skulked there almost sentiently. I couldn't even imagine what primeval geological stunt could have been responsible for it. You couldn't *give* this landscape away — unless, of course, you were Churchill — and it was clear that its current owners hadn't even bothered to see if anything useful could be done with it. *No one* would ever move out there, that much was certain. Those who think a wilderness of trees can be terrifying should consider a wilderness without trees.

Soon, we started encountering more and more oil transports heading in the same direction we were. You can tell if an oil truck is full or empty. Full ones sit low, move slowly, and tilt back when accelerating.

"Are we sure they're carrying oil?" I asked Watson.

We both craned our necks to observe the one we were then overtaking. Black and greasy, the vehicle could have just driven out of a swamp.

"I don't think that's milk in there, do you?" he replied.

The significance of these transports — and there were many, many of them — was complex. Jordan usually received oil *from* Iraq; why would it now be sending oil *into* Iraq? And where would the oil be coming from? Since Iraq's refineries were being systematically demolished even as we spoke, the country could no longer supply itself with oil, let alone give any away. Were Jordan's own refineries now returning a supply stored for such emergencies? Or was there another vast consumer of oil somewhere between Amman and the Iraqi border?

The border closed each day at 2:30 p.m. anyway, at which time the entire area was cleared by orders from on high. A dozen or so of the oil transports we'd passed on the way were now parked a mile or so back from the border, near a high-security compound. A number of different flash luxury sedans with Iraqi plates came and went between these two points while we were hanging around.

We had to hang around for quite a bit, too. Without permission from whoever was in charge of this top secret shanty town, we wouldn't be going much farther. Taped over the border commandant's door was a jumbo poster of Saddam Hussein. In Jordan this was not an especially unusual sight — I just didn't expect to find one in an army base, the way I wouldn't expect to find a portrait of the U.S. president hanging on some Canadian general's office wall.

The commandant turned out to be a major in one of King Hussein's crack Bedouin special units. You don't want to fuck with these jokers — it would be your very last deed on earth — so the border was the best place for them. Although the buckled, shanty town shack exterior of his HQ would have made a Calcutta rat scoff, inside it was amazingly opulent, with sheepskin couches and a desk the size of a squash court. The major, wearing army uniform, keffiyeh, floor-length sheepskin abaya, and a huge silver belt with an even huger dagger lodged inside it, got up as we were ushered in. Then he left for half an hour. A kerosene heater provided us with the non-option of either choking to death inside or freezing to death outside. Feeling we were being subjected to all manner of arcane tests — including the one involving our passports — and still lumbered with the sepulchral Abdul, we refrained from commenting on the startling array of wacky objects and uncommon paintings furnishing this five-star hovel. Only after some time did it occur to me that the decorator had made the place look as much like a tent as possible.

When the sinister major stalked back in, his moustache appeared to have grown an inch or two longer. Without saying a word, he sat himself behind his prodigious desk and stared. Behind him, an eight-foot oil painting of King Hussein, Bedouin Warrior, seemed to be supervising the proceedings. Whatever they were. Bedouin have a thing about staring, though: they like to stare. They like you to stare back, too, but not for that long. I've been told that they can read your intentions by the length and steadiness of your stare; and that, conversely, you can convey your sincerity and humility in the face of their superior manliness by staring a bit, then admitting defeat. So I stared back at the major.

I was wondering whether anyone had told *him* about this staring tradition — since I'd looked away three times now, then gone back to staring again when it seemed to produce no results — but he suddenly bolted to his feet in a cloud of dust and grimy sheepswool strands.

"Instead I will execute you," he announced.

Not.

"You may now go on your way."

Our way wasn't much of a way or that far away to cause such a fuss, as it turned out. We simply wanted to take a look at the border itself in order to get some idea of whether or not there was a mass exodus turning into a mass murder on the far side. Many thousands of migrant workers were thought to have fled Baghdad after George Bush indicated its potential impermanence, and although Prince Hassan had told me many of them had crossed the border, causing a gigantic problem in Jordan, it was still believed that many more were being denied exit visas and forced to camp out in appalling conditions on the far side.

The border, however, told us nothing. Wind blew through it, scattering old newspapers, dust, hailstones, and garbage. A vista of chain-link and barbed wire, there was something unspeakably awful about it. It reminded me of Auschwitz. And the no-man's-land between the two Husseins' realms turned out to be three miles long — so, given the swooping thunder clouds and their rich assortment of precipitations, only Superman would have been able to check out the Iraq-side action. The icy wind and the pervasive gloom seemed to be clotting around my bones by now. I just wanted to go home, or to a home — anyone's home. Traveling isn't all it's cracked up to be, and I don't recommend eastern Jordan in January as a fun alternative to Jamaica.

Heading back west, rain turned to snow, then to white gravel, then to granite Ping-Pong balls, then to gobs of iced phlegm, then to the kind of porridge your grandfather claimed he made the *traditional way* as taught him personally by Robert the Bruce. The secret was to add fermented goats' hocks, gunpowder, and pine resin. Whatever was falling from the low-slung butts of these obese purplish-black clouds, the stuff certainly put you off ever wanting to eat it. I learned much later that, contrary to popular belief, dropping 96,000 tons of explosives on a major city like Baghdad is not particularly beneficial to the general ecology of the surrounding area, and that all kinds of shit goes up into the air after the specific shit comes down, and this ragout of urban detritus can often get carried many hundreds of miles before finding a change in air pressure to make it yearn to be back at ground level once more. How often do you see tar-like blobs in the scoops of brittle snow spattering like eggs on your windshield?

Abdul had seemed unusually alert and anxious when we threatened to take a walk around the Bedouin major's compound, where the big trucks had also pulled over. Which was why I suddenly let out an inhuman warble of pain and demanded the driver to stop instantly so I could unleash a bladderful of sulfuric acid. Near the oil transports. Clutching my guts, I hobbled toward the privacy of some man-sized boulders.

Behind them, and behind the oil tankers, well out of sight from the road, were camouflaged army trucks obviously packed to the gills with *something*. Soon I smelled why. There's no mistaking the odor of high-octane airplane fuel — which was most definitely what these parked tankers contained in superabundance. There were batteries of SAM launchers all along the hills, which conveniently concealed most of the landscape on either side of this road for a good fifty miles, and these batteries had been unusually active during the last hour or so.

There had been a mystery concerning the whereabouts of Saddam's air force since the war began, but it was suddenly becoming a little less mysterious. Jordan had been a haven for Saddam's planes during the Iran-Iraq war, after all — and it clearly was again. No wonder Prince Hassan's ulcer was shaking its booty: his brother, the little king, might have gotten himself in a little too deep this time. And the CIA weren't about to save his skin now. In fact, no one was — except his namesake down the road a thousand miles.

There was more: the lifeline between Baghdad and the port of Aqaba had not been cut, as was being claimed. Scratched maybe, but not cut.

Betrayed by old friends in the past, King Hussein was not about to betray an old friend himself. The old friend might now be an international pariah, but he was the only friend Ziggy had. That week.

Over the crest of a small hill, gleaming in that sinister light you get from a searing sunbeam briefly blasting through thick black cloud, lay Tent Town: several hundred khaki tents pitched in orderly rows on flat, muddy land. Soldiers asked for our permits (which I had gotten from Amman's press office), then told us we could stay for only twenty minutes. A Red Crescent official, sitting in a tent warmed by a butane pita bread pan, visibly winced when we asked where the most recent refugees were housed. Hunched over a ledger, he looked like someone engaged in solving a problem that had no solution. *You* try feeding three thousand people with one crate of tinned sardines.

"They're in section C," he snapped.

"Where's that?"

"You get A, then B, and it's after *that*."

Simple enough. Yet with every tent marked by the Red Crescent symbol — which, oddly enough, is a red crescent — it wasn't as simple as it sounded. Because, stamped or stenciled crudely on canvas, a red crescent looks exactly like the letter C.

Cruising up and down the rutted tracks between crowded rows of sodden tents, I watched anxious faces peer out of flaps at our sputtering cab. The worst example of Mercedes technology left on the roads of this planet, the accursed shitbox seemed ravishingly opulent here. It embarrassed me. Indeed, I embarrassed me: socks, shoes, coat, wallet, *Presidential Suite* — what had I done to deserve all this? I'll never make it in capitalism, will I?

I got out of the cab to wander the little rows of canvas alleyways. Blue-black men stood chattering in small groups, storm-cloud-colored men with decorative tribal scars to keep some shred of their ancient dignity even in the depths of their modern misery. There is no mistaking peoples of the Sudan, a country vast — over one million square miles — yet unable to care for even half its population now.

Most of these men were a head taller than I was, yet their manner was strangely stunted, cowed. They weren't sure the horror was over yet.

They were cold and hungry and frightened and uncertain what the future would hold. Everyone — except Sheikh Jaber — knows what a bitch *that* can be. Unlike most foreign nationals fleeing the war, the Sudanese had been all but disowned by their government and had been informed it was the duty of the Red Cross to get them home. Yet no one had seen the Red Cross in eastern Jordan. And home meant a civil war combined with what was then shaping up to be the worst famine in history.

Not that anyone cared. No multinational corporation had been stupid enough to build a vested interest in the Sudan — so no Western shareholders could be losing money. *No one's listening, sorry. You'll just have to starve to death, guys. All four million of you.*

"Speaking as one human being to another," said a gentle giant of a man with what resembled a page of Braille patterning his face, "what do you think of all this?"

"I think it's terrible."

"Yes," he said, nodding grimly. "Is truly terrible. Why people do this to each other? Why?"

"I don't know."

"No one know, sir. No one know. You must *help* us here. We have *no* food here. A man can't live on one tin of fishes a day, can he, sir?"

"No. Is that all you're getting? Sardines?"

"Leetle fishes. I want to go to my home, sir. Yet they say only Red Cross takes us there. We see no *Red Cross*. *You* must help us, sir. We have no voice in all this world. *You* must be our voice, please. *You* must tell this story, or world never going to hear."

I have been asked this twice in my life, and both times the request was achingly poignant and desperately sincere.

I asked another man what the bombing in Baghdad had been like.

"Like the rain," he said.

And I could hear the African monsoon thundering down upon the tin roof of that little shack, in that little village he wanted to reach now more than he'd ever wanted anything on earth.

The great rains of Africa: They are the tears of God.

HOW MANY BODY BAGS PER GALLON?

> — *U.S. anti-Gulf War-for-oil bumper sticker*

WHERE THE SUN SETS

The West Bank, whatever else it was, wasn't a place anyone wanted to visit. Getting there from Amman wasn't particularly difficult, however. It's only a few miles away. But getting back was harder. Members of the PLO picked me up and put me down not much later right in the heart of what was soon to become the Palestinian Authority. When Arabs look after you, *they look after* you. They were looking after me so well, in fact, that they reminded me it was the Israelis I had to worry about now.

Basically, during the 1991 Gulf War, the West Bank was still a Palestinian concentration camp policed by Israel's armed forces with such severity that its inhabitants had more or less given up leaving their homes. The place looks like a troll's metropolis built out of old concrete blocks by thousands of five-year-olds for a school project that was either still under way or had been abandoned long ago. It was a dump, in other words. There were some parts where the Humane Society for Animals wouldn't have allowed you to keep a pet stoat. Most Palestinians and Israelis don't like each other, in case you haven't heard, but since Israelis ran the place (although they weren't supposed to according to the United Nations), Palestinians didn't win many arguments. They were treated marginally better than the Jews of Germany were during the thirties. Admittedly, it wasn't a great idea for Palestinians to cheer in the streets as Saddam's Scuds began falling on Israel. But it wasn't a great idea for Chaim Weizmann, on behalf of world Jewry, to declare war on Germany in 1933, either — and the German Jews begged him not to.

The politics of the Israel-Palestine problem are so involved and convoluted — like anything politicians get their paws on — that they're not even worth getting into. But we'll have to get into them soon, I'm afraid. Again the root lies back in the days of the Mandates. With the PLO as my hosts, however, obviously my guided tour had a slight bias to it, a barely concealed agenda.

I asked a man named Aziz Odeh — who'd worked in a Jerusalem bank until recently — if he thought his people would ever be reconciled in some form with the Israelis.

"No," he said.

There's nothing like positive thinking.

In a hospital that looked like something out of a Florence Nightingale movie, I was shown "victims of Israeli brutality." Lots of them. No doubt, and not that far away, there was a hospital full of victims of Palestinian brutality. I only began to really dislike Saddam Hussein after he started whining about civilian casualties, having done nothing but bomb residential areas of Tel Aviv himself for two weeks. Yes, the atrocities against Palestinians *are* awful. But has anyone come up with an atrocity that isn't awful?

As the European Jews flocking to Israel gradually become Israelis, they also — and increasingly so, it seems — become more like the Arabs in whose midst they now live. Even the medieval horrors perpetrated by Palestinians against Israelis and Israelis against Palestinians are beginning to resemble inter-Arab feuds. Considering their deeply hideous nature, look how quickly they are water under the bridge — and Palestinian lies down with Israeli, as the time under heaven allotted for the purpose of negotiation arrives. You get nowhere in the Middle East by taking sides: it's like a grade three teacher making one obnoxious little bully her pet and the other her pet peeve. A little patience, along with a lot of education, is the only final solution — unless someone wants to use an earlier precedent for final solutions. And you hear talk of such an abomination *as if it had worked out for Hitler.*

"A European colony," said one Arab when I asked him about Israel's right to exist. "An anachronism that must go."

Go where? I wondered.

Having tea with a certain Mahmud Assad and his family in their West Bank hovel, I became terminally weary of hearing the same old arguments. *You're all right,* I wanted to scream. *You're all right — everyone's right. Now just shut up, sit down, and work it out, for crissakes!*

"And we have no gas masks," Mahmud Assad complained. "Though Israel court, they say they must give us gas masks."

On TV in Amman, I'd watched the Allied pilots, who'd obviously just been efficiently beaten up, read condemnations of the war from cue cards. Some men were clearly tied to their chairs in case they collapsed from the effort of confession. Chilling, repugnant, yes. Yet villagers, not Iraqi soldiery, had beaten them up (authorities the world over are trained not to leave visible marks), and, when all's said and done, the pilots *had* just been trying to bomb these very villagers into oblivion. If I were an

Israeli cop, I probably wouldn't give Palestinians gas masks either — court or no court — and if I were an Iraqi villager, I'd probably beat the crap out of an Allied pilot who was trying to bomb my family.

As I watched the exquisite sonata for technology and pyrotechnics involved in a Scud missile getting intercepted by a Patriot for the first time over Jerusalem, I imagined the spectacle might be a topic for a little idle conversation with Israeli Border soldiers. It wasn't.

"Did you enjoy it?" one asked.

"What?"

"Israel under attack."

"No. But it did look sort of pretty, didn't it?"

"Fucker!" another Uzi-toting eighteen-year-old shouted at me. "You fuck your mouth, you fucking big fucker!"

You need to be familiar with languages before you can swear in them. Hebrew isn't that useful a language for mundane cursing — which is why, happily, Yiddish will survive. No language can top the sheer richness and inventiveness of Yiddish when it comes to terms of disparagement.

"What's your name, soldier?" I asked the kid.

"You fuck you, ash-hole!"

His buddy obviously pointed out that I hadn't merited *quite* this much abuse, and that for all they knew I might be head of The Mossad.

"Here my name: Avi Halevi. Okay?"

"Avi, you ever hear of Rabbi Hillel?"

"I don't not believing in bulls-shit religion. There is not any God."

"Hillel didn't say there *was*. But he could recite the whole Torah standing on one foot, you know?"

"Yeah, well thass fucking good for him!"

"Know how he did it?"

"I don't giving no shit how he's doing."

"It's a good trick: you could do it at parties."

"Yeah? So what he doing then?"

"He said: 'That which is hateful unto you, do not do unto others — this is the whole of the Torah. The rest is commentary.' Neat, eh?"

"Yeah. Fucking neat bulls-shit, uh?"

"*Shabat shalom*," I said, for it was the eve of the Sabbath.

At the other end of the Allenby Bridge back to Jordan, things were a little more relaxed.

"A journalist?" asked a very elegant Jordanian Army officer wearing expensive Italian Chelsea boots instead of army issue.

"Historian. Nabatean civilization."

I dropped Prince Hassan's name a few times, with enough detail to convince the officer I couldn't be fibbing.

"I have to go back into Amman myself now," he told me. "Can I offer you a lift?"

"Sure. Thanks a lot."

"Good. I'll meet you outside the customs shed. Just go and get your passport stamped. Amir!" He shouted to one of his men. "Get the professor's passport rushed through for me, would you? Just follow him, you'll be done in no time," I was informed.

The thirty people ahead of me didn't seem to mind in the least that I jumped the lineup.

"Have you any Ishraeli visa or schtamp?" asked the immigration guy.

"Nope."

"You have effer visit Ishrael, sir?"

"I have never been in Occupied Palestine in my life," I replied quite truthfully.

Thwump-thwump: My passport was stamped and returned with a "Welcome to the Kinkdom of Shordan."

This was the third time I had crossed from Israel into Jordan by the bridge, and the situation never failed to amuse me. There isn't anywhere a person coming into Jordan across the bridge could possibly have been *but* Israel, yet anyone having an Israeli visa or border-entry stamps in his passport was inadmissible — even his Jordanian visa, if he had one, was declared null and void. Since no one wants Israeli anything in their passports, the Israelis don't even seem to have stamps. At Ben Gurion Airport, I once saw someone demanding a stamp for their collection —no one could locate the thing. Yet since this whole situation is a nuisance to all concerned, the Jordanians go strictly by the book, and the book doesn't say they can *assume* visitors have come from anywhere. They have to ask, and the book says that, seeing no evidence in their passports to refute the visitors' answers, they can admit anyone they choose to admit. And so they do. It's rather charming.

"So," said the officer, as we drove off, "tell me all about how things are in Israel. I'm dying to know . . ."

KIDS! STOP FIGHTING AND CLEAN UP YOUR MESS!

— U.S. parents' anti-Gulf War bumper sticker

PROMISED LAND

You could hardly pick up a newspaper in those days without encountering that specious platitude, "Truth is the first casualty of war." In reality truth had been mugged, buggered, and beaten up long before this war started. There's only one casualty of war: human beings. There's only one Truth too: Don't fuck around with other people if you don't like other people fucking you around.

Back in Amman, I rose before dawn the next day and took a cab out to Mount Nebo for the sunrise. I highly recommend the spot for those who enjoy the occasional moment of communion with the Eternal.

> Moses climbed up from the western plains of Moab to Mount Nebo, to the top of the cliff facing Jericho. God showed him all the land of the Gilead as far as Dan, all of Naphtali, the land of Ephraim and Manasseh, the land of Judah as far as the Mediterranean Sea, the Negev, the flat plain, and the valley of Jericho, city of dates, as far as Tzoar.
>
> God said to him, "This is the land regarding which I made an oath to Abraham, Isaac and Jacob, saying, 'I will give it to your descendants.' I have let you see it with your own eyes, but you will not cross [the river] to enter it."
>
> It was there in the land of Moab that God's servant Moses died with the Divine kiss upon his lips. . . .
>
> No other prophet like Moses has arisen in Israel, a man who knew God face to face . . .[11]

The place hasn't changed much since Moses' time. I stood exactly where he had, "on the top of the cliff facing Jericho." It's more mountain than cliff, though, and the land of the twelve tribes way down, beyond the river Jordan's silvered ribbon, still looks as if it's unfurling from the ethers before you. But even though we're told Moses' eyesight was still good at the ripe old age of 120, he wouldn't have been able to see as far as the Negev or Mediterranean that morning.

Dawn was more like a terrible wound oozing thin blood and the angry puss of infection through an expanse of bruised and battered flesh. The clouds hung in a thick, undulating fungus across heaven's door, as if a material manifestation of human gloom, depression, and despair. A vicious wind worried the trees and slapped at my hair and scarf. This was, I reminded myself, where all the problems started, after all.

I sat there, gazing now upon the inner landscape of vast silence, where neither world nor wind could reach. And I asked God if he'd really intended to cause such trouble for Moses' descendants by telling them this land was the promised one and would be theirs until the end of time. This was the reply:

I promised I'd leave you alone and I have. Work it out. Whatever you see is what *you* have created, not me. God is good.

It's not a good idea to argue with Him, though.

Jordan has always struck many people as the area having a more solid case for being considered the Palestinian homeland than Israel does. This is a touchy subject out at the little royal court there — after all, there are very many Palestinians already living in Jordan, and more than once they've tried to file their claim to the entire place rather forcefully. Now another possibility had arisen. It was advertised all over Amman by a spurious press release:

Officials at the United Nations have announced that a choice parcel of real estate will soon be unoccupied, and will be available to become an official homeland for a Palestinian state. Eviction proceedings against the current occupant have already begun, and are now expected to be completed shortly.

According to the UN spokesperson, the parcel, situated between Kuwait and Syria, may be considered to be an ideal location for the foundation of a homeland for a Palestinian State.

Officials from the PLO and other Palestinian support organizations were not available for comment.

They were with their real-estate agents.

That afternoon, the "Gulf Peace Team" returned from Baghdad and held a press conference in a curious place that called itself a "training hotel." Presumably it was very cheap, but it looked merely very ugly. Every journalist in town showed up: this was the biggest news in days — although under normal circumstances it may have attracted a *Yoga Journal* stringer and some school kids reporting for the *Grade Six Echo*.

The Gulf Peace Team consisted of various old hippies who'd decided to make a gesture against the war by camping between the Allied and Iraqi forces — on the Iraqi side. The Team clearly hadn't worried that this might make them a useful propaganda tool for Saddam; besides, they'd first been denied permission to camp on the Saudi side of the war zone. Obviously, things had become a little hairy, and they'd decided that being the war's first casualties might not be a very pleasant, let alone effective, way of stopping a war that had already started. Iraqi officials had moved them to safer territory as well, wisely speculating that Gulf Peace Teamers resting in peaceful body bags wouldn't make any better propaganda than had "An Evening with Allied Pilots Who've Been Beaten into Blood-Puddings by Peace-Loving Iraqi Farmers."

But propaganda is a trial-and-error business. Even Josef Goebbels found that the movie about Jews he'd blown a fortune on making had to be scrapped after test audiences complained that it went so far overboard in showing how the average German Jew lived — in a small sewer or time-share rat hole, through which he scuttled looking like a mad troll — that it made even Nazis feel sorry for them. The current Baghdad Goebbels had been similarly stunned to learn that Western public opinion's pendulum had not exactly come swinging back in a resounding endorsement of Iraq's cause after watching his pilot-talk-show's pilot. (No doubt it would have become a series, had it got better ratings.)

Yet with a hit series running in prime time seven nights a week on all three U.S. networks, and twenty-four hours a day on CNN globally, Saddam's propagandists were becoming fast learners. Unlike the hippies.

After all the hype and with the eyes of the world upon them, the Gulf Peace Team didn't do much with their two hours, fifteen minutes of fame.

"Yuh, wull, like, 'ullo! Me name is Nobby Bird, see . . . und I were born in Alnwick, wha issnear Nukassel, innit? Inny a'yuzz 'ere Nukassel Yewnitted sporters? Noo wun? Ritt, like . . . um . . . datt meerks me wha we call a Juddie, see . . ."

Thus began Nobby Bird, Geordie, Newcastle United fan. His autobiography went on for twenty minutes *before* we reached the epiphanic moment that made him decide to join the Gulf Peace Team. I think. Nobody can understand the Geordie accent, which seems to give even Geordies problems communicating with each other. The world's media kept looking at each other to see who was still taking notes. All had pens poised over spiral pads, but rarely did ballpoint meet paper.

"Ahscoosah me," said Akira, a Japanese TV reporter I'd come to appreciate for his guileless honesty. "Ba whaat rang-gridge he spikken thah man?"

I explained that no one knew. It was from a part of England where one heard strange tales of interspecies couplings, of werewolves, of grendel-shanks, hogmen . . .

"Ah-hogmaan?"

"You've heard of Hogmanay?"

"Ah-na-not ah-hear this."

"Scots' New Year, see?"

"Ah-hah! See now, ah-yes. See!"

I wondered what he'd seen — but if he was happy, so was I.

After "Nobby Bird: An Ideological Autobiography," we moved right along — to "My Remarkable Life by Terry Biggs." I must confess I did find it quite remarkable that nothing at all remarkable had *ever* happened to Terry Biggs. Even this heroic venture had not been particularly remarkable, the way he told it. He did, however, tell the disturbing news that the bombs currently being dropped on Iraq apparently destroyed buildings and weren't very popular with the average Iraqi citizen. Terry had also found that, no matter what anyone said, war itself wasn't especially pleasant.

Next came a handsome woman who seemed still to be on an acid trip that had started back in the sixties. "War is an obsolete form of conflict resolution," she announced.

"What exactly do you mean by *that*?" some prick asked her.

You don't need this when your brain cells have been like a skullful of Christmas lights for twenty-five years, do you?

"It's fairly obvious what she means, isn't it?" I felt I should tell him.

"Oh really? Well, why don't I interview you?"

The flower person seemed to think she had said as much as was required, fortunately, and she floated away like an old moth. The next act, a woman who looked as if she'd pick a fight with anyone after half a glass of Hungarian claret, informed us that only men start wars, because there's something wrong with men, but not anything that couldn't be treated by a series of massive injections of female hormones. Every time a woman had become successful in the male world, she said, men had plotted her downfall. Joan of Arc, for example, or Cleopatra. With women at their helms, the ships of state would sail smoother seas. There would be no more war.

Oz One's unmistakable voice could be heard to ask: "Joan of Arc? Cleopatra? Katherine the Great? Elizabeth I? Indira Gandhi? Golda Meir? Margaret Thatcher? Yew oughta do a bit-ah revision, young lady."

"Very typical reaction from a backward Australian misogynist like yourself. Now *shut up* and let me finish."

He did, wisely.

The cameras and notebooks absorbed this guff from several more team members before questions could be asked. Since no one could think of that many questions to ask, however, the team members soon continued with more details about their origins, their neighborhoods, their bookshelves, their dreams, and how they'd come to be in Iraq.

A young Scotsman with extravagant hair said he'd been involved in "Enterprise Training" and that coming to the Gulf seemed like an enterprising thing to do. No one except the Brits present knew what "Enterprise Training" was. It's a British government-funded scheme, in fact, to pay unemployed people while they learn a skill, develop a business, upgrade their two O-Levels, and so on. It would be fun to know which subversive bureaucrat considered that joining the Gulf Peace Team satisfied these requirements.

At one point, an unidentified Australian voice called out from the doorway, "Leave some time fer th' Austraalians, 'kay?" And then, when the Gulf Peace Team had wrapped up this enlightening conference, a middle-aged man who looked and dressed as if he could have sold insurance or mortgages sailed like a coal barge through the crowd and sat himself down at the now-vacated microphone-littered table. Then he began to read an overwrought statement about "beautiful Iraqi children" suffering and "a war crimes trial for Henry Kissinger and George Bush." Much as I'd like to see Kissinger on trial for something — *any- thing* — you couldn't pin this rap on him, however.

While the Emotional Moment was proceeding, camera crews packed their equipment and reporters milled around in groups questioning individual Gulf Peace Teamers. I walked over when the Australian had finished and asked him if there was some sort of problem between him and the team. "Bloody Americans hog all the media," he grumbled, effortlessly working himself up into a spectacular rant about egomaniacs, lesbians, know-it-alls, dope fiends, pansy-boys, college-freeloaders, work-shy nancies, manipulators, and pretty much every social caste in Sydney except the one he belonged to, whatever it was. Referring to a woman who'd evidently remained in Iraq when they chickened out, he told me, "If she wants to get run over by a tank, I'd be happy to *drive* it." Perhaps feeling he was giving a bad impression of himself, though, he then added, "most of the team are beautiful people, nah question. It's juss a few with these gigantic ee-goes and this damn *lesbian* thing, see what I mean, mate?"

"Clear as crystal, cobber."

Peaceniks really should make a pact to get on with each other in public. If *they* can't get along with each other, what makes them think anyone else can?

THE GULF WAR GIVES ME GAS
— *U.S. bumper sticker protesting war-for-oil*

THE WHEEL OF FIRE

It wasn't all fun and games in Amman. With a couple of the less cynical, more diligent, and better informed media shamans, I scoured the town in search of good restaurants and found three — one of them with a maitre d' who played a mean game of chess, too. But all good things have to come to an end (though I'm not sure *why* they have to), and my last outing with my international colleagues was a visit to Amman's Baq'a Ghetto for Friday prayers at the Amir Alley mosque.

It wasn't the prayers that interested us, it was the imam's sermon. Diplomats used these Friday meets as a barometer of the Palestinians' general mood weather. Baq'a is one of the grimmest places I can imagine. It doesn't defy description, exactly, but it can be described utterly in seven words: low, crumbling concrete boxes, stinking, muddy lanes. All the men living there not only look as if they want to kill you, they frequently *offer* to kill you — and sometimes they actually do kill you. Twenty-odd years of anger, resentment, and hate tend to take its toll on the human psyche. Baq'a was erected as a temporary camp for a temporary problem. But many living there now have known no other world than this "temporary" camp.

The Palestinians, let's face it, have been shafted by almost everyone. Many Arabs will confess that it's not the Palestinians they're concerned with but the *Palestinian Problem.* Others voice deep misgivings about Palestinian identity: who are these people? They're not Arabs, that much is certain. No Syrian will hear the suggestion that they might be stray Phoenicians. They could conceivably be some sort of prodigal Jewish tribe — after all, we've lost ten of them. Most likely, though, they're one of the earliest truly multicultural peoples, a mélange of Mongol, Crusader, Egyptian, Ethiopian, Bedouin, and — you name it. Every Palestinian probably has a Scot, a Swede, an Oriental perched somewhere in his family tree. A pioneer freewheeler who came and saw and quite liked the place — or liked its remoteness from whoever he didn't wish to see again for whatever reason — and stayed.

The biblical relationships between tribal peoples in the area reveal how fractious and fragmented the land was four thousand years ago, and it has remained so more or less constantly. To the local Canaanites, the followers of Moses were just another crew of thieving foreigners, no worse, no better than all the others. There was war and there was peace, a time to sow, a time to hack someone's head off, a time for every purpose under heaven — as long as you kept your able-bodied men fighting fit. As Native American history shows, you don't need a concept of land ownership to develop a territorial imperative.

If it is possible to identify how and when the current problems in Israel began, they can be traced to a period early in the First World War, specifically to October 24, 1915. This is the date of a second letter from Sir Henry McMahon, the British high commissioner in Egypt, to Hussein, the sharif of Mecca, who had indicated his willingness to lead the Arabs in revolt against Turco-German forces, in exchange for British backing in his claim to leadership of all the Arabs, and of a clearly defined Arabia. In the letter McMahon pledged British support for Arab independence in areas that had previously been proposed by the sharif, but subject to certain reservations:

> The districts of Mersin and Alexandretta, and portions of Syria lying to the west of the districts of Damascus, Homs, Hama and Aleppo, cannot be said to be purely Arab, and must on that account be excepted from the proposed delimitation.
>
> Subject to that modification, and without prejudice to the treaties concluded between us and certain Arab Chiefs, we accept that delimitation.
>
> As for the regions lying within the proposed frontiers, in which Great Britain is free to act without detriment to the interest of her ally France, I am authorized to give you the following pledges on behalf of the Government of Great Britain, and to reply as follows to your note:
>
> That subject to the modifications stated above, Great Britain is prepared to recognize and uphold the independence of the Arabs in all the regions lying within the frontiers proposed by the Sharif of Mecca.[12]

McMahon went on to say it was understood "that the Arabs have already decided to seek the counsels and advice of Great Britain exclusively; and that such European advisers and officials as may be needed to establish a sound system of administration shall be British." Then he added that he also considered it was agreed that:

> as regards to the two Vilayets of Baghdad and Basra the Arabs recognize that the fact of Great Britain's established position and

interests there will call for the setting up of special administrative arrangements to protect those regions from foreign aggression, to promote the welfare of their inhabitants and to safeguard our mutual interest.[13]

If you find this somewhat vague and ambiguous, so did the sharif, who was shrewd enough to be aware of the reasons for it being that way. He protested the exemption of the Syrian Mediterranean coast from the area of Arab independence, maintaining that Aleppo and Beirut could not be regarded as anything but Arab. Yet he knew the war — and specifically the swift removal of Turkey from it — was a more pressing issue, so he agreed to put this problem on hold for the duration, declaring his trust that Britain would subsequently persuade "her ally France" to hand the disputed territories over to the Arabs. With regard to the Iraqi vilayets (provinces), he was more ready to compromise, recognizing the all too tangible reality of a British military occupation there, but he still pointed out that, because they were part of the former Arab Empire, seat of the caliphs and the first major center of Arab culture, it would be "impossible to persuade or compel the Arab nation to renounce the honorable association." The end of the occupation, he agreed, would be worked out through negotiation, but "without prejudice to the rights of either party or the natural wealth and resources of these parts."[14]

But what's all this got to do with Palestine? The short answer is: Nothing. The name wasn't mentioned, either by Sir Henry or the sharif. This, however, was because Palestine was not an Ottoman administrative division — although, as a geographical term, it was employed throughout the Christian world. In discussions by ministers in the British cabinet, Palestine is most certainly referred to, and by no stretch of the imagination could McMahon's exemption of "portions of Syria lying to the west of the districts of Damascus, Homs, Hama and Aleppo" — which, in reality, was a feeble attempt to accommodate French interests in Lebanon — have referred to the *sanjak* of Jerusalem, an area that covered two-thirds of Palestine and was situated well to the south. It has been argued that the sharif either understood or should have been aware that Palestine was excluded, but there is no proof of this and he certainly never accepted it. The situation could have easily been clarified by Britain simply by saying that Palestine needed a special status because it was sacred to the three major religions, but Britain decided against doing this. Clarity was certainly not the point nor the objective here.

In any case, the British were dealing with the French behind sharif Hussein's back, concluding the Sykes-Picot Agreement, in late 1916, which more or less resembled the proposals in McMahon's letter. While the sharif's claims to a leadership of all Arabs were somewhat flimsy, his Arab Revolt proved quite successful. And it would have been more so had not one of the British officers sent out by the Arab Bureau in Cairo to assist the revolt, Colonel T. E. Lawrence, picked the sharif's third son, Amir Feisal, as commander of the Arab forces. Amir Abdullah, the highly intelligent and patently capable elder brother, would have been a far better choice, but Lawrence didn't find him as irresistibly handsome as Feisal. (For those who've seen the movie, in reality the first Allied troops to reach and liberate Damascus were a body of Australian cavalry. Lawrence, however, made an arrangement for Feisal's camel corps to make the official triumphal entry and install their own governor. Movies aren't always historically accurate.)

Without the Arabs, though, the Germans would have probably been able to cut off the Red Sea to Allied shipping, which would have altered the course of the war. It was something else that altered the course of Anglo-Arab relations. When the Bolshevik Revolution pulled Russia out of the war, papers relating to the Sykes-Picot and other nefarious backroom deals were found among the imperial archives and the information was immediately forwarded to the Turks. Jemal Pasha, of course, wasted no time relaying details to the Arabs, as proof of the treachery against Muslim peoples by wicked Christian powers. Sir Reginald Wingate, McMahon's successor in Cairo, came up with some fairly inventive and plausible reasons for the sharif not to worry himself over what became known as the Petrograd Papers, but the sharif was no fool. Besides, evidence of Britain's real intentions for the future of the Ottoman Empire was beginning to mount up. A few days before Jemal Pasha told sharif Hussein about the secret Anglo-French accord, a letter from Britain's foreign secretary, Arthur Balfour, to Lord Rothschild was published on November 2, 1917.

His Majesty's Government views with favour the establishment in

Palestine of a National Home for the Jewish people, and will use their best endeavours to facilitate the achievement of this object, it being clearly understood that nothing shall be done which may prejudice the civil and religious rights of the existing non-Jewish communities in Palestine or the rights and political status enjoyed by Jews in any other country.[15]

The reverberations of this document, now known as the Balfour Declaration, are still being felt, and will continue to be felt a century from now, no doubt. Whereas the consequences of the Anglo-French agreement were eliminated within a few decades by the demise of British and French imperial power.

The last attempt to restore Jewish independence in Palestine had failed back in AD 134. After this date, the Jews had been scattered like leaves in the wind throughout the world, leaving only a few thousand of the ultra-devout in Jerusalem and small communities elsewhere in the Holy Land. The rest were persecuted just as often as they prospered; they knew tolerance just as they knew discrimination. Yet with the economic expansion of western Europe in the eighteenth century and its concomitant movement toward religious toleration, Jews suddenly benefited to a point where liberalism and assimilation were a greater threat to their survival as a distinct cultural group than the earlier persecutions had been, particularly in those areas where the concentration of Jewish population was greatest, such as in Russia and Russian Poland. The Jewish prayer "Next year in Jerusalem" — recited at the close of a Passover seder — was never a political slogan but rather the expression of a spiritual or Messianic ideal. It took nearly two thousand years to nurture the idea of a mass return of the world's 12 million Jews to re-create a Jewish state in Palestine.

And it was largely due to the nature of new anti-Jewish movements that arose in the nineteenth century and, influenced by the nationalist temper of the times, emphasized race rather than religion. In response, and on account of their environment and the pressures of persecution, the Jews themselves began to think in terms of a new Jewish nationalism. From the latter half of the century on, there was a steady movement of eastern European Jews to settle in Palestine. Many, many more, however, emigrated to the United States and western Europe; yet all the same, by 1914, there were some 80,000 Jews — counting the indigenous communities — in Palestine. But there were 650,000 non-Jews. They were termed Arabs at the time, but they were actually the antecedents of today's Palestinians, many of whom are, of course, ostensibly Arabs, though few could claim anything like a pure Arab blood line.

The first Jewish settlers founded little colonies to work the land. These were the pioneers of "practical Zionism." "Political Zionism" — the concept of turning Palestine into a national Jewish state — came later, with the publication in 1896 of *Der Judenstaat* (The Jewish State: An Attempt at a Modern Solution of the Jewish Question), by Theodor Herzl. Not a good title. Herzl was a prominent Austrian political journalist, and in his book he declared that the Jewish question was neither social nor religious, but national. He maintained that assimilation had not worked out, and that anti-Semitism was growing, although he himself was a highly assimilated agnostic Jew. He didn't feel that all Jews should be forced to emigrate to a new Jewish state, but simply that it was important for Jews to have sovereignty over a stretch of land to suit their national requirements. It's impossible not to agree that this was a perfectly good and necessary idea. Herzl didn't say it *had* to be Palestine, but, he pointed out, if it *were* Palestine, the European Jews would help to civilize the surrounding region.

It was this last bit that appealed to the British.

Herzl organized the first Zionist Congress, which was held at Basle in 1897. During its proceedings, delegates called for the colonization of Palestine by Jewish agricultural and industrial workers and — more significantly — the organization and binding together of the whole of Jewry.

For tactical reasons, the early Zionists talked of a "home" rather than a "state" in Palestine, although they had yet to secure Ottoman consent for this. Theodor Herzl's request was rejected by Sultan Abdul Hamid. So he busied himself with alternative locations, considering at one point Sinai and Cyprus, which were denied him by Egypt's Lord Cromer and the British Colonial Office. In 1903 Herzl was offered Uganda by the British government, but the offer was less than solid and Herzl was less than enthusiastic about it. He still agreed to consider it, however, but the idea was rejected by the sixth Zionist Congress in 1904, just prior to Herzl's death.

After this, the focus of Zionist activity shifted from Vienna to Britain.

Ironically, the staunchest opposition to Zionism came from highly placed Jews — though admittedly because they probably feared Zionism's consequences for assimilation generally. But even Vienna's chief rabbi had declared that Zionism was incompatible with Judaism, a view still shared by some factions of ultra-orthodox Jews, including the mettlesome crew in Jerusalem who throw rocks at anyone driving a car on the Sabbath.

Thus it was that British Gentile Zionists, like Balfour and C. P. Scott, editor of the *Manchester Guardian*, were as instrumental as Jewish Zionists, like Lord Rothschild and Herzl's leading disciple, Chaim Weizmann. Balfour, who was foreign secretary, along with people like Lord Milner, the former imperial consul in Africa, and a sizable group of Foreign Office officials and government advisers that included Sir Mark Sykes (of the infamous Anglo-French accord), all saw enormous advantages in a Jewish Palestine as part of the Empire.

A subtext to these imperial convictions was the romantic appeal of a return of the Jews to Zion. This was founded on the Old Testament Christianity that had been very much a part of their Victorian upbringing. Although not then in the cabinet, Churchill found this same attraction in Zionism too. Back in the heady days of the Empire, romance and possibility did not seem so far apart, as the work of writers like Tennyson and paintings by the so-called pre-Raphaelite Brotherhood so clearly show. King Arthur and Moses, viewed through the imperial tint of Victorian eyeglasses, were interchangeable figures — jolly good chaps both of them.

The 1917 cabinet, inevitably, veered further and further away from the Sykes-Picot Agreement to international control for Palestine. "Britain could take care of the Holy Places better than anyone else," coalition Prime Minister David Lloyd George told C. P. Scott, and a French Palestine was "not to be thought of." The most outspoken opponent of the Balfour Declaration was Sir Edward Montague, secretary of state for India, and the only Jew in the cabinet. His American counterpart in many ways was the Jewish anti-Zionist, Henry Morgenthau, Sr., former U.S. ambassador to Turkey. The position of both men is understandable, but the forces aligned against them had far more reasons to *support* the Zionist cause — few of which had much to do with Jews or Judaism.

The British congratulated themselves that support for Zionism had brought the United States into the war in April 1917, although this conviction stemmed from a greatly exaggerated view of the wealth and influence in Washington of American Jews during that period. But belief is always more important than reality in politics. Even the Germans were aware of the possibilities up for grabs by winning Jewish sympathy, especially among the many American Jews of East European origin who loathed the Russian government with a passion. Which was why Germany had been trying without much success to get the Turks to lift their objections to Zionist settlement in Palestine. Britain also hoped its adoption of Zionism would win over the Russian Jewish socialists who were then attempting to influence the Kerensky inter-revolution government to take Russia out of the war.

An awful lot of threads in the many hues of practicality and idealism were thus woven together to make the Balfour Declaration. Rothschild and Weizmann were invited to submit a draft, and their version said that "Palestine should be reconstituted as the National Home for the Jewish people." This was deemed a little too obvious — a little too *honest* is what it was — and the diluted version we've seen was used.

If anything, sharif Hussein's alarm about the Allies' intentions was exacerbated by the vagueness of this document. He'd seen enough vague British documents by now to know that vague meant trouble. He'd also become king of Hejaz — the vital strip of what's now Saudi Arabia between Jordan and the Yemen, containing the holy sites of Mecca and Medina — and he had an awful lot of people to answer to if a Jewish state sprang up in Palestine. Commander D. G. Hogarth, head of the Arab Bureau, was sent to bamboozle Hussein with anything that came to mind. His report stated that "the King would not accept a Jewish state in Palestine, nor was I instructed to warn him that such a state was contemplated." Whatever Hogarth told the king instead worked, for Hussein next became positively enthusiastic about the advantages that Jewish immigration would bring to the Arab countries.

By 1918, though, when Weizmann had established the Zionist Commission's headquarters in Palestine, it was painfully clear to the Arabs what was really going on. They believed the Zionists aimed to take over the country and place them in subjection. Although "Arabs" formed 90 percent of Palestine's population, the wording of the Balfour

Declaration was unambiguous in referring to them as the "existing non-Jewish communities" whose civil and religious rights — though not *political* rights — were not to be prejudiced.

Weizmann and his Commission became increasingly concerned, however, that the British were not being forceful enough in driving home to the Palestinians their intentions of fully implementing the terms of the Balfour Declaration. Without this, they knew that it might well prove impossible to achieve their goal, which was, unquestionably, to turn Palestine, whatever the boundaries that entailed, into a Jewish national state with a substantial Jewish majority. Weizmann himself admitted how surprised he was at how "non-Jewish" Jerusalem and Palestine had become, and he left after a few months, convinced it was probably impossible to prevent Palestine from becoming an Arab state.

For their part, the British were largely oblivious to both the Zionists' real aims and the actual situation in Palestine. They certainly had no idea they were in the process of creating one of the least soluble political problems in history. Some did register their apprehension when reports from British officials on the spot noted the total incompatibility between Zionist aspirations and the overwhelming feelings of the indigenous non-Jewish population, but the vast majority could see little of importance beyond the interests of the British Empire.

Few now recall the letter written two years after the Balfour Declaration by its author, yet it encapsulates the whole story leading through this century to the Baq'a Ghetto and Islamic Jihad:

> The four great powers are committed to Zionisn, and Zionism, be it right or wrong, good or bad, is rooted in age-long tradition, in present needs, in future hopes, of far profounder import than the desires and prejudices of the 700,000 Arabs who now inhabit that ancient land.[16]

Even the Baq'a mosque is ugly: bare concrete and corrugated tin. From numerous loudspeakers with the audio fidelity of a Baby PeePee doll, the imam's near-hysterical voice came scraping, rattling, and rasping through the chill damp air to batter my eardrums. The whole scene resembled a crazed attempt to produce the Nuremberg rallies on a shoestring budget. Looking at the scowling scornful faces around me — perched on rooftops, walls, hanging from lamp posts and chain-link fences — I didn't fancy Lord Balfour's chances of success with an audience of today's Palestinians: *You have to understand, chaps, that what we want is far, far profounder and more important than your pathetic little concerns. Do you see? Now run along and do stop bothering everyone . . .*

The gist of the imam's sermon was familiar enough: go forth and kill Americans, Israelis, and anyone else you don't like the look of. His idea of a parable was a story concerning an Iraqi peasant who comes across an American pilot who's just parachuted from his wrecked plane. Should the peasant turn the pilot over to authorities and collect the reward now being offered by Iraq's government (so pilots could make better propaganda videos)? Or should he do his duty as a Muslim and kill the murdering infidel? Here was a tricky one, I thought, feeling certain, however, that the solution wouldn't be especially ingenious. It wasn't, either: the peasant chops the pilot's head off and takes that in to claim his reward from the authorities. It didn't even make sense — unless the authorities thought the head was still alive.

An inspiring thought for the Sabbath, though. I tried to picture the Anglican version of this. But there isn't one.

The street outside the mosque had filled up with dozens of TV cameras and a good hundred-odd reporters. La Belladonna from RAI did a stand-up before her camera, briefing RAI's viewers somewhat idiosyncratically on the situation at hand, while a still photographer rolled in the mud at her feet to get both TV star and a minaret in the same frame. Other teams huddled in packs on rooftops and balconies, some which appeared on the verge of collapse.

Vendors suddenly materialized with carts full of oranges and fresh-baked flat bread. Show me an angry mob and I'll show you big profits for the fast-food business.

When the TV cameras come out in places like this, it's always time to leave. They create what they think they're recording. They provoke acts that wouldn't have been performed for a local audience. When the eyes of the world are upon you, you have to perform. And there were far too many global eyes here, in a place that needed little provocation at the best of times. From a nearby street, trucks appeared, sloppily but gaily festooned with images of Saddam, King Hussein, and Yasser Arafat. In the back, they held forests of placards — the very ones I'd seen at Sheikh Tamimi's bunker — and from speakers roped to anything suitable came tinny, rasping, Munchkin voices shouting out, "Victory for Saddam!" "Death to America!"

In deference to the needs of an international audience, perhaps, many placards were in German: TOD FUR AMERIKA. It looked like a U.S. company that sold garments made from tod fur until the lexicon kicked in.

The streets filled with keffiyeh-shrouded men and, as the howling-banshee trucks moved off, video cameras pointed from all directions, motor-drives whizzed, and some journalists even leaped into the back of trucks. Why not? After all, they *were* the demonstration — for this was now indeed an official and verifiably authentic *Palestinian Demonstration*. No matter that virtually half of the demonstrators were journalists. They became what they beheld and filed copy. As it is with Hollywood movies, a handful of weary extras, artfully framed and edited, becomes a numberless horde of The Oppressed, ready to rip out the foundations of the world and the lungs of the oppressors. *They'll be outside your door by tomorrow*, that's the message.

I saw it on CNN that night in the Al Hanah. Had I not been there, I would believe to this day that Baq'a had erupted, that many thousands of gun-happy Palestinians had massed in support of Saddam.

It wasn't like that, though. It was a few dozen people, whose homes and lives were shit, clinging to the carrot cynically dangled by Saddam for his own purposes. They weren't being helped by being presented as a potent and massive threat, either.

ANOTHER FASCIST TERRORIST FOR PEACE

> — *U.S. anti-Gulf War bumper sticker referring
> to the illegality of Bush's actions*

"APOCALYPSE NOW, PLEASE . . ."

When the sky is rent asunder; when the stars scatter and the oceans roll together; when the graves are hurled about; each soul shall know what it has done and what it has failed to do.

— THE HOLY KORAN 82:1

Utter darkness. Snow. The combination made it seem the stars were indeed falling from an empty sky, that paradise was drawing close to hell, as predicted for the last days of the Koranic Cessation. Once again, this time in the freezing night, I stood at the edge of Red Crescent 1, the tent city near Ruwaishid. There beneath the storm, after a bone-chilling, four-hour cab ride out of Jordan's capital, Amman, I felt again that I should probably be trying to get back home — like all those poor invisible wretches huddled together for warmth in the night. But I wasn't heading home. I was waiting in the flecked charcoal silence at three in the morning to meet Muhie and Abdul-Khaliq, Bedouin smugglers who plied their trade between Iraq and Jordan, moving any illicit commodity — for a price. With the war on, I was a little more troublesome and certainly more illicit than gasoline, guns, or booze, but, for $6,000, Muhie felt his outfit could handle the job.

Anne Collins had come through. It seemed almost miraculous that I could walk out of Amman's Amex branch a rich man — yet I did. Had I known the money was drawn on Anne's personal account, though, I might have been a little more frugal with it.

I'd lived with the Bedouin while researching the book on Egypt. "You could trust them with your life," I'd written of them. I never thought I'd have to, though. I wasn't really sure what had brought me back to their world once more or what made me think I had to bear witness to the destruction of Iraq. But I'd watched CNN at home that first night back in January, as a demons' firework-party ripped across the Baghdad sky, and had felt desolately sad, as if a vast injustice was about to consume that world in its flames.

Materializing from the snow-spattered shadows, Muhie beckoned silently. Tall, lean, fierce-looking, he had a moustache that looked in the gloom like a black skylark dangling from his croissant of a nose. His intricately embroidered abaya was lined with sheepskin and floated out like wings as I followed him down the mud track toward the main road — the forbidden highway to Baghdad. Abdul-Khaliq was waiting in the truck, its heater full blast, engine running, headlights off. Muhie's brother, Abdul-Khaliq, couldn't have looked *less* related. In a frayed black overcoat many sizes too small, he resembled an OPEC fat cat fallen on hard times.

I'd never asked the brothers exactly *how* we'd get to Iraq, but I'd presumed it would not involve driving through the main border post. Some twenty minutes later, we bounced off the highway over igloo-sized boulders, Abdul-Khaliq handling the steering wheel as if it were an obdurate Frisbee. We finally hit something soft but unyielding.

"*Al hamdu lillah ala as-salimah,*" yodeled Muhie.

Roughly: "Thank God we arrived safely."

From somewhere in the splattering sleet-riven murk came a familiar noise. No other animal on earth sounds like a bored camel — I'd learned that in Egypt, where the camels are more prone to boredom.

"Now you must be Bedouin proper," Muhie said.

A keffiyeh that smelt of wet dog was wrapped around my head, an old brown abaya thrown over my shoulders. I said to Muhie that I now looked more like a Bedouin than either of them, and he laughed. I came to understand that whenever Muhie laughed it had nothing to do with his finding something funny — it meant, generally, that he was amazed at my stupidity.

The three of us rode off into an icy void, the camels treading delicately around invisible rocks, snorting objections to the lashing sleet and the inconsiderate humans on their backs. Muhie led and Abdul-Khaliq stayed behind me, absurd in his wino's coat.

"This Syria now," Muhie announced some time later, standing in his stirrups and gesturing at a universe of black ink. We weren't in Syria for very long, for Muhie's next words were, "There place Iraq."

No sooner had he said it than we heard an eerie roaring noise somewhere below the ridge of a hill ahead. Our camels heard it too, and didn't like it at all, twitching, hissing, waving their huge necks, unwilling to proceed a step farther. As Muhie whipped his mount to goad it on, something resembling a gigantic welder's torch rose over the horizon, boring into coal-black clouds that glowed briefly as it slid past them and quickly out of sight. We could still hear it, though — an alien howl fading off into the night. The camels bucked and hooted with fear. The three of us jumped off our saddles, gripping reins and slipping over mud and rocks as the animals thrashed around, not believing a word we said to reassure them, sensing our own lack of reassurance, our wealth of panic. Dragging the camels to a crest of the hill a short distance away, we looked down on a sprawling collection of Iraqi military equipment and some thousand-odd soldiers scuttling like gnomes around it. The camp hadn't been there when the brothers had passed through the area a few days before.

Stumbling over slimy rocks, we pulled our camels northeast away from the camp until the beasts had calmed enough to allow passengers back on. In the dark distance, we could hear the rumble of trucks and the muffled shouting of men. We rode in silence through a bleak, metallic dawn. All around, the great Syrian desert gradually emerged from night. Muhie muttered something to his brother and urged his camel to a trot, leading us in a weaving path until we reached a small, crude road. Here we jumped down and walked a short distance to a bare, pathetic tree, the sight of which sent the camels into a frenzy for some reason. Feed-bags were pulled out, and the animals chomped noisily while we humans shared a round of flatbread. The sudden noise of an engine in the distance sent my heart flying against my ribs.

"Allah!" Muhie said.

The old truck, soon bouncing toward us, was expected. Its driver exchanged *salaams*, and swapped his vehicle for our camels. Soon, soaked and aching, I watched steam coming from my old abaya as I fell in and out of fitful sleep between the brothers in the welcome warmth of the truck's powerful, clattering heater.

Passing through somewhere called Nukayb, we'd left the Syrian desert and were headed toward the fertile plain between the Tigris and Euphrates once called Mesopotamia ("between rivers") by the literal-minded Greeks. Muhie and Abdul-Khaliq led complicated lives, full of complicated arrangements. Twice we crossed rivers in leaking rowboats, picked up by alternative transport on the other side. Landing in the icy mud of one river bank not far from a bridge, Muhie grabbed my wrist and indicated something with his ample, majestic nose. Beneath this bridge, surrounded by several untidy, chain-smoking soldiers, was a flatbed truck that had obviously been converted into a mobile missile launcher. Its cargo reclined, half-concealed by tarpaulins, in what resembled a section of metal sewer pipe.

"Sometime truck fall over when beeg bullet fire," Abdul-Khaliq explained, smirking. "Make truck for farmer people not soldier. Big problem for heem."

The art of our necessities is definitely fucking strange and can indeed make the vilest of things precious. We all laughed at this failure of Iraqi adaptive technology. Fear makes you laugh — until it doesn't, that is.

We reached the outskirts of An Najaf, one of the Shia Muslim holy cities, in the early evening. Here, in central southern Iraq, I got my first glimpse of what this war meant. Whole areas that looked like industrial suburbs had been flattened.

"Must wait here," Muhie announced, turning into a rubble-strewn street of low concrete houses, many partially collapsed. As his brother switched off the truck's overheated engine, I heard the sound of children crying the way children cry when something really bothers them. Any parent knows that cry.

I was led into a dark house where, by the smoky light of oil tapers, we were given tea and bread by a large woman veiled in black, only the pungent smell of old sweat giving her more substance than a bulky shadow. A little girl followed her in and out of the room, screaming intermittently and often clutching at chairs and walls for support. I asked the woman's husband, Ghanem, if the child was all right. A thin, haggard-looking man, he wouldn't speak directly to me.

"Her ears bad from bomb noise," Muhie said. "Hurt too much her ears now."

A doctor later explained to me that bomb blasts can damage not only children's lungs, but also the little canal in the ear that controls balance — besides fracturing the eardrum itself. Many Iraqis will never hear properly again. Nor will I. I asked about civilian casualties, and the woman embarked on a tirade of oaths.

"She say Saddam and the Bush all killers," Muhie told me. "Say why people must die?"

From An Najaf, I was hidden in the back of a larger truck behind crates of irritable chickens smelling of ammonia and wood. Occasionally, we were pulled over by soldiers standing near small fires — the only lights on in Iraq — and given a cursory inspection, usually accompanied by crackling laughter. The brothers up front knew how to handle these situations. As we bumped off, I often saw, through wooden slats and feathers, the wedges of Scud launchers and other such equipment concealed beneath bridges or makeshift arrangements of canvas, wood, and stone.

Al Hillah was the end of the line for both us and the chickens. A quiet little town of single-storey dwellings and narrow lanes, it was the only place I saw that the war hadn't affected yet. Here some incredibly covert arrangement provided us with horses — old, worn-out beasts that would rather have gone to sleep than head off cross-country in a biting wind that spat frozen rain like tracer bullets.

It soon became clear why we'd left the road: skirting low hills, we saw a buzzing hive of military activity concealed in a small valley. Generators powered little circles of flickering lights within which many people worked on large pieces of equipment — tanks, launchers, and such. Repairs, I initially assumed, until a ladder or piece of temporary scaffolding appeared to collapse, to distant cries of alarm, crushing a tank as it fell.

Tanks don't usually crush that easily. Presumably, this was one of Saddam's vaunted mock-weaponry workshops. Muhie growled sharply and angrily as I attempted to take a photograph, making it clear this was a very, very bad place to be caught. Before long we'd reached the river again, receiving tea in another gloomy house, jumping into a small, disastrously battered motorboat, and heading off into mist and sleet.

Then it came.

First, a thunderous roar that seemed to shake the very riverbed. Next, a thousand vast streaks of vague light that twisted down in streamers from tortured wedges of cloud, exploding a mile or so from the eastern bank of the river and creating incandescent mushrooms of purplish-orange light. Blinded and deafened, we communicated by gestures as the brothers landed the boat with a thud against a rock. It took only minutes. It wasn't silence that remained, so much as a ringing split by shouts and screams and sirens.

"This Al Musayyib," Muhie said, his hot breath pouring in my ear.

There was smoke everywhere in the chaotic little streets. I followed the brothers past houses where people wailed and screamed around various kinds of wreckage that had recently been a solid part of their lives. If you've only ever seen this kind of thing in movies before, it will shock you to the core. It's horrible.

"You stay night at imam house," Muhie told me.

"What?" I assumed shell shock had made me mishear.

"Imam," Muhie repeated. "You know imam?"

"Mosques, prayers . . . that sort of imam?"

"Yes, yes. Shia mosque. You know Shia?"

I nodded, visions of spending the night with "Hanging" Ayatollah Khalkali flooding my mind.

"Good man, this one," Abdul-Khaliq added, noticing my concern.

"*Best* man," elaborated Muhie. "*Absolute.*"

"You never thought hell would be this cold," said the imam, in English so unaccented it startled me.

His home was adjacent to a small white mosque, its dome glowing faintly orange in the light of nearby fires. We had been shown into a study — a shelf of books, three fat old armchairs, a low table — where the imam sat, face wreathed in the white mist of his beard.

"Whose hell is it?"

"Yours and mine," he replied, waving his robed arm. "Sit. Relax. You are my welcome guest, and, as we say, the guest of Allah."

Coffee was served, along with dates as tough as shoe leather. Imported, no doubt. We sat in the silence that frequently accompanies Arab gestures of hospitality; then the Bedouin brothers, telling me we'd move on at dawn, rose to leave.

In the conversation that followed, the old imam made it very clear that neither he nor God wanted anything to do with Saddam Hussein.

"His piety is a sham," he said. "Like all the Ba'athists, he was and is an atheist. This war is not a holy war, it is a war of selfishness, ignorance, power, greed . . ."

The imam had memorized the entire Koran, he informed me modestly, adding, "the holy book has much to say on war, for peace comes from war. Yet the war about which Islam teaches is a war in the human soul, not . . . that abomination of guns and blood for the sake of mere oil and money."

As more coffee was being served and the imam continued his virtuoso sales job on a faith that concerned peace and tolerance above all, a couple of maimed sirens sounded somewhere outside. Seconds later, that awesome, ominous, and now familiar thunder swept above us. The room lit up, the building shook. Seizing my arm, the old man virtually dragged me from the room and down a crumbling flight of stone steps into a musty cellar colder than most fridges.

The place wasn't empty, either. Before my eyes adjusted to the gloom of a single taper, I heard and felt many little bodies around me. Clutching blindly, screaming with fear, a dozen or so children had just been woken yet again that night. The noise of explosions above us was unimaginably terrifying. The whole world seemed about to collapse, to fold up, give in, go home. Yet in the midst of this, accompanied by some women who were also there in the dark and the cold, the imam started singing what I presume were children's songs, loudly and tunelessly. The louder the explosions, the louder he sang, until everyone was singing.

These fragments shored against my ruin . . .

It was over quickly. What followed was worse. Upstairs flashlights waved, voices called out. The confusion was absolute, the raw terror total. In the imam's hallway lay a small girl whose left leg had been ripped off above the knee; standing over her a woman in torn clothes screamed unintelligibly, beating the walls. Then a man in some kind of nightshirt slapped this woman hard around the face twice, shouting and pointing at the girl, who lay mute, staring at the cold stone, thick blood pulsing from her leg.

"Get a fucking *doctor* here!" (I'm pretty useful at such times.)

"No doctors," the imam said, calm, almost stern. In moments, we'd carried the girl to the study and propped her leg up on a chair, tying a belt just above where it now ended. Boiling water arrived; grit and dust were swabbed off the stump. My holdall was still almost full of medical supplies. And you don't take the upriver heartland trip, the highway into endless night, without finding out how to do those things you never need to do yourself in that other world, that parallel universe that watches the imam's one on TV. It was more like Last Aid than First, my medical expertise, but it encompassed the basics.

I tipped out my grime-spattered bag, poured a whole bottle of iodine over the maroon and yellow mush of meat, tubes, threads, and bones, and ripped open a wound pad.

Nothing conveys either the eerie calm or the plummeting sense of an utter and terminal horror felt during those minutes. Nothing.

More people arrived, most with minor wounds, all with shock. Mothers moaned to themselves, nursing babies who cried like sick cats. Men chain-smoked in huddles, often raising their palms to heaven and saying, "Allah," grateful not to be dead, but uncomprehending. On the cusp of dawn, the metal-and-starlight voice of the muezzin rang out above us, "*Allahu Akbar.*" God is great — in spite of everything, still great. But not one of us.

As the little mosque next door filled up with murmuring shadowy forms, I stood outside, exhausted, breathing in air toxic with spiteful fumes — cordite, rubber, shit — gazing around at smashed buildings, listening to the cries of children and the odd loaded silence. No, I thought, I imagined hell would at least be warm.

When We decide to destroy
A population, We (first) send
A definite order to those
Among them who are given
The good things of this life
And yet transgress; so that
The charge is proved true
Against them: then (it is)
We destroy them utterly.

— THE HOLY KORAN, XVII, 16

On the morning of January 29, 1991, I was in the back of another truck, this one carrying bags of fertilizer, and we were heading into the eye of Desert Storm. Approaching Baghdad's industrial suburbs, fertilizer dust irritating tears from my eyes and tickling my nose and throat until they burned, the devastation of nearly two weeks of constant Allied bombing appeared on all sides. In places, not a building was left standing for as far as I could see. By the roadside at intervals, lying on makeshift beds in the misty, freezing damp, lay casualties crudely swaddled in bloodstained bandages. They were waiting, I learned later, for the few ambulances that daily made rounds, either treating the wounded where they were or carrying them off to overburdened, understaffed hospitals. Most doctors and nursing staff had been sent to the eastern front. So had all able-bodied men. We were bombing the defenseless, the old, women, and children.

As we skirted the city's perimeter, heading northwest, military checkpoints became more frequent — though just as lazily inefficient as before. Beyond the rubble of factories and low-rise housing, the scattered towers of the city's modern center were occasionally visible, were still *there* at least. What we passed, however, was not there. It had gone. Everywhere, people picked through what had gone, arms full of ragged clothes, lamps, vacuum cleaners, pots, and pans — the remnants of lives they'd worked their lives to build. Faces seemed stunned, frozen, neither alive nor dead. Ghosts of those they had been.

At yet another stop, I attempted to blow the biting dust from my nose on my sleeve, noticing how silent this vast city seemed now, recalling those days an age earlier when it had seemed invulnerable — tacky, despicable in many ways, but *invulnerable*. The past is a very foreign country.

The present was about to become one, too. I should have been more observant. Before I could even register what was happening, two Iraqi soldiers flung aside fertilizer sacks and hauled me from the truck, shouting, pointing battered old Kalashnikovs, pushing. Numb with shock, I was frog-marched to a large, shuttered bungalow, then goaded with rifle butts down creaky wooden stairs into a dark subbasement. A door slammed behind me and voices above — among them Muhie's — yelled at each other. After some minutes, two soldiers appeared, ordering me to strip. At gunpoint, I handed over my watch and underpants . . . and wedding ring. Oddly, it was removing the ring that made me feel truly naked.

Gathering everything into a pile, the soldiers angrily shouted things I couldn't understand. All I could notice was the state of them. One lacked much of his nose and the ends of three fingers; the other limped badly and had an ear that looked as if a chain saw had recently gone through it. Their uniforms were filthy and ragged; one man had no laces in his mud-caked boots, another had only a huge old safety pin to hold his fly together. For some reason, I felt sorry for them.

I felt less sorry for them after an hour alone, however. The room was completely bare and its stone floor damp, so I hopped from foot to foot like a mad cockatoo. Weak gray light stole through chinks in the outside shutter of one narrow window just below the ceiling. After I'd thrown up uncontrollably, the Big Fear kicked in. Images of the captured Allied pilots I'd watched on TV in Amman kept floating before me.

That's what you'll look like soon, kiddo . . .

It was the British pilot I saw — the one who resembled a mangled hunchbacked elf. Pacing and hugging myself for warmth, I next realized I'd be *lucky* to get off that lightly. I wasn't a POW, the Geneva Convention didn't *mention* me — I didn't even have an Iraqi visa. Such thoughts and infinite variations on them went round and round my head, as my head and the rest of me went round and round the room. It truly is fear itself we have to fear. Knowing *anything* would have been better than imagining everything. You can't imagine death, for a start. But how about torture? How about the prods, the clamps, the wires, the amateur surgery? How about the broken bottle up your ass?

It was when I had started to think freezing to death might be all fate had in store that the door at the top of the stairs burst open. Sudden noise and light startled and blinded me. All I'd heard for hours was the occasional car, the odd muffled voice, the frequent clip-clop of horses. Instinctively, I retreated into the farthest corner, hands shielding my face. *A poor, bare, forked animal . . .*

But it was Muhie and Abdul-Khaliq who came down the stairs first, followed by soldiers. Everyone was laughing heartily.

"Beeg problem finish," Abdul-Khaliq announced, winking. Behind him a soldier crouched to deposit my clothes in front of me. He was also clutching the bottle of Chivas Regal from my medical supplies — and it wasn't full anymore.

"Too much cold," Muhie stated, pointing at my clothes. Cagily, I dressed. The soldier with the sawed-off ear pulled my ring and watch from his pocket, saying "*As-salamu Alaikum.*"

"*Wa Alaikum Asalam.*" Peace was upon us . . . or so I hoped.

"I tell this men you doctor," Muhie said. "Beeg mistake happen. Now these man too much sorry. I tell you give medicine. One man he have too much bad ear." He pointed at the ear in question.

Another soldier stumbled down the stairs with my bags in the only hand he owned. A light I could probably have turned on myself was flicked into throbbing generator-life. The whiskey was passed around — it has never felt so good — and cigarettes appeared. Soon, I was dressing the soldier's ear. It was a mess, that ear, finished, gone. The Bedouins nodded approval each time I performed a doctorly move. I fished out the antibiotic vials I'd purchased in Amman, breaking open a disposable syringe. The vials weren't easy to break, and I wondered how many doses a vial contained. Presuming "one" was a reasonable answer — and hoping that no one had ever died from too much penicillin — I dabbed the soldier's arm with Chivas and stuck the needle in his knotted muscle, pressing its plunger.

This looked painful to me, yet, watching the process in rapt fascination, the other three soldiers demanded injections too. After three hours, about ten other soldiers had joined us, along with three or four civilians. For soldiers in the middle of a war, these men didn't appear to have much pressing business that needed their attention. And if they did, they weren't in any shape to attend to it anyway. Almost all of these men, I learned, were veterans of the Iran-Iraq war. Only soldiers who still possessed most of their bodily parts were deemed worthy of being dispatched to the Kuwait front.

After examining my tape recorder suspiciously, one soldier had put the Chris Isaac tape I'd offered him in it. By now we'd listened to "Wicked Game" — everyone's favorite — about thirty times. Not only that, as I stitched and dressed and daubed and injected, we'd all become pals, buddies, *guys*. It was only when someone said he hoped Saddam got a bullet in his head, "before everything gone," that I realized what incredible pals we were. Although a deadly silence followed this remark, it then unleashed a flood of grievances: Saddam, Bush, Baker — everyone loathed the scheming, bloodthirsty lot of them. These men, my buddies, were not the "war-hardened vets" speculated on by Pentagon experts. They were war-weary wrecks, people who wanted to have normal lives again before they forgot what normal lives even were.

It *had* crossed my mind that there must be more comfortable places than a bare, cold concrete crypt to have this party-cum-free-clinic — but after a few drinks, I must say, medicine gets to be more fun. Only when the bombing started did I realize why the subterranean room was so popular. My left ear still reminds me of that night. It's finished now, too, that ear. It's gone for good — it'll never hear music again. And it liked doing that.

When CNN reported that air strikes appeared to concentrate on the outskirts of Baghdad, it was right. The noise was stupefying and the cellar rocked at times like a storm-tossed boat. The generator died — shock, I think. Through the shutter, laser-beams of magnesium light shot into the smoky darkness in which we crouched. From what I recalled of outside, there hadn't seemed much left to destroy, but some-one wasn't taking any chances. After all, *we* were still there.

The smell of fear filled the room — and my fear smelled much like anyone else's. It defies description, in truth. Fear. So does war. So does what followed.

After thunder, screams. Perhaps the description should be as *surgical* as the bombing was said to be. One girl, aged ten or so, with shrapnel wound to the abdomen, holding lower intestines in hands like snake's nest. Teenage boy, unconscious, head like half-eaten boiled egg. Old woman coughing out spray of blood. Old man whose eyes and forehead appeared to have been Kentucky-fried.

We did what we could — not much — and, while we were doing it, another wave of bombing arrived. By dawn there had been three. There had been three or more each night since the war began. I hate to think how many more there were after I left.

Blood, corpses, smoke, screams. I staggered around outside, oblivious to the fact I shouldn't be staggering around *outside* at all. My head throbbed and, gong-tormented, it rang too. It hurt. I felt a hand grab-bing at my sleeve and saw the soldier whose ear I'd dressed — my pal, my buddy. Penicillin hadn't killed him yet; but something was bother-ing him. He pulled me down a smoke-veiled side street where the remains of a camel that looked as if it had swallowed a live hand grenade lay half-pinned to bits of wall. Beyond this wall lay the remains of a bungalow. A family of ten date farmers had lived in this house — or so I heard later — and now a family of seven date farmers was homeless. Laser-guided projectiles may be smart enough to avoid some buildings in favor of others, searching for ingeniously disguised chemical-weapons plants, but they're not smart enough to avoid camels or date farmers. A little later, Muhie and some of the soldiers showed me an obliterated hi-tech death-factory cunningly arranged to look as if it had been an elementary school. Scraps of kids' art projects fluttered beneath crumbling concrete slabs and twisted metal rods. A little exercise book lay stained by fire and rain, with the universal language of children's art and words etched in rudimentary English that were just too apt and too heartbreaking to be ever repeated.

Those who reject Our Signs
And the Meeting in the Hereafter, —
Vain are their deeds:
Can they expect to be rewarded
Except as they have wrought?
— THE HOLY KORAN, VII, 147

The trip out of Baghdad, north to Samarra, wasn't so much anticlimax as overkill — too much more of the same. But we're resilient creatures, perhaps *too* resilient. No one needs nerves of steel. Tiny, garage-like stores stayed open, although their owners had little to sell. People did what they always did, pointless as it might now be, merely to hang on to some shreds of normality. Merely to *remember* normality, if only to pass the memory on as legend, as dreams for another generation.

Takrit, site of Saddam's first murder and most enjoyable lunch, Bayji, Al Mawsil. Each northern Iraqi town looked the same in the late evening of January 30. Years spent building would now be followed by years spent rebuilding — a Zen master's lesson in the futility of human endeavor. Delirious with fatigue and hunger, I watched an endless stream of trucks and cars pour in and out of a whole mountain. As night fell we paused to eat bread and sleep. It was too cold to sleep. From the mountains a huge missile burned slowly up into swirling clouds like a flaming drill. Not fifteen minutes after it had disappeared, a monsoon of fire dropped from the night, splashing down the mountains. Another appointment at the end of the world, I thought. How many more do we have left?

Kayf, Dahuk, Zakhu — Kurdistan in the deep of the night. Saddam had razed some of these places himself. This was Kurdish territory, or at least Kurds thought so. I wish I'd said goodbye properly to Muhie and Abdul-Khaliq, but I didn't realize they were going until they'd gone — after introducing me to Barzan. They'd even paid Barzan whatever he charged, which was sufficient for him to give me a pair of gloves, as well as to lead me through his exhausted, shabby homeland into Turkey.

Wearing all my shirts and T-shirts, plastic bags wrapped round my feet, I walked for the rest of the night behind Barzan through the snow and rocks, up hills and down steeper hills. Our breathing, our heartbeats echoed around those mute, observant towers of stone. As a sick and feeble dawn leaked through night's black flesh, the resolutely silent Barzan showed me what looked like the entire Turkish army camped far in a hazy distance, and pointed out the wisest route to follow next.

"Goodbye," he said, formally shaking my hand. I owed him my life.

Then pulling down his sheepskin hat, he turned back — back to Iraq.

Late that night, after only five days and nights in the war zone, I was in Istanbul, watching CNN and eating food. Food. It seemed not much had happened while I'd been away. The war was going according to plan. It was a triumph of technology. Civilian casualties were minimal. Bombs were smart, better educated these days, it sounded, than most American citizens. Bombing by bombs this smart was *surgical.* If they get any smarter they might quit the armed forces, go straight, grow rich.

They were George Bush's "Thousand Points of Light" — except, for once, a politician had far exceeded his promised munificence. The message, cleared by countless censors, was really this: *Don't worry, the war's doing fine. Carry on with your lives, while you can . . .*

I emptied half a bottle of vodka into a glass, and when George once again reassured the world that his weapons wouldn't, couldn't, and hadn't damaged so much as one civilian target or even one innocent hair on a civilian's head, I said out loud, "George, you are one fucking lying son-of-a-bitch."

And I threw the bottle at the TV screen.

It didn't break, but the picture turned to gray and silence — which was all I wanted it to do.

In the Torah We decreed for them a life for a life, an eye for an eye, a nose for
a nose, an ear for an ear, a tooth for a tooth, and a wound for a wound. But if a
man charitably forbears from retaliation, his remission shall
atone for him. Transgressors are those that do not judge in accordance with
Allah's revelations.
— THE HOLY KORAN, V, 45

PAX AMERICANA

PART THREE

Inferno
1995

"Father: our pain," they said,
"Will lessen if you eat us — you are the one
Who clothed us in this wretched flesh: we plead
For you to be the one who strips it away."
— DANTE, *Inferno, XXXIII*

Simple, plain Clarence! I do love thee so
That I will shortly send thy soul to heaven,
With lies well steel'd with weighty arguments.
— SHAKESPEARE, *Richard III*

The worst of evils and the greatest of crimes is poverty.
— GEORGE BERNARD SHAW

NEL MEZZO . . .

War ages you. You find yourself using phrases like "before the war," phrases your parents used when they wanted to seem especially old or venerable or *experienced.* But if I felt the chill ache of middle age suddenly — okay, *finally* — what did the Iraqis feel? They were still on the wrong road, lost in the dark woods. It's tangled, rough, and savage *describing* those woods. Just *thinking* about them brings back the fear that hits my guts like one of death's 1,000-volt cattle prods. The only aspect of it all that makes writing the story even vaguely worthwhile is the good I found there: diamonds of good glittering in lakes of burning tar, golden ingots of goodness gleaming deep beneath a hundred million tons of dull, dead black rock. Even a few pearls of great good cast before teaming herds of bristly, oil-streaked, shit-caked hogs.

For the best don't lack all conviction in Iraq: they *run* the place.

THE PRODIGAL SON-IN-LAW

The invitation came as something of a surprise. Beneath an unassuming letterhead, its eagle crest looking more like Batman in leg casts, I read:

> *The Embassy of the Republic of Iraq presents its compliments*
> *and has the pleasure to extend to you the invitation of*
> *Mr. Hamid Yousif Hammadi, Minister of Culture & Information*
> *in Iraq, to attend the seventh session of the*
> INTERNATIONAL BABYLON FESTIVAL

which will be held in the ancient city of Babylon/Iraq
for the period from September 22 – October 6, 1995.
And also to attend the conference on ancient history which will be held during the
period from October 1–4, 1995 focusing on the following subjects:

1. Medicine in Mesopotamia.
2. General Atcheological and Phiological Subjects.

At first I thought the subjects in the last line were typos and were really archaeology and philology, but now I'm not so sure. The range of festival activities did *promise* to be fairly eclectic, though:

This tourist, artful and cultural festival comprises of different activities such as;
Music Songs, Folk dances, Poetry and Drama gathering from different parts
of the world, as well as Fashion Shows and in addition to all that; organizing
Cultural Conferences concerning Geology, History, Music and Art Affairs.

It had been nearly four years since I'd thought much about Iraq, let alone thought I'd be back in Baghdad. A response was requested within a mere three days, but "any suggestions" were heartily welcomed, ". . . knowing that the administration of this festival will cover all travel expenses from Amman to Baghdad and vice versa & all accommodation expenses inside Iraq only. Awaiting for your kind reply, we remain, Mohammed T. Fakhri, Attaché."

Mr. Fakhri clearly did not wish to spoil the upbeat tone of his invitation by explaining why one had to fly to Amman in order to reach Baghdad, an exercise comparable to heading for Mexico City when Washington is your destination. Baghdad's Saddam International Airport had not seen much activity lately, however — a problem no doubt faced by any airport that suddenly finds itself situated in a "No-Fly Zone." A handwritten sign taped to the padlocked door of Iraqi Airways' offices in the Al Rashid Hotel summed up I.A.'s concomitant situation: "IT IS OUR PLEASURE TO INFORM ME YOU THAT IRAQI AIR WAYS IS ARRANGING SMOOTH SURFACE SERVICES FROM BAGHDAD TO AMMAN . . ."

When an airline is suddenly in the bus and taxi business you know there are problems.

Against the advice of both British and Canadian governments, and family and friends, I accepted Mr. Fakhri's invitation — and a commission from *The New York Times* magazine — wondering why I would do this again, and what the invitation was really about. A joker usefully suggested that Iraq might need more hostages. After all, cultural festivals were not something that I could imagine Saddam's Revolutionary Council had placed high on its agenda for at least five years. Perhaps he'd *really* enjoyed my war reporting? The *Times* felt the invite was a useful Trojan horse — I'd cover the Festival while uncovering a "real" story.

The answer — or at least a hint of hidden agenda — arrived by a fax a few hours before I left for the airport. Framed by an inch-wide floral border that made it resemble a menu, this document was signed by Hamed Yusuf Hamadi himself, Baghdad's Minister of Culture and Information (in a variant transliteration of his own name). "A nationwide referendum for the nomination of President Saddam Hussein for the post of the President of Iraq will be held on 15 October 1995," I learned.

> *The occasion will be both a historic and major event that takes place in Iraq*
> *for the first time. We have the pleasure to invite you to visit Baghdad*
> *and to her Iraqi cities to see the conduct of such a large activity along with other*
> *politicians, parliamentarians and journalists who will come from*
> *different parts of the world.*
> *We will also be pleased to meet any programme your wish for during the visit.*
> *Arrangements have been made with the Iraqi Embassy in Amman*
> *for your reception on arrival at Queen Alia airport and for you road passage to*
> *Baghdad. Accommodation will be provided with one of Baghdad's luxurious hotels . . .*

After fifteen hours in the air, a twenty-six-hour bus ride straight from Amman's airport to Baghdad is not precisely what the much lagged and weary traveler needs. Yet this was what a dapper, doleful, and very bald man seriously proposed, holding up a hand-scrawled sign reading, "BAGHDAD-BABYLON." I assumed he was from Jordan's Iraqi embassy, but later discovered he was a retired Lebanese electrical engineer and active poet from Rexdale, Ontario. My blank refusal to hop straight on the bus had him all but weeping, and I would have caved in to his pleas if the waiting vehicle had not looked better suited to ferrying schoolchildren around the city than it did to cruising across eight hundred miles of desert wastes. Fear was also a factor, I confess. Yup, fear was back in the game all right. With or without my government's blessing, I still wished to register with the British embassy in Amman before plunging back into Saddam's republic of fright. At least someone would know where exactly it was that I had vanished — if I did eventually vanish.

"We don't advise it," said a starched British consul the next day from behind six inches of plate glass, within the spacious manicured grounds of Britain's modernist fortress overlooking one of Amman's pleasant valleys. "We can't help you *there*, you know."

"I know."

"Yet you're *still* going?" He seemed incredulous.

"Yes."

"If you lose this," he waved my passport at me, "you're in trouble, you know. *Trouble.* Possibly the Russian embassy in Baghdad could help you. They're looking after our interests now."

"The *Russians* are?" (What a difference a decade makes.)

"Yerse. Good luck, old chap."

I told him I'd check back on my return so Her Majesty would not lose sleep over lost subjects. He gave me what sounded like a special phone number to call when — or if — I returned.

"You won't be able to call from *there*, though," he added. "We've no communication links with Baghdad now. *None.*"

The statement seemed to please him unduly.

By contrast, the Iraqi embassy far across town resembled a Harlem liquor store, with an Hispanic-looking hood dispensing indifference or abuse through a tiny window to various surly customers gathered in the street. Beyond the creaking meat safe of a door was a waiting room furnished with several tattered politburo sofas and monster armchairs, all of which faced a huge oil portrait of Saddam in a dusty, gilded frame of astonishing opulence. He was wearing what could be described as a Victorian hiking outfit — very Alpine chic — and he was standing by a tree upon some sort of snowy eminence, gazing: Master of All He Surveyed.

The Rican hood took my passport and placed it next to his brimming ashtray, then continued to smoke, read his newspaper, answer three vast old telephones held together by duct tape, and ignore or bark scorn at those supplicant faces constantly appearing beyond his window. Occasionally — very occasionally — he buzzed open the squealing mighty steel door for a privileged few. There were two black-and-white TV monitors on a busted shelf, and they revealed a blurred, grimy view up and down the street outside, but neither he nor anyone else so much as glanced at these hi-tech security features.

Considering the traditional Arab indifference to Time, it was astounding to find that, within thirty minutes, a withered, solicitous man appeared and ushered me through what resembled a military common room from the Gulags, then into a neglected courtyard and up some steps to a comparatively opulent office, where a suited official was prodding the guts of a grimy photocopier with a screwdriver the size of a rapier. The official shook my hand and the usher urged me to sit down. Then the official informed the usher in Arabic that, happy as he was to meet me, he was merely repairing the office photocopier and was not the room's true occupant. Deciding against offering any explanation for this blunder, my usher took me back to the waiting room.

An hour later I was finally seated with the opulent office's real occupant, a suave, oiled man who appeared to have some vague knowledge of a Babylon Festival, some vaguer knowledge of another bus heading to Baghdad that night, and very exact knowledge of what a taxi would cost to get me there in half the time and thrice the comfort. He then arranged for such a taxi personally — and presumably also arranged for its owner to charge me what I later discovered was precisely twice the going rate for an Amman-Baghdad run. He may, however, just have been dealing with the financial insecurity caused by recent strains in Iraqi-Jordanian relations.

Two leading Iraqi generals, who also just happened to be sons-in-law of Saddam, had recently made use of this run, "defecting" with their wives and, apparently, some billions of dollars belonging to their father-in-law. As transport, they'd used a convoy of mine-proof Mercedes limousines, seeking and obtaining refuge in Amman by cell phone on the way. A week before I arrived, King Hussein himself had publicly agreed with one of these generals, Hussein Kamel, once virtual satrap of the South and architect of Iraq's nuclear weapons program, that Saddam should now be deposed, sent packing immediately. This restored the little king's image in the West somewhat. Saddam was suddenly out of favor, could not come knocking on Jordan's door again. One can only speculate what General Kamel had told the king to effect this drastic change of heart — and, since Jordan is basically the only route out of Iraq, it's surprising that he hadn't heard it before. The Saddam lapel buttons, posters, and official biographies, conspicuous during Desert Storm, had now all but vanished from Amman's stores, too — especially those stores situated in its major hotels.

But remember Boutros Boutros-Ghali's wise conclusions after studying Arab disputes — they pass like sandstorms, forgotten when their fury abates — and also do not forget that Jordanians and Iraqis are cousins. Because the glow of virtue had been rapidly fading from Hussein Kamel's public image since he'd arrived. Not every member of the so-called Iraqi Opposition in exile saw him as their best hope for inspiring the nation's army to rise up and depose Saddam. There were now rumors that Kamel had butchered sixty thousand people in Kerbala, hiding corpses in the mosque housing Imam Hussein's tomb — the holiest spot on earth for Shi'ite Muslims. These rumors were more like hard facts in Kerbala itself.

Hussein Kamel therefore had the spin doctors and image surgeons in a frenzy. The very morning I set off through "Churchill's hiccup" to Iraq, for example, The Jordan Times reported that the general had just deposited $35 million in a Jordanian bank. The Times, usually a fine newspaper, made no attempt to analyze this story, which was clearly a press release from the ER of Kamel's PR people. Did it indicate his commitment to Jordan, his faith in the local economy? Did it hint at ongoing expenses in Amman, such as wages for an organized opposition and the training of crack guerrilla units? Or was The Times slyly alluding to the alleged billions appropriated from Saddam's off-shore bank accounts, suggesting that the $35 million probably represented Hussein Kamel's pocket money, a few measly bucks to keep him in the style to which he'd become very accustomed, and of which his annual Iraqi military salary would have funded about five minutes.*

Uncertainty reigned, as usual, then as now. Uncertainty was virtual Regent of Iraq. Western media were mentioning reports of rogue army units roaming the South and looting villages, hijacking buses and cars to survive. Other rumors suggested a burgeoning civil war on two fronts, another Lebanon in the making. All over Amman I'd heard tales of "Sand Pirates," dune warriors swooping out of the great Iraqi desert upon unwary travelers, willing to murder for an old pair of shoes or a cigarette; happy to cremate an entire coach full of people on the highway in broad daylight and escape with ten bucks in small change, a cluster of fresh dates, and all the melons they could carry. The Travelers' Advisory was not optimistic about conditions for those off to Baghdad. It rarely has been.

For me, getting out of Jordan, with all the appropriate documentation and visas any border bureaucrat could wish for, seemed harder than getting into the United States would probably be for an Iraqi assassin with no papers whatsoever. It took three long hours.

The three-mile stretch of no-man's-land at the very end of "Churchill's hiccup" that takes travelers from the realm where King Hussein's

* When Hussein Kamel returned to Iraq in 1996, Baghdad media reported that he was promptly murdered by his own blood relatives to atone for the shame he'd brought upon them. However, I was told by people in Baghdad that this was bullshit, that the defection had been a ruse to begin with and Hussein Kamel, Saddam's right-hand man as well as son-in-law, had undergone plastic surgery on his return, and would soon assume a new identity outside the country. He'd faked defection in order to make some covert financial transactions that would have been impossible in Baghdad, moving some nine billion dollars probably appropriated from state coffers. The stay in Amman had also allowed him to assess the strength and nature of the anti-Saddam Iraqi exiles' movement. Friends in Jordan close to the Royal Court had also ostensibly confirmed this, saying that General Kamel spent most of his time meeting delegations of foreign bankers or traveling to various centers for off-shore banking himself. He seemed uninterested in the exiles' movement and had only met with its leaders once. Furthermore, King Hussein made no secret of despising the general and never once saw him privately. It made sense. Hussein Kamel was no idiot, and if he'd absconded with Saddam's money and daughter, he would not have returned under the impression that a simple apology to his father-in-law would heal the rift. But an alternative scenario portrayed him as the victim of a classic Saddam double-cross: he faked defection, did what Saddam wanted done, then returned, but neglected to ask himself how Saddam would explain to his people the prodigal son-in-law. They knew Saddam shot people across conference tables for disagreeing with him — a botched defection would not go unpunished.

ubiquitous portraits are replaced by Saddam Hussein's ubiquitous portraits is truly a bridge across worlds. Even my dull, untalkative driver seemed suddenly animated — distinctly edgy, in fact — as we drove through a grandiose arch emblazoned with the titanic image of Saddam. This time The Leader was costumed as Sheikh of Araby, with fancy keffiyeh and gold-edged abaya, perhaps in deference to, or competition with, the slightly more genuine Arabian potentate whose protection we had now just forfeited.

Instead of officials dressed like British Tommies or Yasser Arafat, here there were officials wearing virtually any street garb they felt like wearing. The sole mandatory sign of office was still the Saddam moustache, though, badge of the Mukhabarat and Amn, the Secret Police. Those who guarded the guardians, who epitomized Fear, were, I had heard, more powerful than ever. Their presence was still a more effective deterrent now than any legal code. But in a speech apparently delivered to his latest Minister of Justice in 1988, Saddam himself defined the role of the Law: "The application of justice is a direct doorway that leads without guards or barriers to the values of Almighty God."

Iraq is full of direct doorways opened by "justice" and leading into a one-way corridor that goes straight to the next world.

We were immediately waved over into a parking lot beside a building labeled "EXECUTIVE GUEST LOUNGE." A moustache in a shimmering brown mohair suit seized my papers and, with considerable courtesy, suggested I take a seat inside "for a few moments."

The place was quite an improvement on the dusty wooden pews within a corrugated tin shack that Jordan had provided for travelers waiting on the vagaries of its bureaucracy. Thick broadloom, padded armchairs, and sofas; fat swags of gold brocade silk curtains; and vases exploding with sheaves of radiantly artificial flowers. In the entrance hall there was a touching poster of Saddam many years ago cradling his baby son, Uday; and, at the far end of the lounge itself, a fine gilt-framed portrait of The Leader solo wearing a white three-piece disco suit and an affably rakish grin. His necktie involved gold squares and white polka dots on a field of thrashing diagonals.

The most obvious feature of this Executive Guest Lounge was a live band and a troupe of some dozen singers and dancers. They all clapped their hands vigorously, performing a rather hectic variety of folk dance.

It was good to see that Iraq still knew how to welcome visitors, even if the caliber of hospitality out here in the desert seemed a little excessive. I clapped and hummed along.

Offered tea by another moustache, who also presented me with an Iraqi entry form, I quickly discovered that the in-house entertainment was, in fact, a group of Armenians rehearsing for their upcoming gig at the Babylon Festival while they, too, waited for returned passports and Iraqi travel permissions.

The entry form seemed far more interested in my mother's maiden name and my grandparents' surnames than it did in trifling issues like passport numbers and birth dates. I wondered who had ever ticked "Yes," to "Are you bringing weapons or explosives into Iraq?"

ANOTHER IRAQI MILLIONAIRE

The road to Baghdad had been more than repaired since its Gulf War thrashing: it was now a brand-new six-lane interstate, straight as an airport runway and just as empty. We encountered possibly six other vehicles in as many hours. No one had cause to use three hundred miles of pristine highway, since for all intents and purposes, this road led only to the Jordanian port of Aqaba, and Aqaba wasn't receiving visitors from Iraq these days. In Iraq if you don't have a reason to travel, you simply don't travel.

The brightest lights in that vast, dark desert were stars, a pulsing web of fiery diamonds shining through unsoiled air, high black air like obsidian. The constellations, however, seemed jumbled or unfamiliar, several resembling celestial blueprints for pyramids or huge Pythagorean solids. The sky even possessed its own version of the desert's cruel mirage trick: heaven's dome had walls so low here that often I saw the shimmering costume jewelry of a distant city appear on the horizon, only for it to recede endlessly, or disappear entirely, or metamorphose into another arcane blueprint of the gods. These dream cities aggravated the sense of isolation and helplessness that felt as if it were pouring up through black sand like oil, the deeper into Iraq we drove.

It may well have *been* oil, too, since the world's second largest exporter of the stuff had been banned by a UN embargo from exporting fossil fuel

— another punishment for Saddam's military sins. A similar situation in New Zealand would have the South Island looking like a sheepskin comforter by now. One consequence of the embargo for Iraqis was that gasoline remained inflation-proof. Gas was cheap, cheaper than water in fact; gas was the only commodity everyone could afford. If cars were similarly affordable, Iraq would now be a nation of cab drivers. My taxi even had a homemade extension to its gas tank, enabling the border-Amman-border leg of any trip to be achieved without the help of expensive Jordanian gas. At first I thought we had a water cistern stashed in the trunk, which as a consequence barely had room for a toilet bag and some postcards. I only learned the truth at a truck-stop pump, astounded by the gallon-counter's mounting digits and the time our refill was taking. Had I then known what this jumbo-jet-load of fuel cost I would have been still more astounded: less than seven cents.

In the meantime, I'd spent far more than that on a glass of mint tea served from the doorway of a furnace room adjoining the truck-stop's restaurant-and-shopping-arcade complex. From the darkened highway, this sprawling structure had appeared as a miniature Las Vegas of flickering colored neon — the first man-made lighting we'd seen in two hours. Close up, however, it was a shambles of epileptic fluorescent strips coated in peeling spray paint and cracking like bug zappers. Haggard, unshaven men with bloodshot eyes crouched with dominoes and cigarettes, or shuffled back and forth to the parking lot with blackened rags, wrenches, old tin cans — whatever was available for gonzo Band-Aid engine repair.

The arcade of open stalls, most of them illuminated by kerosene lamps, was a similar study in hopelessness and despair. Iraq had changed. Some twelve one-man operations all sold identical wares, their proprietors either too depressed to solicit trade, or convinced that customers were matters for Fate to worry about. It was all the will of Allah: so sit back and stare at the concrete. Every stall had a tray of Sumer Filters, Sumer Mild, and Al Rashid Filters, "Made in Mesopotamia" — as if "Made in Iraq" might prove a deterrent to exports. There were also many aluminum cooking pots and pans, several thicknesses of bristly rope in coils, a couple of sad gelabias hanging like thin headless ghosts, a turret of enameled copper plates decorated with "Thanks, God" in Kufic script, and four or five foxy nylon body stockings in dry cellophane packages bearing the image of a sloe-eyed, busty babe clad in cobweb catsuit above the legend "OPEN CROTCH." There were razor blades of the old type, shampoo, tooth-paste, photo frames, "Playboy Brand" sunglasses — and everything a King of the Road might need for both his outward journey and his return to the little lady. When a man starts taking home aluminum stew pots instead of crotchless body stockings, he must be aware that some great watershed in life has been crossed. But no one had been taking any of this merchandise anywhere for some time, judging by the look of it.

The restaurant was either closed or saving electricity, but a managerial figure resembling Douglas Fairbanks, Jr., sat behind a stately desk in its lobby, prodding a calculator as if testing roadkill for signs of life. Beneath the desk's glass top were pressed low denomination examples of every currency on earth. He seemed like the right man to ask.

"Change money?"

"Amerkan dollar?"

"Certainly."

"Hundred dollar's bill?" He perked up.

"What rate?"

He consulted the roof of his skull from inside before concluding that "Twenny-ones" was a reasonable answer.

I mimed vacillation, trying to detect any signs of flexibility.

"Give me twenty-two," I finally tried.

"Okay, frenn," he agreed, instantly.

As I handed over the crisp, self-assured bill, I wondered just how much more flexibility existed. The official bank rate was 600 Iraqi dinars to the dollar; he was changing at 2,200. Back in 1990, there had been 6 dinars to the dollar. Not so many years before that — when oil flowed and Saddam was a major customer for British and French armaments — the dinar was worth more than the dollar. Now inflation was reported at over 1,000 percent, something no one can really grasp. Something that speaks to the reality of paper money.

I certainly hadn't grasped its implications then, however. When the manager returned with a plastic shopping bag full of banknotes in classic rubber-banded slabs, I assumed that he'd brought the entire contents of his safe with him, perhaps to bank next day. Instead, he nonchalantly handed me the bag.

"Two 'underd twenny towsand," he sighed. "Okay, frenn?"

There were twenty-two slabs, each containing one hundred pastel blue-and-violet 100 dinar notes. They bore the images of Saddam disguised as a conservative banker on one side, and on the other, a view of the modernist architectural eyesore known as the "Baghdad Clock," above which was proudly emblazoned "CENTRAL BANK OF IRAQ." Many of the notes were suspiciously new and printed on paper crisp and frail as a dead moth's wings. But they were genuine: no one would bother to counterfeit Iraqi currency. Until a few weeks earlier, 100 dinars had been the highest denomination there was, but now a 250 dinar note had appeared in circulation. Even a 5,000 dinar note, however, would cost more to forge than it would purchase.

Tipping out the cash on my cab seat, I felt furtive, illegal. No one ever carries so much cash. It looked like a dope dealer's haul, and I felt certain that any official finding it would arrest me on the spot. Every one of the fifteen major pockets in my Tilley vest contained a high roller's wad, and yet I still had a foot of bills left to conceal somewhere else. (But by the time I was once more changing U.S. for Jordanian currency — I JD = $1.35 — looking at the meager sliver of limp bills thrust back for my $100, I missed my high roller's wads, missed being a millionaire.)

The only obstacles to cruising at a steady 120 miles per hour all the way to Baghdad were "check points." These generally comprised a wood fire burning near a ragged old tent pitched just off the shoulder, and two messy rows of large rocks, each row positioned across a different half of the route north — probably to suggest that braking might be better than attempting the hairpin zigzag around them. Such check points apparently existed solely to support the nicotine habits of the soldiers manning them. Nothing was "checked." A bleary-eyed blank face merely peered in through the driver's window, then a hand seized the four or five Sumer Filters thrust out instantly and wordlessly. These weary faces never even glanced at what their hands retrieved; they just nodded, backing away into flickering shadows as we navigated the rocks and sped off.

When I first saw the dozen-odd packs sitting neatly in my driver's plastic "Auto-Organizer" tray (next to a glass tumbler, a bag of grapes and dates, and a carton of cookies), I thought the man must be a dedicated chain-smoker, a pro who knew the Amman-Baghdad run was a twelve-pack job. And at the first check point, I thought he was fumbling to hand over papers, permits, insurance, license. He couldn't — or wouldn't — tell me what problem the tobacco bribe was sparing him or us from, however. And whatever it was, how serious could it have been if five smokes solved it?

Iraq is a topsy-turvy world, though, and to comprehend it you need your mind in a headstand. Like that Beatles' song, Iraqis even say "hello" when they mean "goodbye." But they say "hello" when they mean "hello," too. After a while, however, there are things about the place that you don't even want to comprehend anymore. It's like having a conversation with the insane: first you worry because it doesn't make any sense; then you worry because it's *beginning* to make sense.

HALLOWEEN IN HELL

Compared with the highway, Baghdad was bustling. But compared with what the city once had been, it was almost deserted, the broad streets bleak, forlorn, and dark, except for the odd ice cream parlor or café whose proprietor had a fetish for exterior novelty lighting.

The official back at Iraq's embassy had told me I was booked in at the Meridien Hotel — in my experience, a chain of exceptionally luxurious five-star establishments. The driver had trouble finding it, however, something which I found hard to believe and intensely irritating after such a long drive. Downtown Baghdad is not a big place and has few buildings higher than ten storeys. It seemed to have fewer buildings than I remembered generally, and many of these were now lower than one storey, thanks to some of the 126,645 air sorties, 322 Cruise missiles, and 96,000 tons of explosives employed to make Desert Storm's forty-two-day-long point to the Iraqi people.

Our trouble, it transpired, was largely due to the Meridien having changed its name to the Palestine Hotel — probably when the original owners, glued to Peter Arnett's daily CNN damage updates a world away, decided that neither they nor most of their regular guests would have much reason to visit Baghdad again for a very long time. With its offset polygonal balconies, the Palestine's tower resembled a honeycomb fashioned by bees the size of ostriches. Unexpectedly, there was a hive of human activity inside its lobby, too. A mob of Orientals thronged at the reception desk, shouting and waving passports like stock exchange hustlers. To one side, a table swathed in Babylon Festival posters propped up three men who looked like school teachers at the annual fête.

"Country?" one inquired briskly.

"Yes, Canada!" another exclaimed, hearing my answer. "Good. You are welcome, my friend."

The Canadian "delegation" — which turned out to be me and two Lebanese poets from Rexdale — was indeed booked in at the Palestine, I learned.

The Meridien people wouldn't like to see what's become of their hotel under its new management. Outside — at night — it seemed fine, grandly imposing even; but inside, with the benefit of lighting, it looked as if it had been hauled up after a few years on the ocean floor and dried out.

"Rooms are even worse," one of the teachers confided, when I asked if any other hotels were available to my "delegation."

"Sheraton better," another confessed. "Sheraton much better. Rooms there *good*."

"Can I go there?"

"Of course. Why not?"

It wasn't the sort of response I'd expected from officials of a maximum security state, and to encounter such a freewheeling attitude cheered me immensely.

The Sheraton's tower rose up directly across the road from the Palestine. It was now called the Ishtar Hotel, though, but its lobby looked far more user-friendly than the previous one had, rising in an atrium through ten of its twenty floors, with three elevators sliding up and down inside glass tubes that were framed by flashing lightbulbs.

Here, too, was a Babylon Festival table with officials behind it. One of them, an effete little man with a Hitler moustache, greeted me as if we were old dear friends, handing me his business card. It announced "Hassan Al-Shamari, Journalist/Translator, Ministry of Information." There was no address or phone number.

"I will be your *guide*," he stated, as if the news would have me weeping with joy. "Also I want to make an interview with you for my newspaper."

"Can I check in first?"

It was 1:00 a.m. Actually it was 2:00 a.m., since Iraq is an hour ahead of Jordan, but I didn't learn this for two days. I'd been traveling for thirteen hours and needed to wash, eat, sleep, not be interviewed (about what?).

Handed a key, I carried my own bags to the elevator and soared up through the roof of the lobby atrium to the fourteenth floor. Below it, I was happy to see, was the thirteenth floor, which allayed any suspicions that I'd been assigned to its bad luck. This superstition apparently hasn't made it to Iraq.

The fourteenth floor was very dark. At first I thought the lights were merely off, but it was the lightbulbs that caused this problem: of some fifty in sight, only four were functioning.

The room had some problems, too. It smelled of dead air conditioner, sickly plumbing, and robust mildew. A shuttered balcony was coated in fine ocher dust, its wooden slats looking able to survive perhaps another year or two without a paint job before they started in earnest the business of actually disintegrating. The carpet was badly patched in areas, and someone had once rebuilt a car engine or slaughtered a goat near the foot of the bed. What must have been a large cigar had melted a half-inch shute into the television's plastic roof. Between the two bedside lamps, one out of eight lightbulbs functioned, thus the only real source of lighting was a terrifying four-foot plastic tower containing two searing fluorescent strips that turned the room a ghastly shade of twitching green. The furniture was worn and weary: it wanted to go home.

Normally, none of this would have bothered me. Nor would the huge gaping hole above the bathtub, where some amateur plumber had clambered through the ceiling to have a word with troublesome pipes, dislodging in the process a pound of cement rubble and dust that still lay in the tub. But the *faucets* bothered me. The faucets were the last straw. It wasn't the sebum-like scum, thick as smeared toothpaste, that coated them: it was the fact that, when turned, no water emerged from them.

"Then take the room next door," suggested a night manager. "Or the one next to that. Or any other one you like." He handed over about twenty keys.

Unlike the Palestine, which I'd learned was overbooked (hence the Asian scrum), the Ishtar seemed to be entirely empty.

The room next door was a through-the-looking-glass version of the one I was in, but its faucets produced water. With all the keys at my disposal, however, and the entire fourteenth floor to scavenge, I soon had bedside lamps with eight glowing lightbulbs between them; I had two full rolls of what appeared to be miniature toilet paper installed in the appropriate twin holders, and I had two more spare rolls above. I had a television whose picture was not just a multi-colored blizzard, and I had a fridge with actual ice rather than very cold water in its ice trays. I had extra pillows, none of them bearing the imprint of a head that sweated nicotine, and I had two sets of bath towels that had not only been washed that year, but were also far larger than face cloths.

After standing beneath a shower powerful enough, with all the pressure of twenty empty floors behind it, to clean the soot off old buildings, I turned on the television to find Disney's *Aladdin* playing within a light rainbow snow storm. An in-house movie feature to remind guests where they were now, perhaps? In fact, it was not: it was merely another project by the same coincidence specialists who had once scheduled *Alexander the Great* to be broadcast the moment I entered a hotel room in Alexandria.

Throwing open more rattling desiccated shutters, I gazed out over the broad curve of the river Tigris at an oddly familiar, but much more spread-out skyline. There was the structure like a gigantic squashed onion on a two-hundred-foot golf tee — a copy of Kuwait City's Martian spaceport mosque — then the sloping ziggurat of Ba'athist founding father Michel Aflaq's mausoleum (also the ruling party's official museum), the four great bridges without which Baghdad would grind to a halt (and virtually did when the "Allies" managed to bomb only one of them), and the scattered towers of various government buildings rising out of what looked like a lush forest covering much of the Tigris' west bank. It was the CNN skyline, background to the "Allies Kick Butt" segment of the great *Desert Storm* maxi-series — that was why it seemed so familiar. It wasn't the Baghdad that I remembered. Television creates false memory: we think we've been everywhere, done everything, but we haven't. It's all a dream.

Far to the south, on the east bank where I now was, blazed a strangely levitated bonfire, its writhing ectoplasmic flames stretching and receding like a vast burning claw trying to rip stars from the sky. It turned out to be the burn-off chimney of an oil refinery that Saddam had decided to build right in the city, feeling that locating this monstrosity near a densely populated area would spare it from enemy bombs — even if this also meant greatly assisting the city's air with its ambition to become entirely unbreathable. Baghdad's air was unusually humid for the time of year, too, heavy and unwholesome with the weight of rot and toxins. You could *see* it. It looked and felt like poisonous ghost-earth covering a living graveyard. Above this pollution blur, stuck like a silver dagger in the dark flesh of night, was a very beautiful Islamic crescent of moon.

There was no sign of Hassan, my guide and potential interviewer, down in the lobby, so I walked over to the utterly deserted coffee shop and sat in an alcove wondering if a waiter would appear. One did quite soon, so I asked for a beer and a menu.

"Beer finished now," I learned.

"Wine?"

"Wine finished also."

I'd been imagining this beer for around thirteen hours now, thus was grief-stricken to hear such news. Had they run out, or was it merely after hours?

From what I could grasp, it seemed possible to have this beer in my room, so I asked for the menu's club sandwich to be sent up as well.

"You must pay esstra for the room-coming," said the waiter.

I nodded assent, and slipped him what seemed like a handsome tip at the time, but which I later estimated at the equivalent of a third of a cent.

"Nice cold beer, OK?"

He appeared to understand.

I was fighting with the television — to tune in what had to be a French-Canadian movie dubbed into American — when the same waiter arrived bearing something covered by a wok lid on a tray also containing a spoon and an empty salt shaker. But no beer.

"The beer?"

"Finish," he replied, sadly.

I could hardly ask for my third of a cent back, so I inquired about water, which was "No problem" — an overly optimistic statement as things turned out.

The club sandwich had become a sort of schnitzel made from the flesh of an old horse or camel roadkill coated with a batter made from sand and custard. It reclined on a bed of slippery French fries next to one pale little broccoli floret. Everything was cold, too.

Baghdad: *Strange days have found us . . .*

THE WASTE REMAINS

Baghdad is not just the capital of Iraq these days, it is a state within a state, a security zone within a security zone, evidently organized for some final last stand, some apocalyptic siege — as it has usually been for over a millennium. Movements of citizens are even more restricted than they always have been. Everyone has to carry several different ID cards. Baghdad is now the very core of Saddam Hussein's rapidly shrinking world, and in many ways it must resemble his mind. Here the secret police and various security networks — Amn, Mukhabarat, Estikhbarat (the military intelligence), and Jihaz al-Amn al-Khas (a private security force for the military and industry) — have drawn their lethal webs so tight that the city is a maximum security cage, impossible to enter or leave unless you are permitted to enter or leave it: thus it is impossible to forget that you are imprisoned within it. Here freedom is not just another word for nothing-left-to-lose, because most of Baghdad's inhabitants have nothing left at all, yet they no longer even know what freedom is, let alone what freedom *feels* like. Many even believe their Leader still when he tells them that his military dictatorship has made Iraq "the most democratic nation on earth." They need to believe in something. With six thousand years of continuous, recorded civilization behind you and your land, you don't just give up. You just go on. You just make do. No one ever said it was a rose garden . . .

Dawn revealed a green, sluggish Tigris sliding past overgrown parkland, where crumbling structures, which proved to be fish restaurants and cafés, squatted untidily amid groves of drooping trees. A legless man in rags sold newspapers from a makeshift platform positioned right in the middle of a four-lane road following the river's bank. The baleful barking of countless dogs had awakened me, and it continued relentlessly until sunlight finally appeared. The early morning air reeked of decay and sewage. Wherever I looked there were tattered, crumbling buildings, so long neglected that it was hard to believe they weren't boarded up, let alone that they were still occupied, still in business. Rubble of many varieties sat in piles or splashed across rooftops or cascaded onto balconies. Some of it had been bulldozed into jagged heaps that were even, on closer inspection, impossibly *still dwellings* which had just suffered particularly unconscionable neglect or abuse. Wrecked but not ruined.

I was shocked to the core. Those who won't give peace a chance should see what war actually achieves. What was once a rich and vibrant city, full of ambition, hope, discotheques, and grandiose construction projects, was now an ugly, battered Third World slum, with not a single redeeming thing of beauty to be found anywhere throughout all its many miserable square miles. Except the human spirit, which seems to thrive under such circumstances.

And no city's circumstances — not even Calcutta's teeming cesspit, not even the sweating diseased toilets of West Africa — can hold a match to those circumstances now endured in Baghdad. Here the outer circumstances pale in comparison with the inner carnage and horror. Not just the city has suffered from neglect and physical abuse: the minds of its inhabitants have been tampered with in an infinitely crueler, probably irreparable manner. For over twenty years, what has been happening to Iraq amounts to a psychological holocaust, an atrocity that almost no one in the West seems to grasp fully in all its awful scope and complexity, since we are continuing to help make it even worse than it already was before Saddam Hussein attained demonhood in 1990 and caught our media's attention.

On Iraqi television, adults dressed as animals — cats, a crocodile, badgers — were cavorting laconically on an amateurish set. They had ill-made body suits and grotesquely large masks, yet they spoke with normal human voices, as if not realizing they were now animals. I left for breakfast.

Hassan waylaid me the moment I stepped out of the elevator, not to commence his interview — a subject he, in fact, never again raised — but to furnish me with four postage-stamp-sized coupons that could be exchanged for "Breakfast," "Lunch," "Dinner," and "Liquer" (which had a line drawn through it and the word "Coffee" substituted by hand). No beer, no wine . . . *now this*? Iraq wasn't dry, or wasn't dry the last time I'd passed through; it wasn't an Islamic state. Perhaps Saddam was still trying to curry favor with some of the richer and more pious Arab states? Or even with an infinitely more potent entity? He certainly needed to curry favor with someone very influential, and do it very soon, too. I couldn't get a straight answer about the booze out of anyone.

The coffee shop was at least no longer deserted. Three men and a woman of indeterminate nationality sat together at a central table. The woman wore jeans and a vest of many pockets, like my own; she also clutched a spiral notepad. If she wasn't a journalist she was definitely disguised as a journalist. From some twenty feet away, it sounded as if she spoke Turkish, which shifted into broken English as she began an argument with the waiter who'd brought her a cup of something she didn't want.

"Fry yegg or ommylette?" I was asked.

I ordered the omelette, which arrived thirty seconds later, but had clearly been created much earlier. Thin as dandruff, it must have contained half an egg stretched with water, and it was accompanied by a tiny leaf of some sort, three matchsticks of carrot, and a bread roll baked not that long ago then deep frozen and thawed out several times — probably on account of power cuts, or for ideological reasons.

I faced an identical breakfast every morning for many days, until I could no longer handle the sight of it. Lunch and dinner were invariably dry, crumbly rice crowned by a cubic inch of meat in some form, occasionally supplemented by a tiny salad plate of vegetables diced into pin-head flecks to create an illusion of quantity. No other food was available — the menus were merely decorative. The hotel's budget (if its management even bothered to make one with inflation at 1,000 percent) did not extend further than basic commodities.

Grim as it was, compared to most Iraqis, though, we had food fit for kings. But nutrient-deprivation takes time to adjust to, and my very cells were crying out in protest before long. True, the food *was* free, but then, relatively speaking, so were the meals in restaurants outside that still served real food to those who could afford it. You can't call $2 for three people to eat ten different dishes exorbitant, can you? Unless $2 represents nearly two months' salary.

GEORGE BUSH: WAR CRIMINAL

Twenty dollars for a new matched set of Waterman ballpoint and fountain pens in a leather case seemed reasonable, too. This bargain was on sale in a corridor of the Al Rashid Hotel that now housed a small bazaar with some thirty vendors of antiques and upscale goods who had their wares spread over folding picnic tables. There were hundreds of new luxury pens available — Montblanc, Cross, Cartier, Shaeffer — and even a glass case containing rare antique models in solid gold and filigreed platinum, many inset with jewels or Burmese jade. There were also hundreds of new and nearly new Dupont or Cartier cigarette lighters. There were dozens of cases containing silver and gold knives and forks and spoons, too, and many more with just teaspoons, every box bearing the name of some prestigious firm in either London or Paris. All the antiques were from France and England as well, I noticed. There were dueling pistols, swords (*lots* of swords), monogrammed hip flasks and cigarette cases, unattractive bronze statues usually involving a horse, crested silver goblets, and countless other items of upscale Victoriana, including sets of silver Indian rupees bearing the old queen-empress's plump and disapproving profile.

But what was it all doing *here*?

"Soldiers they bringing from Kuwait."

It was loot, in other words, spoils of war. It looked exactly like the sort of stuff every rich or royal Kuwaiti would have storerooms filled to the rafters with: tacky yet definitely expensive gifts from obsequious deal makers or would-be deal makers in Europe, Japan, and America.

I'd come to the Rashid for memories and because the Ishtar's lobby was depressing, its arcade of sad dusty shops with little to sell not even open, and not a newspaper or magazine stand in sight. After the war, it was widely believed that one of Saddam's more important secret bunkers was situated beneath the Rashid Hotel, which was why he allowed CNN to remain there: his insurance policy against a direct hit on the refuge where he apparently sat out much of the bombing himself, a hundred feet beneath the man reporting it to the world. Although typical of Saddam's cunning ploys and riotous sense of humor, I never thought there could be much truth to the speculation, however, until I saw the Rashid myself again with the benefit of hindsight.

Its unmarked black glass entrance doors now slid noiselessly open to reveal a five-foot-square mosaic tile image of George Bush's face with the legend "BUSH IS CRIMINAL" beneath it. Visitors must walk over George like a doormat to reach the main lobby. I liked this idea. The clunky symbolism reminded me of those ancient Egyptian reliefs that show the pharaoh with tiny enemies subdued beneath his huge divine feet. I now have a Saddam Hussein prayer mat in my doorway.

Where any other hotel would have a main lobby, the Rashid had a vast, empty marble cavern with no discernible function — unless, of course, it was to allow people to enter the building and use certain areas without having to encounter hotel guests. The main lobby lay beyond this mystery space, which was now not quite empty: it contained a little Babylon Festival table staffed by a glamorous society matron who worried with her compact mirror whether or not her hair was working today. I inquired if Babylon Festival "delegates" could stay at the Rashid, too, if they wanted. The lady looked baffled; she didn't understand what either me or her hair wanted from her, but she smiled — as she'd no doubt been brought up to do. Her lips weren't working either, unfortunately, so the effect was quite frightening.

"Ask at the reception desk," she decided. "I'm very happy to meet you."

This was a bald lie.

"Yes," replied a haughty desk clerk at reception, hesitantly. "But you must *pay*."

"How much?"

Thirty-six dollars a night for a suite was how much. It would be $700 at the Pierre. But 79,000 dinars — the translation — was outrageous: over two years' salary for an average middle-class Iraqi. Eighty thousand dollars a night would be steep even in Europe.

A Gulf Arab in white keffiyeh and gelabia crossed the lobby holding two Marlboro duty-free bags crammed with banknotes. Another small bazaar was encamped at the far end of the lobby, selling old kilims, Liberace-style rings, and much made from ivory — including whole six-foot elephant tusks.

"Take it, friend," urged a high-pressure-sales artist, as I handled a giant milky white tooth.

He was asking a mere $25.

"I might have a bit of trouble getting it through Canadian customs."

"What *trouble?*" he exclaimed, hurt. "This ivory . . . *pure* ivory, friend. Not *bone.*"

"*That's* the trouble."

"No, my friend. You listen to me: this *IVORY*, not *bone.*"

I explained that my government had a problem with IVORY not BONE, and did not think it wise that elephants should become extinct just because their tusks were valuable. He didn't have a clue what I was going on about, not a glimmer. When the survival of your family is threatened, the fate of animals does not seem that important, though.

In the Rashid's coffee shop — still a black-and-white pharaoh's vault of Italian marble — four men took half an hour to prepare a glass of fresh orange juice, while I stared through the angled windows at the garden's maze of hedges. The place didn't even *feel* like a hotel anymore. It was impersonating a hotel, and its staff were impersonating staff — but resentfully, like undercover narcs working as busboys in a biker bar. They wanted to arrest the customers, not serve them.

Back at the Aladdin's cave of loot, a vendor came down 80 percent from the $40 he originally wanted for a $2,000 fountain pen. Then he confessed he'd take "what you wish" for it: his license to vend at the Rashid expired that day and the police would be on his case if he stayed a minute longer. The potential punishment for expired vending licenses appeared to be awful beyond imagination. If this was a sales gimmick, it certainly worked. It wouldn't anywhere else: because there is nowhere else where it *could* be true.

Samir al-Khalil writes: ". . . the object of torture is the erasure of difference; it is the business of surgically intervening in the biological fact of irreducible individuality so as to 'disprove' it in reality."[1] What I think he means is that having a bottle broken in your ass isn't good for the ego.

SADDAM HUSSEIN'S IDOL

That evening was the Babylon Festival's grand Opening Night. Sturdy, functional red buses arrived at the hotel, and Hassan herded me and many other people into what seemed to be his personal bus.

"Thirty-six nations participating," he'd told me when I inquired.

"Fifty-five were approached."

He nodded proudly at these figures.

Considering Iraq was the host, nineteen refusals seemed negligible. Who were they?

Hassan couldn't recall, but added that he was still expecting Australians and Swedes to show up. None ever did. Who, then, were the thirty-six that had allegedly arrived?

"Italy, Germany, Portugal, Russia, Yugoslavia, er . . ."

He became distracted by one of his sheep about to stray.

I took this international participation with a pinch of sand, since, knowing what the "Canadian delegation" consisted of, I could imagine how close to the inner circles of official power these European participants probably were — *if* they'd showed up. And anyone on our bus whom I initially took for a German or an Italian or an ex-Yugoslav invariably turned out to be from somewhere in that panorama of ethnicity now called "Russia" for convenience.

You need a fertile imagination to get excited about Babylon — that much I already knew — since little remains of the second-oldest city on earth. On the other hand, too much remains of Iraq's reconstruction of the second-oldest city on earth.

Still, I will admit that there's definitely something bizarrely thrilling about passing a standard green highway sign that reads, "BABYLON 8." Some form of sign has been around the same spot for nearly five thousand years, because Babylon was trading goods with the great cities of the Indus Valley back then, and those early Indians regarded it as an equal to their own mighty city states — indeed, it was the only competition they faced that was worth mentioning.

Babylon: Where Hammurabi assembled the earliest known legal code; where Nebuchadrezzar held the Israelites in captivity; where Belshazzar had his feast and saw the writing on the wall; and where, a millennium and a half after Hammurabi, Alexander the Great died at the age of thirty-three, having already conquered the known world and been declared a god by the priests of Egypt. The span of time is breathtaking. But nothing else about Babylon, if one looks closer, has much at all to brag about. Hammurabi's city was completely destroyed after a savage Hittite raid, so it is, in fact, the remains of a Babylon rebuilt by Nebuchadrezzar a thousand years later that we see today.

Hammurabi can at least claim his legal code as a lasting achievement — or he can *try* — but it was his fostering of a powerful priesthood around the cult of Marduk that actually gained him potent fame in his own time. Even the mighty Assyrian kings were so overawed by the power of this super-god that they felt it essential for the success of their reigns to be crowned before Marduk's towering statue in the great temple of Babylon.

Although Hammurabi's code is the earliest that has survived, it is not exactly one under which anybody would now wish to live — or die. Although the O. J. Simpson trial provided (to many Iraqis as well, by the way) that there really is one law for the rich and another for the not-so-rich, at least this parallel justice is not actually *written* into any legal code. Yet.

Hammurabi, for example, decreed that if a man beats to death the daughter of a wealthy man, that man's own daughter will be executed. But if the man kills a peasant's daughter, his punishment will just be a stiff fine. And if it's merely a slave girl whom he kills, the fine will be a good deal limper. On the other hand, any man accusing another of manslaughter and failing to prove his case is to be executed himself. A man caught copulating with his own daughter is to be banished from the city; yet if, after his father dies, he's found in bed with his mother, both of them are to be burned alive. Setting slaves free was a crime punishable by death, too. And if one of your slaves was ever surly or rude to you, Hammurabi's code decreed that you should cut off his ear on the spot. The code does indeed contain, word for word, the eye-for-an-eye, tooth-for-a-tooth concept later adopted by Jewish law, but back in old Babylonia, there were certain caveats: "If a wealthy man knocks out the tooth of a wealthy man, then that man's tooth will also be knocked out. . . ." But "if a wealthy man knocks out the tooth of a peasant, then that wealthy man shall be fined . . ." about ten bucks. At least the Father of Legislation was honest and straightforward about his double standard.[2]

Most of the code protects property rights quite equitably, it's true, but there's also a lengthy section dealing with Hammurabi's opinion of himself. It's hard to imagine any president getting this piece of legislation past the house: "I am the king who is pre-eminent among kings; my words are choice; my ability has no rival."

Saddam Hussein also faces no obstacles to his amendments to legislation and, speaking in the third person — a vice I've noticed he often falls prey to — he once summed up the essence of Iraq's legal code thus: "Saddam Hussein has the authority to cancel or commute a sentence. Sometimes I abolish a capital punishment against someone and order his immediate release . . . so that his new humanity might assume its full dimension. If we commute the death sentence to life imprisonment he would not enjoy his humanity as we wish and want. . . . Therefore most of the pardons we give are full ones."[3] Modesty obviously prevents him from adding that he also has the authority to throw anyone he likes in jail, and sometimes order them tortured or executed without burdening the courts or judges with the nuisance of a trial, or even troubling bureaucrats with the task of recording charges, arrests, convictions, and so on. This principle (efficiency) itself is extolled in a section of Saddam's book on socialism that is headed with admirable clarity, "The Best Use of Time and the Cutting Down of Formal Written Correspondence." Comparisons with other dictators are welcome.

But Nebuchadrezzar is Saddam's supreme role model, his idol. Their two profiles appeared superimposed — with Saddam above, naturally — on the poster for the Seventh International Babylon Festival. Beneath them was placed a phrase that began, "From Nebuchadrezzar to Saddam Hussein . . . ," then deteriorated into drivel about "glorious jihads." But from Nebuchadrezzar on, the history of Babylon is actually an ignominious saga of internecine bloodshed, constant war, and sieges so tenacious they occasionally forced the Babylonians into cannibalism. If there was ever a lull between bloodbaths, some self-aggrandizing construction projects got under way. Nebuchadrezzar made Babylon feared and famous only because he eventually won the wars that he'd also invariably started in the first place. The Babylonians themselves probably could have done without these victories if it meant avoiding the carnage that preceded them, and the powerful priests of Marduk seem ultimately to have felt the same way, branding Nabonidus — last of the dynasty created by Nebuchadrezzar's father — a heretic. This, however, merely gave the Persian emperor Cyrus the Great carte blanche to cakewalk his way over and take Babylon lock, stock, and throne, without even firing an arrow.

Saddam never mentions this end of Babylon's history, unsurprisingly, but he's certainly obsessed with the earlier period, with the triumphs of his idol over Assyrian scum, with the destruction of Jerusalem, and particularly with the Captivity of the Jews. French architects working on the Babylon reconstruction project two years earlier had told me that Saddam frequently paced up and down all night in the facsimile version of Nebuchadrezzar's palace, apparently conversing with the late king's spirit — perhaps exchanging suggestions for organizing a second Captivity.

History isn't Saddam's real forte, though. He makes it, why should he read it? But, to be fair, no one with the equivalent of a grade four education — which is all that can actually be traced for Saddam — can be expected to know much about anything they have not personally experienced. Thus Saddam's view of Babylon circa 700 BC bears an eerie similarity to his view of the world in general circa the last twenty years.

THE FAT LADY SINGS

Our bus turned north off the Baghdad road at the Gate of Marduk, having halted several times for military check points with sunken video cameras that scanned the vehicle's chassis for dubious objects. From a parking lot that spanned ten acres, we walked toward yet another check point, where X-ray scanners and an airport security archway had been set up right across the road. Banks of electronic gadgets hummed and beeped; many people were frisked or brushed down with hand-held metal detectors. Beyond this barrier rose the circular walls of a repro Alexander the Great's Amphitheater, where hundreds poured in a wedge toward one narrow stairway leading up to a tiny little door.

Hassan had this problem under control, though. He herded his people over to where a pair of wrought-iron gates led into the amphitheater's tangled gardens. But no one wanted to go into this gloomy jungle with him.

"VIP entrance," he kept announcing.

A Lebanese poet took Hassan's side, reassuring us this was a far, far better route. Indeed, within thirty seconds, it got us into the arena through another door. Once inside, we found ourselves facing a gigantic stage upon which the garishly amateur set of some high school Shakespeare effort had been erected: a massive but fragile-looking white throne, several crooked pillars, and a clam shell the size of a small car. Rising up the entire rear wall, there was also an inexplicable forty-foot-high translucent polythene tube as wide as a sewer pipe.

Hassan had earlier doled out large enameled metal badges bearing the Babylon Festival logo and much very blurred Arabic script. Seeing these emblems pinned to our chests, various ushers started rounding up Hassan's people, encouraging us to ascend the steep stone stairs leading through row upon row of packed humanity seated in ever-widening horseshoes up to the very lip of this vast terraced stone bucket.

"You are from?"

"Canada."

"Ah, yes. Good. Welcome, friend."

"Thanks."

"You are delegate or dancer?"

I really do not look like a dancer. "No. Poet, in fact . . ."

"Ah," the man trilled. "Then you sit there: Media Section."

The "Media Section" was front row, stage right — an even better deal than the Diplomatic Section directly behind it. Some of Hassan's people glanced scornfully back at me, as I left them clambering up to the Delegates' Section and eased myself onto a foam cushion in front of a man who turned out to be the Indonesian ambassador.

As the place began to fill up like a nightmarishly overcrowded fairground's Wall of Death, I attempted to identify the thirty-six different nations that had deemed it worth their while to show up for what had to be just Saddam's pre-phony-referendum propaganda jamboree. After Ghana, the Sudan, Armenia, Turkey, Pakistan, India, Bangladesh, Jordan, Russia (probably good now for ten separate nations), Mongolia, North Korea, and Somalia, I gave up.

"I *say*," said the most Etonian of accents behind me. "Where are *my* people performing, old chap?"

"Indonesia is in Neboo-shaad-dresh palace, you exshellence," a more important-looking usher than mine replied, clearly familiar with the immaculate little man behind me.

"Oh-*ohhh*," the Indonesian ambassador responded, not particularly interested in his own question. "So there are several *different* venues, am I right?"

Almost: There were three different stages offering simultaneous performances. One in Nebuchadrezzar's palace, one where we sat, and another no one ever seemed able to locate.

"Good *stuff*," the ambassador decided. "*Excellent*. Well, *well*. I am most *terribly* anxious to see the show."

The usher tried to inform His Excellency that this anxiety would not be quelled by remaining at the wrong venue, but eventually learned that the ambassador was not referring to the Indonesian dance troupe. It was the main event, the Official Opening here in Alexander's amphitheater, that he was so terribly anxious to see. I imagined how terribly disappointed the dance troupe would be to find their own embassy ignoring them. Then I considered how incredibly thoughtless it was for the Iraqis to have scheduled any other event to coincide with the Official Opening.

Pakistan's consul looked like a vintage English cad or bounder from the Terry Thomas era, arriving with three stunning daughters dressed for an all-night techno-pop rave. Smoothing the surface of hair so lavishly greased it appeared solid, an obsidian skullcap, he sat looking about and nodding at various acquaintances while he slowly screwed a cigarette into a clarinet-sized gold and tortoiseshell holder. The action seemed as obscene as the impossible pleasure he appeared to be deriving from the tobacco smoke itself. Perhaps they weren't *daughters*?

There was a sudden hush in the vast buzzing arena, and I realized that dozens of very serious-looking Iraqi solders — the Republican Guard, in fact — had started pouring through previously hidden lower doors, and were ascending the two stairways on either side of a conspicuously empty five-row square directly facing the stage. All armed with fully automatic submachine guns, their uniforms and red berets flawless, they fanned out until the empty patch was entirely surrounded. Several others had positioned themselves at the rear of the stage itself. Craning to look up at the amphitheater's crescent walls, I realized that they, too, were now a virtual barracks of army personnel. Some soldiers clutched walkie-talkies, others, powerful hand-held searchlights; several had belt-fed light machine guns attached to monopods yet still nimble enough to also feature pistol grips; and many packed automatic rifles sprouting massive magazines. On the actual walls and upon the roof of a structure housing TV cameras were mounted five large combination mini-missile launcher machine guns — ones with the kind of compressed gas-powered magazines capable of releasing a hundred armor-piercing bullets a minute. From the tell-tale ruby sparkle above their barrels, it was obvious these toys were also fitted with laser-sighted night-vision scopes. No one was taking any chances here.

Milling around near the stage were what I assumed to be the elite of Iraq's moustachioed secret police. Their suits were expensive, their shirts and ties were of silk, and they never once relaxed from the task of scanning the audience slowly and methodically. They had been *trained*. A few held Mac-10 machine pistols (a thousand rounds a minute) and several had silver handguns shoved into the waistband of their pants.

This was a far, far different crew of guardians from any I'd seen before. Here was the army that the other army — the ragged, skinny, confused one — would have to take out before it ever took out Saddam. It seemed very clear that the only outfit that could even dream of taking out The Leader and his crack elite of deadly personal Praetorians was these boys themselves. And The Leader was obviously well aware of the fact, since senior military and security officers were purged more regularly than Elizabeth Taylor's husbands. Over a hundred had been jailed after Hussein Kamel's flight to Amman, along with some four thousand subordinates. And "jailed," of course, has another meaning in Iraq.

When the trained professionals had determined that all was as it should be in the amphitheater, a corridor opened in the crowd of moustaches packed at one lower entrance, and through it came a whole column of Saddam Husseins. Convinced the Man himself was actually here, I soon realized that this troop of lookalikes was led by Tareq Aziz, now the token citizen and all-purpose international voice of Iraq. He was nearly invisible in his donnishly crumpled suit among all these pristine uniforms. Widely touted as the next president, if Saddam ever relinquished the post willingly for any reason, Aziz would not have been heading the parade if his boss were coming. The Saddams following him were twelve generals from the Revolutionary Command Council and the National Security Council, one of which councils — no one seems entirely sure — is, theoretically at least, still the supreme authority in Iraq.

In the hierarchy of command there are now two of everything, it appears, a major characteristic of the system Saddam has refined, a system that now also permeates all of Iraqi society — right down to frightening divisions deep inside the individual human mind.

In theory, of course, Saddam is a humble servant of both councils and the Ba'ath Party's cabinet of ministers. In theory, he could be voted out of office, too. In theory, someone could travel back through time and prevent his mother from ever conceiving him . . . Iraqis, however, tend not to be comfortable with abstractions and theories. They're desperate for a few little concrete realities to pit against the crumbling concrete reality of their misery.

When all the generals were seated, it occurred to me how foolish it was to place almost the entire Iraqi governmental hierarchy in the same building, let alone in such close proximity to each other. Then, watching their faces, it occurred to me that this thought was also occurring to them, and that, furthermore, it could be interpreted as an indication of their current irrelevance and eminent dispensability in Saddam's scheme of things. Their eyes betrayed the terrible toll taken by years of expecting a bomb or bullet with your name on it to arrive at any moment.

These were not young men by any means, either. They had to average seventy-five. All possessed the pale pink skin that everyone in high positions had here. They were all northerners — people of the mountains, not the plains. In a speech, Saddam had once claimed that all true Iraqis were of the mountains, not the plains, which seemed to bode ill for those who were certain that their origins were the plains and not the mountains. Caste — as the word originally meant — is always based on color, it would appear, and I have found that racism is as rife among despised peoples as it is among those who despise them.

A sudden and deafening explosion had everyone jumping in fright, then, when we found out that it was merely a fireworks display erupting beyond the front wall behind the stage, laughing nervously at each other's hair-trigger paranoia. It seemed uniquely ill-advised to let off exploding rockets under such circumstances, yet the shock released a bilious tension that had been mounting steadily. The presence of so many men who were so close to those few dark figures who controlled utterly their lives and minds made this crowd of mainly ordinary middle-class Iraqis edgy and scared, or so it felt to me. They'd come for distraction, not to be reminded of what awaited them later and tomorrow, and perhaps forever.

But before the distraction there had to be a tiresome speech. It was not by Tareq Aziz, however. He seems to be the only convincing civilian within a mile of the hard-core rulers, which is why he's been so busy over the last five years showing the world that Iraq does not look remotely like a military dictatorship. He seems kindly, too, but apparently he's not — or so many Iraqis assured me. Kindliness is not what it takes to survive around Saddam. Saddam likes to surround himself solely with family, but he also seems to trust minorities, and Aziz is a Christian. He's Don Corleone's consigliere, in fact.

Instead of Aziz, a wicked-looking little man did a creditable forty-minute impression of Sheikh Adolf at al-Nuremberg. It was a virtual parody of a tyrant's speech, too, ranting on about Washington, Zionism, Clinton, Rabin, Jihad, Baghdad, and a whole polluted river full of dribbling invective. This was followed by a list of preposterous predictions for Iraq's glorious future, largely based upon the unexplained premise that both America and Zionism would somehow soon vanish from the face of the earth, leaving Saddam Hussein in charge of the planet and the golden age that this would inevitably usher in. I tuned out this radiant nonsense; it seemed to me a lot simpler to send Saddam and anyone who wanted to accompany him off in a space shuttle to run Pluto — but I could just be a victim of Zionist brainwashing.

At every mention of "Saddam Hussein" (and there were many, many such mentions), someone summoned up an artillery barrage of applause and incited lupine howls of what might as well have been "Heil!" It was not unlike the off-camera enthusiasm prompted from audiences at the taping of a TV yack show, except these operations cannot afford so many audience *plants* to aid in the process of tailoring reality to fit their needs.

When this tirade of fantasy and crazed vitriol had finally boiled itself dry, the nasty little general trotted back to his perch, while a plump lady in a skinny lady's gown announced that the entertainment would now begin. And it sure did.

With Adolf Hitler — who made it through grade twelve — as your genial host, you got five hours of Wagner. But with Saddam Hussein you got . . . well, three hours of a high school pantomime penned by a collaboration between Andrew Lloyd Webber and Mother Goose.

The *entertainment* concerned the collapsing moral standards that had once prevailed in Babylon and turned its kings into crapulous lechers or wimps, mere shades of real men, who would rather drink themselves mad as bats and then dance with loose women until they passed out than they would attend to manly things like warfare and crisis management. It looked like fun, though, a helluva party.

The audience definitely shared this view, needing no prompter now to let loose howls of approval for every new chorus line of Mesopotamian minxes, whores of Babylon, knockouts from Nineveh, dames from Damascus, and maybe even sheilas from Sheba. Ordinary Iraq was having a whale of a time, letting off steam that had perhaps been building up for years in the mind's pressure cooker. I've never seen such rapture in the faces of an audience.

As will happen with amateur events, though, costumes fell apart, wigs flew off, sequins spun into orbit, a six-foot spider got trapped inside the giant clam, and a two-headed dragon actually caught fire. But the pace never let up. The pace *couldn't* let up, since the dancers danced, actors played, and singers sang along to a taped soundtrack that kept up a breakneck disco pace, whether or not wigs flew off and dragons burned.

The plot was straightforward enough until some prancing monarch in a satin mini-dress and Beatle wig decided that the whole of Babylon should party till it dropped. After this, events became slightly baffling. Big spiders kept showing up to perform big song-and-dance numbers with big scorpions, and a pair of young lovers had to flee from the two-headed dragon, which often appeared to be fleeing from itself as the two actors inside its four-legged body differed over every stage direction in the script — if there *was* a script. At one point, something like a python wrapped around a six-foot turnip came skipping on stage to perform a highlight from *Swan Lake*, until five fat cross-dressers with hats like baroque lampshades jumped out and hacked it to pieces with broadswords for no discernible reason.

The massive polythene tube was there to simulate a waterfall. It simulated one very convincingly, too, since it split in half as a ton of water was poured down it from the amphitheater's ramparts. The resulting torrent cascaded out over much of the stage, wreaking havoc on another big song-and-dance number that involved Marduk's priests and either leprechauns or giant leeks. There was also chanting shrubbery that hopped in circles when it felt the urge, losing many leaves.

Not long after the waterfall, someone had his throat slit in the big white throne, which dripped with blood for the rest of the performance. While the throne bled to death, five 300-pound ballerinas in metallic tutus thundered and splashed across the stage in a *Stomp of the Sugar Plum Hippos*. Ballet and square-dancing are not as far apart as they seem. The murderous cross-dressers reappeared now, evidently entranced by this dance — so entranced that they joined it, broadswords and all, nearly decapitating one Sugar Plum Hippo and knocking another into some delicate scenery, which vanished beneath her bulk as if by magic.

A mature woman with a Himalayan chest, looking as Elizabeth Taylor probably would in *Cleopatra Part II*, floated out to ecstatic applause and shrieks of adoration. A big star, clearly, one whose youthful beauty age could not hope to wither — at least, not as far as this audience was concerned. Even the soundtrack stopped until hysteria wound down into the odd yodel or wail of yearning. Then it became apparent that this vintage national treasure was the love interest for a young lad who bore as striking a resemblance to Saddam Hussein as was possible for some makeup wizard to create with a lithe and delicate twenty-two-year-old ballet dancer as raw material. Besides being a little on the young side for his *gal*, our guy did not give the impression that he'd ever had much interest in gals at all. And for someone supposed to be Nebuchadrezzar — as I soon realized — our hero didn't even look as if he could get *into* an army, let alone *lead* one.

As if to prove that appearances can be deceptive, young Nebuchadrezzar was soon locked in mortal combat with the clumsy two-headed dragon. This was a major production number, with several interested parties we had never seen before participating in an anguished chorus-commentary on the Big Fight. No one wanted the dragon to win. The dragon had no friends. Even the spider and scorpion wanted nothing to do with him, and the turnip-python had vanished long ago. The dragon's character development left much to be desired, though. Besides *being* a dragon, he hadn't done anything especially evil to merit our hatred. And he looked a bit like Dudley the Dragon as twins. Not that this stopped Young Neb, for whom the slaughter of stuffed toys seemed about the right pace.

When the dragon finally keeled over — in two directions at once — Neb freely plunged his little sword up to its tip in one of the beast's two chests. The tip suddenly ignited some sort of blinding explosive flash, to the audience's utter delight. Next Neb lunged at the other chest, but to no immediate effect, forcing him to tickle the dragon with his sword tip in search of whatever set off these flashes. The galloping soundtrack wasn't waiting for technical hitches. In the meantime the dragon's other chest had been burning away merrily, and by now the fire was spreading across its furry scales, releasing dark vapors filled with tadpole-like flecks. Though dead, the burning half of the dragon began to beat its chest, succeeding only in setting an arm on fire. The crowd found all this highly amusing, and at first I wasn't entirely sure whether or not the fire was deliberate — a comic interlude, perhaps?

As Young Neb danced on and the various of types of chorus sang, many cast members began casting worried glances at the blazing dragon, now thrashing around in an attempt to gain some fire-fighting cooperation from its inner other half. It wanted to roll over or stand up; neither of which was possible without a solid partnership. Only when the flames had spread to its second chest, setting off the recalcitrant other flash — which clearly shocked the hell out of whoever played that half — was a rapid unanimity of purpose reached. While Young Neb had his arms nearly ripped from their sockets by a swooning Cleopatra II, the dragon managed to stagger upright and, sweating fire rather than breathing fire, it zigzagged unsteadily across the stage, stumbled, then fell right over the left apron. Fortunately, a group of ushers caught the floundering creature. Unfortunately, discovering fire is hot, they quickly let go. You could hear the thump from where I sat. Last seen, the blackened dragon was weaving away, wisps of steamy smoke curling up from fur that now dripped sooty water on all sides.

Two hours later, I jumped up with everyone else and clapped my hands sore, as Young Neb and his ageless bride ascended the white throne, Babylon's future was assured, and scores of dancing girls and dancing guys all waved the Iraqi flag. And everyone lived happily ever after.

Except the Japanese Delegation. As four thousand people began to leave the arena, a gaggle of Kabuki girls shuffled out on their little feet and began arranging small props on the stage, while the twangs of traditional Japanese strings could just about be heard.

"They want to leave tomorrow," Hassan told me, when I collared him to ask what was happening on stage. "So they have said they will perform even if their performance is not scheduled."

The full story turned out to be that the Japanese were so horrified by their hotel, the food, and Iraq in general that they'd decided to leave the very next day no matter what. Thus with the quiet dignity, grace, and formal charm characteristic of their land, they performed their gig unannounced, so no one could ever say that the Japanese were people who didn't keep their promises.

The audience, however, were rank strangers to good manners — not a Kabuki crowd — and they didn't appear to care who wanted to perform next. The Official Opening's Iraqi spectacular was through and so were they. A bunch of people in white-face and kimonos with small feet weren't about to change their plans for riding on a wave of euphoria all the way home — back to that lonesome beach of the soul where tomorrow would once more find them all stranded.

I haven't walked a mile in the average Iraqi's shoes (I haven't walked a mile in my own shoes for that matter), so I'm hardly qualified to judge their behavior. All they knew, I think, was that they were happy for a moment, and they wanted to hang on to that moment for as long as they could. Classical Kabuki doesn't really light my fire, and I doubt if it would have done anything particularly incendiary to enhance the mood of anyone else that night in Babylon.

MONEY

Hassan kept asking his people if they'd enjoyed the show, and then *how much* they'd enjoyed the show. His cheeks were flushed and he beamed with either pride or pleasure. I wasn't sure whether this joy was caused by the relief that Babylon's first night and his first day of duties for the Festival had been pulled off without a hitch, or whether bonfires of elation had also been set ablaze in him by the entertainment.

"It showed how wine and women were down falling of the old Babylon kings," he explained to a puzzled Ukrainian.

"Downfalls seem like a lot of fun, no?"

Hassan looked at me quizzically, then said in a conspiratorial voice, "Yes. Maybe we can make party in your room one night? I will invite some Russian girls and we drink beer? That will be fun, yes?"

"Beer?"

"Yes. But we will keep this to ourselves."

"Russian girls?"

"Not *all* of them," he assured me hastily. "Just a few who like the good time. Their master is very strict, isn't it?"

"Their *what*?"

He meant the small-time tyrant with a Lenin beard who chaperoned a bevy of ballerinas. Apparently he trained and choreographed them, too — although he looked as if Marxist dialectic had been his first love, and that the temporary collapse of Communism had forced him into ballet.

"Where do we get this beer?" I inquired.

"We can get it," Hassan reassured me, nodding sagely. He pondered a moment, and a moment longer, then leaned over until I could smell steamed rice on his breath, whispering, "If you need to change money — not at bank rate, understand? — I can do it. This just between us, okay? Do not tell the others."

"I understand. Thanks."

Now we shared a secret. I wondered, however, if this were a ploy to trap me into revealing the extent of my own corruption. My down falling. If not, how big a risk was he taking?

By the time I left, however, every other Iraqi I'd met had eventually offered to change money for me at rates ranging from 2,200 dinars for a dollar to well over 3,000.

The currency was going nuts; it confused people. No one knew what to charge for anything anymore, and prices ranged all over the place. A can of soda would be 4,000 dinars in the morning, then in the evening, in the same place, it would be 2,000. Or 5,000. Cab drivers took anything you gave them without a mutter of complaint. Everyone seemed dazed by the very thought of money. Even kids who sold matches on the street had great folded slabs of ragged cash in their ragged pockets. Young and old, relatively rich or positively poor, everyone in business knew how to speed-count banknotes. Cash stacked in 100-dinar blocks was frequently measured with rulers rather than counted — any error couldn't amount to much, except saved time. Cash registers had to be emptied twice an hour, and all over Baghdad there were people ferrying stacks, cardboard boxes, or shopping bags full of money off to banks or vaults or stashes or bins.

Everyone in Baghdad had lots of money.

I wondered where the cash was actually kept: an average office safe would only hold around $200 in dinars. No one was rushing off to change the dollars they received at a higher rate, either: no one wanted dinars at any price. They were worth less than their paper. And they were treated that way: poured into plastic bags like trash, tossed over counters, or just left piled on open ledges. No one was likely to steal them. Bank robbers would need a few dozen partners, some fork-lift trucks, and a couple of tractor-trailers to make crime *break even*, let alone *pay*.

The new 250 dinar bill seemed heinously shortsighted: Iraq's Central Bank needed to seize tomorrow and start printing up a 10,000 dinar note, retitled 10 Saddams, or 10 Georges . . . or 10 *something*. I wouldn't want my name or picture on such torrential currency if I were leader, though.

With inflation heading toward 1,000 percent, the Central Bank of Iraq's lending rate — not that it did much lending anymore — was now 15 percent *a day*! If my interview with The Leader came through again this time — and like one of Pavlov's dogs, I'd naturally requested one the moment I saw a government minder — I wondered if he'd offer to change money, too: "Not at bank rate, *understand*?"

Since it first began in China, paper money has relied entirely upon faith in a strong central government for its value to remain stable. It's not really *worth* anything. After President Nixon took America off the Gold Standard, the money no longer promised "To Pay the Bearer" diddley-squat on demand. Where it used to say that on the old bank-notes, you can now read "In God We Trust": faith alone — in a deity or industrial sector — is all that supports the dollar. Iraq's staple fifty-dinar bill doesn't *say* anything, but there is a picture of Saddam in front of the Big Egg war memorial on it, so one got the point: millions would die before Saddam Hussein allowed Iraq's economic bubble to burst.

But what at first seemed farcical grew frightening. Light comedy became very black. The pantomime at Babylon was soon a little too much like a grotesque parody of Baghdad circa 1995: *Halloween in Hell.*

THE STATE OF THE NEWS

None of the Western countries — none of *our crowd* — had embassies in Baghdad. Only the other kind, *those* countries, the ones always in trouble, debt, and usually Africa, only *they* had embassies here now. It struck me that I was a stranger in a strange and parallel world, one where all the things that didn't matter much at all in mine were almost *all* that mattered — all there *was* to matter. It was a world where national differences assumed a transcendental importance: *Here is our national costume; this is our national dance; they are very different from yours, which our people, of course, admire very much . . .*

The national costume of the West to most Iraqis was now desert camouflage fatigues; the national dance, one of death. There was only CNN to correct the balance, after all.

And the only ordinary Iraqis who got to watch CNN these days were ones working at the Ministry of Information's Press Center. The Ishtar-Sheraton certainly didn't provide it for guests — it barely provided *anything* for guests — nor did the Palestine-Meridien. Only those able to afford a home satellite dish could pick up the signal. The three main things about satellite dishes in a country where they are ostensibly illegal is that (a) they're prohibitively expensive; (b) you can't smuggle one in under your abaya very easily; and (c) even if you could, while you're in work togs discreetly installing a thirty-foot concave steel dish before some tall grass on the lawn, you might as well erect a billboard on your roof announcing "OCCUPANT INVOLVED WITH DUBIOUS AND PROBABLY CRIMINAL ACTIVITIES." The Satellite Dish Crowd in Iraq was limited to Saddam's inner circle. Baghdad is also, remember, a city of snitches, snoops, and *bassassin* — professional *and* amateur spies.

Ninety percent of Iraqis thus only have access to news that their rulers deem fit for human consumption. It's been this way in the private communications field generally for longer than most even remember. As the Iraqi education system slowly withers up and dies quietly from starvation, the population is already manifesting an alarmingly drastic reverse trend toward chronic illiteracy. The illiterate are more manageable. The great and abiding importance that Saddam has attached to education can be summed up with a sentence from his speech to the Higher Council for Literacy, back in September 1980: "Every Iraqi citizen must be prepared to shed his blood for this nation and his principles." Prepared or not, hundreds of thousands have definitely shed their blood, yet it has done their nation little good. Blood isn't shed for any but Saddam's principles, either — among which is numbered the barely veiled suspicion that literacy is the mother of all dissension. Soon there will only be national television and a nation's rumors to inform the masses how the rest of the world lives and what the rest of Iraq does.

The International News segment that I watched with rapt fascination on Iraq's state television invariably catalogued disasters of various kinds and social unrest of any nature — largely in villainous nations like Britain, Israel, and the United States. This presumably sought to demonstrate how the wicked are punished, and also how the common people hate their cruel oligarchical governments, whose policies no more reflect the national will than the affluent decadence of their members reflects the national lifestyle.

And there are still those who claim there's no such phenomenon as psychological self-projection . . .

Iraqi TV's International News devoted more time to small developing nations that were currently suffering under the same villainous superpowers, usually assisted by *Demon Zionism*, the *Satanic World Bank, Freemasons*, and sometimes even non-specific *Wicked Elements in Iran*. (When I was in Iran the previous winter, I'd noticed that the blame for most ills cited by Iranian state television was usually placed in the lap of *Godless Iraq and the Global Arrogance*, this latter a Hydra-like collective term for the same five evil entities that were pestering Iraq.)

Bosnia was the current main victim of Big Evil in late 1995, naturally, but Rwanda seemed to show distinct promise as a contender for the '96 title — although most reports on the Rwandan situation that I saw aired by TV Baghdad were many months old and thus woefully inaccurate. But state news didn't have to be *new*; it had to be *useful* in some way — for ideological reasons. For exactly the same reason that Ba'athist founding ideologue Michel Aflaq seemed to write endlessly about how the world *should* be, not how it *was*.

Other international events frequently shown were things like development conferences. These were always held to discuss fascinating topics like irrigation in Hunan Province or animal husbandry in Baluchistan. There were also many field reports on speeches delivered by anyone anywhere who at all criticized the United States, Britain, or anything remotely associated with the United States and Britain, such as the "Imperialist Occupation of Northern Ireland" or the "CIA War Crimes in Central America." Or Noam Chomsky on why Noam Chomsky's books accusing American media of a conspiracy to mislead Americans were themselves being conspired against by American media's book supplement editors . . .

"Why else are they never reviewed?" demanded the indignant voice of International News.

And why aren't they on sale in Iraq? I wondered.

In fact, I'd asked Saddam back in 1990 if Noam Chomsky's conspiracy-fueled views of the Middle East — strikingly similar on numerous issues to his own views — enjoyed widespread influence in the Arab world. But it was clear that Iraq's president had never heard of MIT's tame Marxist. Saddam has definitely written far more books than he's ever read.

When this nightly video gallery of international villainy, tragedy, and tedium finally closed up shop for the day, there was always a major exhibition of domestic news to visit. Much of this consisted of what resembled a "Saddam's Diary" segment, videotaped by his own personal television crew. We saw The Leader touring a lot of new construction projects, viewing the latest weaponry purchases, inspecting proud military units in immaculate uniforms, even kissing children, and quite often, as a powerful climax, sitting behind a gilded Napoleonic desk while writing words of immense national importance on a legal pad with his huge gold fountain pen. It was clear proof for Iraqi viewers that Saddam was on the job, always toiling on behalf of their great nation.

Whatever it was that he wrote on this pad, however, he always appeared to have enormous trouble completing its third line. A sonnet, perhaps?

The lion's share of state news time — over twice that accorded any other news — was devoted to sports. Or actually *a sport*.

Soccer seemed to be the only sport that even remotely interested Iraqis. This made it all the more tragic that their national team was having such a truly cataclysmic season, losing matches to the likes of Chad or Togoland with final scores that were, quite simply, *awesome*: 64–0, for example.

Not surprisingly, over half of the team — *seven* men — had been traded over the last few months alone, and the current players all looked to me more like Zulu and Masai warrior princes than they did Arabs. The shortest man had to be around six-three. But the goal nets in soccer, unlike those in basketball, are never beyond any player's reach.

When you're up against a feisty team of five-foot Kalahari Bushmen, whose idea of a warm-up is running from the Indian Ocean to the Atlantic via Zimbabwe, barefoot, being six-eight has disadvantages, too. Yet the Baghdad Butchers (to be honest, I don't recall if they *had* a name) were certainly an impressive and even majestic spectacle to watch as they ran out onto the field, or, for that matter, as they ran off it, always trailing a glistening twenty-foot-long silk Iraqi flag behind them in a blurred cloud of reddish green glory. Before and after, they were the dream team.

It was only *during* a game that they faced problems — perhaps the biggest of which was that not one of them appeared to know anything about the rules and principles of *playing* soccer. For example: The advisability of having a goalkeeper somewhere near *his* goal, not the other team's; of having a center forward who knew to kick the ball *before* he sprinted past it; of having wingers who knew beyond all doubt that the object, the purpose, and indeed perhaps the quintessential *point* of soccer itself was to kick the ball into the other team's net, not their own.

In the case of Togoland's chart-topping sixty-four goals, Iraq could itself claim the credit for scoring possibly seven or eight of these goals. At least the crowd were good losers, though. They struck me as real *sports* — the kind that vanished with Stanley Matthews — cheering every bit as enthusiastically as if *their* team had won. Of course, they also could have known less about the game even than the clowns they were watching play it. Still, it must be confessed, British soccer fans would have beaten the other team's supporters into bratwurst with hammers after such a hideously conclusive defeat. Then burned down the stadium, *then* trashed and looted half the city. They have been known to do far worse things after a *win* . . .

The state news nightly sign-off was also — especially when I think of how they'd achieved it back in 1990 — the finest, grandest, most stirring moment in all the livelong broadcasting day.

In a flashing ten-minute torrent of lustrous burnished images from the glorious past (which as far as Iraq was concerned began in 1979), Saddam could be seen displaying the whole cosmopolitan panorama of his wardrobe. Savile Row banker's suits, shimmering playboy casuals from the Rio nightclub strip, some thirty-odd military outfits (including Air Force and Naval Chiefs-of-Staff dress uniforms), the versatile and perennially popular vampire's cape (as superbly *soigné* with formal white-tie evening dress as it is with the Kenyan Safari suit or the Tweed Alpine shooting jacket *und lederhosen*), a seamless Meccan white linen toga, many manly vests-of-the-unnumbered-pocket (all with sporting functions), a silk blazer with real gold buttons and what looked like the Royal Monaco Yacht Club crest on its breast pocket, several folkloric costumes (including one Balkan with floppy Fez and one Central Asian with Troll King's crown), and finally, of course, the Arab-for-all-regions look, ranging from richer-than-thou Kuwaiti with cloth-of-gold abaya plus million-dollar dagger to the bandoleer, army surplus, and laundry-bag turban of the classical freedom-fighting dune warrior. All these different looks for different moods, all these *disguises*, and Saddam had them all. He probably had many more, too.

Throughout this extreme and uplifting culmination — *Saddam Hussein: Superstar* — frenzied crowds cheered and waved at their glorious Leader, while magisterial buildings shot up under his gaze, spotless new tanks rolled into the sunset, flags fluttered, world leaders were embraced, treaties signed, leading-edge industrial plants opened, super-highways inaugurated, children kissed, Arab potentates thrice kissed, mullahs hugged, brave troops saluted . . . and it fell to the man-in-the-street, who looked upon all he had seen with awe and wonderment, to express the sincere and humble thanks of a sincere and humble people for this divinity at the helm. You'd have been forgiven for thinking that there had never *ever* been two punishing wars, for thinking that Baghdad had never *ever* been bombed "back to the pre-industrial era" (as George Bush so well defined his military intentions), or, indeed, for thinking that *anything at all* had impeded the progress of Planet Iraq.

Officially, though — and state news is nothing if not official — the country's recent history was presented like this: Iraq easily won the war with Iran, suffering few casualties; what happened in the Gulf War, in reality, was a "Stand-Off" — it wasn't a "war" — with Saddam confronting the United States and the Americans finally backing down, conceding they had met their match, after, of course, inflicting many cowardly and criminal attacks on the helpless citizens of Baghdad.

These days a little more explaining was needed, so the current UN embargo found itself cited as the sole reason Iraqis suffered the hardships that were now their daily lot and their constant sorrow.

The people of Iraq must be tired of this by now, I kept thinking. They've heard it before. A lot. And certainly since 1979 — when the future began. For even back during the glory days, in a speech delivered to a massive rally on October 24, 1979, Saddam had announced: "Iraq is a lake of oil: this is the reason for the United States' hatred and for the greed with which the great powers look at Iraq." Any setbacks that might lie ahead could thus be easily explained away and the blame placed where Saddam had always said it should be placed.

Unfortunately, however, he's right about this — and we should be ashamed that he's right.

Imagine switching on NBC to find it broadcasting state-controlled twaddle. We'd laugh ourselves sick. But Iraqis don't laugh much at anything these days. They are no longer really sure what is and what isn't true.

A NEW WORLD ORDER

The next day, Hassan — who never seemed to sleep or change his clothes — announced a trip to the Saddam Arts Center. I told him that I'd been on my way *there* once before . . .

"You will see the excellent modern Iraqi painters," he promised.

"What happened to the not-so-excellent ones?"

The Saddam Arts Center — not far from the Saddam Center for Cardiac Surgery — was fairly predictable. It was also, for a gallery of modern art, fairly heavily guarded by armed soldiers. Like my hotel and many other buildings I'd noticed, it had tracks of six-inch steel spikes embedded in the road to prevent any vehicles without metal tires coming closer than sixty feet. In the lobby, more soldiers stood at ease with drooping automatic rifles, flanking a large canvas depicting Lady Justice wearing a kind of baggy sweatshirt emblazoned with the UN's world-in-a-wreath logo. She was blindfolded as usual, but here by a Stars and Stripes bandanna; she was also gagged, her lips sealed with an X of Band-Aids. On her tilting scales, a bloodstained sword easily outweighed the dish containing a sizable (presumably law) book and, incongruously, a pencil propped near a fat fountain pen like Saddam's. The painting's title was thoughtfully included on the canvas itself, with a legend beneath Justice's misty legs constructed from neat six-inch-high block capitals: THE NEW WORLD ORDER. It would have had definite potential in the sixties, I thought, a big future with the Western college crowd as a dorm poster.

An enormous L-shaped room of Saddam's art center was devoted to the work of Iraq's most revered painter, Faik Hassan, who died of old age in 1991. Faik had evidently experimented with many styles, from a figurative period of (mainly male) nudes, through an Impressionist phase, a dalliance with abstractionism, and a great clunking social realist epoch. This busy time of political fervor was especially well represented by one epically proportioned (and unsalable) canvas from the early sixties that showed a young Saddam standing behind President Bakr, both of them smartly dressed and oblivious to the hectic revolutionary battle raging behind them, hundreds of soldiers firing guns and bombs exploding on all sides.

Faik's "late" period seemed to combine all of these previous adventures in style, producing pictures that now, however, spoke mostly of terminal depression. With a Rothkoesque field of murk, anguished, agonized, or just plain screaming figures underwent a torment so hideous that Faik perhaps didn't feel the need, or didn't have the heart, even to reveal what exactly caused it. One of the very last things to leave his easel merely portrayed this nasty miasma with an Israeli flag floating inside it. He had either lost his talent by this stage or his mind. Perhaps both.

The rest of the gallery displayed more recent work, Saddamian work, which largely dealt with the despicable perfidy of the United States and Israel in symbolism as subtle as a sack of shit. The only exceptions were some rather whimsically erotic paintings in pastel shades of pink and green that hung in a glassed-off area also containing a sizable funeral wreath. The doors were fastened shut by a chain sealed with a huge padlock.

This shrine, I discovered, was devoted to the work of Layla Al-Attar, killed when an American bomb demolished her studio. She also happened to be a good friend of The Leader, who was an enthusiastic collector of her paintings. One large wooden panel of ethereal nudes embracing had a head-sized charred hole in the middle. It was apparently salvaged from the rubble of her studio.

No one could explain why the area was sealed off. It seemed holy.

While examining the work of a man who only painted images of women having curious symbols painted on their vast bare buttocks by other women, I was greeted by an attractive girl in her late teens. She sat watching an aluminum kettle that had been placed on a glowing electric ring on the floor in one corner of the gallery. The rising steam could not be good for paintings hanging above it.

"You like picture?" she inquired.

"Deeply impressed."

"You are welcome here."

"Thanks."

She then rummaged in her purse and produced a fresh fig, handing it to me.

"For you."

"Thanks."

"In my language 'fig' is 'teen,' which is also my name: Tina."

Not a common female name in this part of the world. The Prophet, as far as I know, did not have any Tinas among his large extended family.

"So you'd be 'Figgy' in my country," I suggested.

"Yes, I suppose . . ." She giggled uncontrollably, suddenly feeling awkward.

"You work here?"

"Yes. All day I am here."

That must be incredibly boring, I felt like saying, but instead just threw in more pleasantries. She clearly *wanted* something — her eyes betrayed her — but I'm sure that not even she knew quite what it was.

Many other Iraqi women made it very plain what they wanted: they wanted to marry you and escape from this place. Even girls in chadors

passing on the street would smile shamelessly and shout out proposi-
tions of some sort. What merited a flogging or worse in neighboring
nations seemed to be perfectly acceptable behavior here.

But Figgy wasn't certain what to do with the conflicted feelings inside
her.

"Will you come here again?" she eventually asked, as I devoured the fig.

"I hope so."

"Good. I will bring more fig for you."

It was a firm arrangement in her mind: the fig was a date. I felt unac-
countably sad leaving her there, with her tea kettle boiling on the floor
and her muddled dreams of another kind of life, somewhere, over the
rainbow . . .

STYLE WITH ELSA KLENSCH

I managed to get Hassan's bus to drop me at the Ministry of Information's Press Center, where I sat with the only television, sharing Elsa
Klensch's enthusiasm for the latest underwear collections from design-
ers in both Paris and New York. Underwear was finally getting the
recognition it deserved. Elsa was absolutely right: the big fashion houses
had neglected underwear for too long. It was a pity that most Iraqis
probably wouldn't ever hear about underwear's inspiring assertion of its
rights.

Only Reuters — with Iraqi staff — now had any permanent presence
in Baghdad, although the operation achieved as little as it cost, mainly
rewriting official statements for those few English language newspapers
around the world willing to print statements by the Iraqi government.
The cubicles that the Press Center provided for use by the world's media
stood empty, logo stickers peeling on doors and windows, business
cards of various long-gone staffers taped to the walls like graffiti: *Kilroy
was here . . . for CNN.*

Faris, director of the Press Center, gave me a lecture on Western propaganda, while we watched the brave new underwear. He complained
that every story was full of lies, that no one came to see for themselves
what was going on, that Iraq was open: anyone could go anywhere and
interview anyone they wished.

It was a tired old spiel, though, and Faris was a tired, worn, and frazzled man, old before his time. The rippled black lakes in which his eyes drowned made his face a skull, and his skin matched in tone and texture the cigarette ash he spilled over his shirt and jacket.

"This embargo must stop," he sighed, as Elsa moved on to a man who designed steel furniture. "It is not humane. It's not *civilized* behavior. Why should our people suffer like this?"

"I don't know."

"We have no food, no medicine, nothing! Little babies are dying because they don't get medicine. Infant mortality rates have soared over the last few years. Why don't you people report this?"

I'm not sure why we don't. This wasn't part of his lecture, either — this was from the heart. He was an educated and sensitive man, I came to see; he certainly knew that the job he had to perform was ostensibly a big lie, and as such another form of betraying his own people, too. The strain of it was killing him. Every time he had to fob me off with some nonsense about the complex process required to get permission for this trip or an interview with that person, I could see that it ate away at him.

The one time I lost my patience and told him angrily that his "open country" and its "free access" was a crock, I instantly regretted it. He cast his eyes down and looked ashamed, guilt-ridden, helpless. But jobs were hard to come by, and he had a big family to care for. He had to bite his lip and go on serving the Lie, like everyone else did. Except that Faris, constantly exposed to foreign journalists and CNN babbling away ten feet from his office twenty-four hours a day, knew far more of the truth than most. It made the Lie grow steadily more poisonous to handle, more toxic to harbor. I pitied the man deeply, and I had no desire to add to his already crushing burden.

Occasionally a tiny light within his eyes showed how badly he wanted to have a real conversation with me — with anyone capable of real conversation. But it simply was not possible, especially in his position. The little gestures of friendship that we both made to each other in our own ways often made the silence required of all who served in the Lie hauntingly resonant. I realized how vast that vault in which it resonated must be. It contained an entire world.

"I hope we meet under different circumstances again one day," I told him the evening before I left.

It was as close as I'd ever come since my regrettable outburst to even an innocuous allusion to the truth of what was happening here, what was happening to him. He knew what I meant, of course, but it seemed, as always, unlikely that he could allow this knowledge to take on any other form more tangible than silence and pain.

"So do I," he replied, shaking my hand with heart-breaking sincerity. "I hope for that very much."

The words shocked me, bursting like poetry in the brain.

I hope he keeps on hoping, too. I know I will.

PAUL & ROB'S MOST EXCELLENT ADVENTURE

Midway through my third depressing evening of roaming the Ishtar's grim cautionary tale for hoteliers, Rob Howard, a professional photographer I had worked with often enough by now to consider a friend, arrived from some cushy assignment in Italy. We'd intended to meet up in Jordan, but such arrangements rarely seem to work out. Okay, I couldn't be bothered to wait, assuming Rob would take a cab with all his Manhattan fashion shooter's loot. Instead of a taxi, however — he was a cheap bastard — he'd just emerged from a twenty-six-hour ride in a bus full of Russian artistes similarly bound for Babylon. But Rob was the only kind of traveling companion you want: still able to let such physical and mental torments run off his back beneath a hot shower along with the dust and highway grime that accompanied them.

Vodka had flowed nonstop, unlike the bus, which had halted sixteen times to accommodate its passengers' needs, Rob told me. His lungs now felt as if they'd been through an entire carton of second-hand smoke. It had promised to be hell on wheels. But instead the Russians had turned a tedious and grueling trip into a movable rave, singing all the way, even dancing, and during the frequent desert stops, pulling out balalaikas and harmoniums to perform for that packed house of heavenly bodies above.

Rob's perpetual good humor and sickening charm were hard to re-adjust to initially, but they were exactly the right medicine I needed to fight the creeping Iraqitis threatening every cell and nerve with pincer attacks of fear and sorrow.

"It was so beautiful, man," he kept saying. "So damn cool: out there beneath the stars, with these dudes dancing and singing in the middle of nowhere."

"You got great pictures?"

"No, man. I couldn't be bothered."

I'd forgotten that he actually hated taking photographs. It was a hassle.

A troupe of Mongolian throat singers had even launched into their unique specialty, its eerie, rumbling whale-like music sounding far closer to arias that shadows and rocks might unleash than anything a human voice could sing. This was earth music, ocean beat, sky song. The throat singers were accompanied by a little old Mongolian with saintly eyes, who had also played to that starry desert night on a huge contra-basso. He'd carried this cumbersome instrument all the way from those same wild, distant regions of this world that Ghengis Khan had come from to perform his own unique specialty right here, in a city whose beauty, wealth, and power were legends he, too, had heard and believed since childhood, even eight hundred years ago.

Perhaps it was the Khan's disappointment that made him raze the squalid ruin he found, and slaughter close to a million of its inhabitants, bringing the fabled Abassid caliphate to an ignominious end, as well as reducing Baghdad to barely even a provincial town. The caliphs left history forever, but, although it took seven centuries, their city and its legend returned. Why else would descendants of the Mongol armies be here once again?

Although we lived near each other, Rob and I only seemed to meet up in hell holes, war zones, wastelands where Anglo-Saxons fear to tread. But we weren't Anglo-Saxons — maybe *that* was our problem.

I filled him in on what he'd missed and what he shouldn't miss. I also tried to tell him that this wasn't like any other place we'd worked, that it was *really* dangerous, that walls had electronic ears, and that idle words could mean active trouble.

"These assholes can't run a hotel," he scoffed. "How're they gonna run the CIA? The plumbing doesn't even work, for God's sake: what sort of shape are the telescopic mikes and voice-activated bugs gonna be in? The only bugs in my room are those goddam roaches that gallop under the bed every time I turn around. Man! Did we nuke this place or what? Does the couscous glow? Something's mutating. They're more like turtles than cockroaches. Hey! Were your ears always that green and pointy?"

Some people never change, thank God. Immune to the serious, to the potential for grief, for consequences, Rob was nonetheless never uninformed or unaware. Happiness was a serious business to him, another profession he worked at and promoted. It was another talent, too, a gift. His mood was contagious, with no known vaccine, no available immunity. I felt relieved, glad that this dark place didn't bother him yet. I just wasn't prepared for how quickly it would start to bother him, though, or how much trouble one could suddenly get into without even trying especially hard.

Rob and I found ourselves, the next morning, in Hassan's bus heading through the suburb of low-cost housing named Saddam City toward Big Egg, that giant turquoise tomb.

"What the *fuck* is that?"

"A war memorial. It's where the lights cut out — remember that story?"

"Oh, shit. I thought you made that up . . ."

Babylon Festival Delegates had been scheduled to lay a wreath at Big Egg honoring the dead.

"Hassan," said Rob. "My brother's in the military too."

"Is it so?" Hassan replied.

"Yeah. The Navy. But he's a pilot. The Navy has pilots, you know?"

"Yes, of course: naval pilots." Hassan nodded, confirming this military oxymoron and his broad knowledge of life's curiosities.

"Right, Hassan. He was in Iraq, too, my brother. Well, over it really, during —"

"*Rob!*" I delivered a savage kick to his ankle.

"Just joking . . . I —"

"Zip it up, Robert." He hated being called "Robert." "And stop telling everyone you're from New York City."

"I am."

"No. You're Canadian like your passport, but you live in New York City. No one needs your entire biography. They need you to be Canadian, though, just like your passport. Do you notice many

American delegates around? A few? One even? None, you say? I wonder why that is, hmmm? Maybe it could be something to do with this *war memorial* we're about to visit?"

"Hey, lighten up. He knows I'm just foolin' around."

"No one here even knows what foolin' around is; and I don't know of any place on earth where people laugh themselves sick at the mere thought of relatives killed in a war."

The bus, like the Ishtar now, had filled up with Russians. They were a dour bunch, too, on the whole; nothing like the all-singing, all-dancing, vodka-guzzling party animals Rob had described. There were a few fairly attractive college girls, yet they emanated all the warmth and charm of ice sculptures with hair.

The Lenin-bearded tyrant was actually the cause of this prim and joyless facade. He clearly liked things the way they were when the Party, not parties, ruled, when young Soviets traveling abroad were instructed to avoid contact with decadent capitalist scum. The Marxist ballet master had begun videotaping this outing for posterity; yet, considering the frozen postures and faces of his subjects, he might just as well have employed a still camera.

The Russian guys were something else altogether, though. Capitalism had been waiting patiently for eighty years for these suckers — and it had paid off big. While equally obedient and docile in their Master's presence, they dressed much like any midwest grade-12 kids whose main course of study was thematic unity in *Beavis & Butthead*, or character development in *The Jerky Boys*. Their baseball caps were on back to front; their jeans were several sizes too large and hung as if they'd mistaken their thighs for their waists; some had T-shirts the size of caftans; all wore sneakers that wild dogs had chewed. A few even possessed Walkman clones whose headphones were now surgically attached to their ears, creating that curious phenomenon where white men can move like black rappers, walking to the beat of an indifferent drummer.

Seeing these same boys glammed up as flamboyant Cossacks a few nights later, leaping and spinning, doing the squat-kick and an ancestor of the square-dance stomp, it occurred to me that perhaps we all wear costumes to acquire other identities when we are insecure about the ones we're supposed to have acquired naturally. From Saddam down (or up), everyone in Iraq was in disguise and denial, too, masking a painful or an unacceptable truth.

Big Egg, when we reached it, also seemed to be a variety of disguise, masking the fact that many, many thousands of Iraqis had died senselessly and horribly in wars that achieved nothing but their own horror and misery. Between the two soaring turquoise concaves stood a plinth supporting a bronze monolith of abstract sculpture that was, in its abstraction and size, a fitting symbol for Iraq's war dead. The government had made their enormous numbers an abstraction, too. As Stalin once remarked: "The death of one man is a tragedy; the death of millions is a statistic."

A military band in full dress uniform stood to one side thumping out that variety of music which some find an inspiration, and others merely irritating.

The Russians had by now posed for nine group photos with the Egg as backdrop. Several elegant women I'd taken for Koreans or Thais, dressed as if heading for a fancy evening cocktail event, clicked over the memorial's marble acreage in their black patent stilettos, gazing at everything with expressions of unashamed awe. In fact, they were Mongolians, and one of their number, an older, more matronly woman who could have passed for Imelda Marcos, was accorded the great honor of actually placing the wreath against that twisting five-ton *memento mori.* She had to do this between four overdressed officers with gold swords, enough braid to rig a schooner, and bullet-proof breastplates formed by rows of medals. Soldiers have to take the route to such memorials one step at a time — for ideological reasons — in a stylized walk that the Mongolian lady found quite impossible to copy in her pencil heels and the possessive sheath of a basic black cocktail dress.

There were several photo and video ops for TV Baghdad and the *Saddam Times,* then we were herded down a flight of marble stairs behind the noisy fountain. Everything gleamed with Italian marble. Memories came back of those distant days in 1990.

The place was still about to become a museum, as soon as someone found items to display in the banks of empty glass cases that occupied the largest of the three subterranean halls. A central area was devoted to the presence of a granite plaque the size of a billboard set into the wall. Engraved in the black stone using tiny letters were columns of names;

there must have been well over one hundred thousand names, judging by the few square inches I counted. A similar plaque was situated elsewhere, and a smaller one above ground.

"This is getting like a school outing," Rob complained. "How much more of this are you going to put up with?"

"Take pictures. *Shut mouth.*"

"Pictures of what?"

"*That,* maybe?" I indicated the plaque, where Russian girls were now lining up in pairs to be photographed between two of the more theatrically dressed soldiers, with the plaque as backdrop.

Rob began fiddling with meters, lenses, and the ravenous large-format cameras that go through a roll of film a minute.

"I hate watching you take pictures," I told him. "It's incredibly boring. Did you know that?"

He looked up, unblinking, and after a pause of some twenty seconds, he said, "I bet it's not as incredibly boring as watching you write. Did *you* know that?"

We both cracked up, giggling like kids: not the sort of reaction required from visitors to any war memorial, let alone *this* one. A few disapproving glares were fired our way from various quarters. Hassan suddenly materialized at my side with a man who looked more like a Paris couturier than a museum director.

"This is the museum's director," announced Hassan, introducing me to the man. "Mister Paul is an arch-olly-giste from Canada."

An *archaeologist*? This was news to me.

"Interesting," said the museum director. "History is a hobby of mine, you know."

I wanted to ask what there was to direct in a museum that had no exhibits whatsoever, but instead made the radical suggestion that war was a terrible business.

"Oh, I dunno: Adnan Khasshogi did okay in it," Rob muttered, as he scuttled away to take pictures.

"Tragic," agreed the museum director. "Young lives snuffed out, widows orphaned . . ."

Widows orphaned?

"How many died in the last two wars?" I inquired.

"No one knows the exact figures."

"Roughly, I mean. A ballpark figure."

"It is not known," he repeated. "We have no idea."

"A million?"

"No, no, no," he said hastily. "Not a million."

"Hundreds of thousands, though, yes?"

"No, no. This is excessive. We cannot say quite how many. A hundred, four hundred — we have never known."

I gave him a look usually reserved for door-to-door con artists. "So what are these half a million names carved in stone, then? Soldiers who cut their knees or came down with a tension headache?"

"They are . . . Oh," he saw someone he needed to see. "Excuse me a moment, would you?"

Hassan hopped from foot to foot.

"Why the big secret, Hassan?"

"Figures are not official," he offered. "It is impossible to give exact information, you see?"

"No."

"Very important man, this director," he told me, as if this explained something.

According to a baffling booklet published by the Ministry of Culture and Information's actual "Dept. of Information" itself, and titled "Fao — The Gate of Victory in the Gulf War" (which here meant the Iran-Iraq conflict), from the period of September 1, 1980, to April 18, 1988, "52,948 Iraqis laid down their lives for the defense and then the liberation of Faw." Since the war did not begin until September 4, 1980, one assumes that lives laid down during those three extra days were engaged in covert ops. "Faw," apparently, is the "Fao" of the title, a vital town at the mouth of the Shatt-al-Arab estuary, the oil refining and shipping zone, the ownership of which much of Iraq's squabble with Iran was concerned. When Iran occupied the area for two years — after six years of fighting — the war suddenly intensified until Iran was driven out. Getting Iran driven out also brought an end to the conflict, since invading the area had started it and hanging in for two years had consumed everything Iran had in the way of arms and the men to bear them. The booklet purported to explain why this area of the planet held such significance; a section named "Faw in History" began by stating that this history ". . . dates back to 2500 B.C. Archaeological finds show that the first battle involving human frogs took place in this area."[4]

What exactly "human frogs" were, and indeed where they engaged in their second battle, the booklet didn't say, but history, fascinating as it can be, was not the explanation for Faw's importance. Geography was. In a section dealing with that subject I found the statement that could have reduced the booklet to a lapel button: the Faw peninsula, it announced, "is the main Iraqi sea outlet for foreign trade and oil exports."

Elsewhere were some hints about motivating factors behind Saddam's forthcoming invasion of Kuwait, which was still some years away when "many Iranian officials stated that Iran had become Kuwait's new neighbor." Iraq's Achilles' heel is a tendency to be easily land-locked by any moderately powerful enemy able to gain control of the southeast, and by any silver-tongued charmer able to convince Jordan to close its border.

I showed the fifteen-page document to Hassan, asking why it could state unambiguously that over fifty thousand troops died defending and retaking Faw, while the memorial museum's director had trouble admitting anyone had ever died in a war since Saddam took over the reins of power.

"Department of Information has access only to certain figures" was the answer.

He couldn't explain what "human frogs" were, either, besides suggesting scuba divers.

"Four thousand-odd years ago, Hassan? What were they fighting about? Coral? Pearls?"

"We cannot say much about such distant times."

Few could say much about recent times, either. In fact, few could say much about anything here now.

Rob and I were interviewed next by a reporter from a state television program that employed much of Michael Jackson's "Black and White" morphing video and scenes from some Dustin Hoffman movie in its opening ID sequence, along with various giddily psychedelic Chroma-Key gimmicks. For example: The show's anchorperson, instead of being cut or faded out to make way for the next segment, simply vanished behind her desk as if by magic, reappearing much the same way later, beamed back to her chair from Planet Television.

"What can you tell us about the Babylon Festival?" asked the reporter, having introduced me as "Bob" and Rob as "Williams."

We lied. It was all great, and we were here to build bridges between our governments, and construct monuments to Culture.

"And having a really cool time," Rob added.

Perhaps bridge building hadn't been the best choice of metaphors to use on Iraq's national TV. The only recent activity in that area linking Washington with Baghdad had been the rebuilding of arterial roads spanning the Tigris, after U.S. bombs had reduced one of its bridges to dangling rubble.

The program was replayed around five times while we were there, often enough for people to point us out as the fools who'd come from heaven to improve relationships with hell.

Leaving Big Egg without incident, we now found ourselves at the mercy of a vindictively overheated sun. I hoped Hassan's bus would be heading back to the Ishtar immediately. Instead, however, we all traipsed in a weary platoon over to a distant structure resembling what Nebuchadrezzar would have built himself as a guest cottage or vacation bungalow, had he needed one. It was not the maquette for Michel Aflaq's mausoleum — as I'd also speculated — either. It was a memorial-cum-museum to an old revolutionary buddy and a cousin (or brother) of Saddam, one whom we last met when he was working as an elementary school guard near Takrit during Saddam's great escape. He'd done well, becoming General Adnan, Iraq's Minister of Defense. But then he'd perished tragically when his helicopter encountered a violent sandstorm that none of the occupants of three other helicopters accompanying it even seem to have noticed. Saddam was scheduled to fly back from Mosul — or wherever it was they were — with Adnan, but miraculously changed his mind.

God, no doubt, had a hand in this rescheduling, Saddam himself confessed, in the pamphlet doled out by Adnan Memorial staff and prefaced with The Leader's funeral eulogy to his old comrade-in-arms. Even described by Saddam himself, the events surrounding Adnan's demise sounded highly suspect and were redolent of assassination. The text also reeked of sheer guilt. Saddam felt bad about icing his old pal, but he could not let sentimental attachments interfere with presidential duties. High-ranking generals often needed purging, or just sacrificing to the interests of the state, whose interests were naturally identical to those of The Leader. It was a dirty job — murdering relatives and good friends — but, hey, *someone* had to do it if the status quo was to retain peace of mind, and latent plotters scared back to the straight and narrow path of docile obedience.

The memorial was colder than a walk-in freezer — possibly for the benefit of General Adnan's corpse, which lay in its stately casket on a roped-off dais festooned with plastic floral tributes. The museum, which was only a few antechambers, appeared just to contain whatever of the general's personal effects his widow and children would have otherwise boxed and banished to a forgotten corner of the attic.

"He was like a brother to Saddam," Rob announced, studying his tourist brochure. "Fought side by side . . . weathered many storms . . ."

"But not sandstorms . . ."

"Fought front to back — wow?" He interrupted himself. "Know how long this memorial took to build?"

"Unless it was begun before he died, of course, no more than a few years at the —"

"Nope! Four months. F-O-U-R months. *By decree of Saddam.*"

The Leader's conscience must have been like nitric acid bubbling around his soul until Adnan had been laid to rest. Saddam was, by all accounts, highly superstitious. His mother had been the village psychic — and she confided to a friend, or so I was told, that with Saddam, she felt as if she had given birth to a major demon.

Symbolic gestures meant as much to Iraq's president as they did to Nebuchadrezzar and Hitler: that is, they meant more than real gestures. Baghdad boasted several grand structures built since Desert Storm, most of them in the Big Egg vein, or of the more functional Saddam-Center-For-Theoretical-Studies variety, but all of them devoted to some species of government interest.

Rob refused point-blank to endure another school outing on Hassan's bus. I could see his point, but was wary of attracting any unnecessary attention from the Mukhabarat or Amn contingent now stationed in the elevators and on every floor, as well as peopling the lobby. Although the afternoon's diversion was to a museum built to display gifts presented to Saddam by his global peers, I decided to suffer it, pondering in my spare time the wisdom of embarking on some furtive solo expeditions.

DANGEROUS MEN

Nearly a week had passed — though it seemed longer. We sat in the Palestine Hotel's bar drinking melon juice with a couple of German artists who'd also been on Rob's ten-wheeled Russian cabaret from Amman. A tiny Portuguese woman named Lumina had joined us as well; she was a journalist reporting for what sounded like a Muslim newsletter published on a bimonthly basis for Muslim communities in the northern Algarve. She'd heard terrible things from a Turkish friend about the escalating atrocities committed by Sand Pirates and rogue army units in southwestern Iraq. She'd heard rumors of journalists being arrested and tortured in Baghdad, too. Her Turkish friend had other horrifying tales concerning evil deeds taking place in the northern regions: cannibalism, for instance, and public beheadings, dismemberings, burnings, floggings, stonings, and even public being-torn-apart-by-wild-dog events. Takrit, Mosul, Samarra — the actual locations mattered little, because Evil had no map. All this, understandably, scared the hell out of Lumina; she wanted to leave, to go home. Except she was more afraid to leave than she was to stay: she'd not yet noticed any cannibals and pirates in the hotel's vicinity.

Josef, the German, videotaped everything and everyone, smirking or nodding occasionally, and once in a while throwing out some sort of comment like, "Yah. Thass how it iss 'ere."

This was his fourth visit to a Babylon Festival. An art gallery several blocks away from the hotel always gave him a one-man show for his paintings when he came: something, I realized when I saw them, that no one back in Germany would ever dream of doing.

Rita, the other artist, was also on her fourth visit and her fourth one-woman show. The pair were not married, however, or even lovers; they scarcely seemed to be friends, yet they did always attend the festivals together, and they were huge fans of the Saddam Arts Center school or *genre* of Iraqi painting. Rita's work was quite devoid of anything remotely resembling talent, and her photographs were worse than mine, except far larger.

"Did you feel zee pow-ah?" she asked Rob, hearing we'd just come from Big Egg.

"Where?"

"At zee mem-oreal. Iss really a powe-full place. Big enershies dare. You know?"

"*Absolutely,*" Rob agreed.

Later he admitted he'd forgotten to tell me that she was a complete nutcase. So was Josef, although he had moments of lucidity. I think. He warned me to be careful of Rita's real boyfriend, Saif. Saif was an Iraqi poet with German citizenship, who looked like Rasputin but always seemed extremely friendly whenever our paths crossed. We kept promising to have coffee together, or tea. Or water.

"He iss nod to be trusted," Josef said. "In Chermany he is vun person, bud ass soon ass vee cross sa border 'ere he iss somevun else. He plays boce sides, you know? He bekumce you friend to vind owd vot you really abowd, vot you *really* sink; zen he reports to Mukhabarat every-sing. He hass too many friends 'ere. Effen Uday, Saddam's son, iss his friend. Uday iss a ferry *dane-cherous man.* I sink more danecherous zan hiss fader."

The stories about Uday had recently spread West, when someone called Latif claimed to have been forced to work as Uday's double, even undergoing plastic surgery to perfect an already stunning resemblance. Latif escaped to Geneva, telling tales of such stupendous debauchery, avarice, and cruelty that I'd been certain they were fabrications produced to obtain protection and refugee status. Yet the rumors persisted independently in Baghdad, too. Hearing that Saif was welcome within Uday's private circle, I took steps toward hinting that I would very much like to meet The Leader's son myself, if possible.

"Be care-full," Josef warned. "You haff no idea vot kind off people zeese are. Zay can do anysing zay like to you and day ged a-vay viddit."

"Why would they *want* to do anything to me?"

"If zay vinde datchew are not votchew zay you haar . . ."

"Meaning?"

"If you vur really zare to ride abow-did vor zum noose-paper."

Josef was shrewd — or could be — when it came to seeing who people were behind their masks. Yet he was also overly fond of provoking a reaction, any kind of reaction, and would say hostile, absurd, rude, or just plain crazy things to see how whoever he said them to would respond. He looked down on most as fools and morons — and he also tended to treat them that way. Those whom he'd misjudged badly usually avoided him in future, simply assuming he was disturbed, mad, bad, or merely unpleasant, but definitely not dangerous to know. Just tedious to tolerate. I never felt entirely certain that what he said about Saif was true, and I suspected at times that his dislike for the man had more to do with Rita's relationship. But I was cautious, nonetheless. Indeed, caution was becoming my middle name here — and I started to loathe the very *texture* of the word. Part of me yearned to see what happened if one was not cautious, however, if one threw caution to the wind, or, better yet, cast it into the flames.

COLONEL GADDAFI'S GOLDEN HAND GRENADE

If the contents of Baghdad's Saddam Gifts Museum were anything to go by, The Leader was an extremely popular guy internationally. Even the Government of the State of California had at one time found cause to fork out a fairly sizable chunk of tax dollars in order to purchase a gift that would not appear insultingly cheap alongside other forms of tribute due to a man of Saddam's stature. The French, for example, had virtually shipped over Cartier's entire catalogue by now. Finland felt that a somewhat impractical but exquisitely carved walking cane fit the bill. The old Soviets apparently did their shopping for Saddam-worthy offerings in Leningrad's museums, often favoring the Fabergé wing. Fidel Castro, who never had gift problems, was responsible for the traditional box of truncheon-sized Cuban cigars, its contents invisible, its seal definitely broken. He probably sends crates, not boxes, anyway. Saudis gave the weaponry equivalent of costume jewelry: sabers for drag queens, Liberace shotguns, Elton John pistols. Other Gulf family-business states simply told Tiffany's or Piaget's or possibly even De Beers Consolidated Mines Ltd. to courier out the most expensive item currently in stock.

Only Colonel Muammar Gaddafi had come up with something original, something I felt I could not really live without myself: an eighteen carat, solid gold, fully operational, beautifully engraved hand grenade, in its own custom-made leather and velvet presentation case embossed with the Libyan crest. The Colonel clearly devoted much time and thought to selecting the right gift for the right person. It was touching. I wondered if he had more of them, and if anyone had ever used one: a tough decision, an extreme measure, since you'd spend five years picking up the valuable pieces afterwards. But then a Cruise missile costs $100,000, bringing the Desert Storm smart weapon tab alone up to $32,200,000 — excluding transportation and miscellaneous expenses. Just to impress Saddam — or impress *upon* him.

I informed Hassan that we would not be attending the festival that night. He was no longer certain what was on the program, although others claimed that Armenian musicians topped the bill, preceded by something like Tibetan Elbow Dancers or Croatian Wolf Charmers.

TRADITION AND THE INDIVIDUAL TALENT

As the days passed into a second week, what had once been a flawlessly organized schedule of events — three in progress at any one time — deteriorated into a flabbergasting chaos that had Bulgarian Stoat Jugglers jockeying for attention with the Havana Butter Makers Guild Ballet or with a traditional Goblins' Wedding Dance from Turkmenistan. An elfin fellow from Samarkand, whose talent consisted of playing the same tune on harmonicas that ranged in size from a church pew to a rat's tooth, even stormed off stage angrily; he'd only reached his toolbox-sized model when a legion of Indonesian drummers had started battering out a traditional tribal war dance behind him.

The range of national entertainments still thriving out there somewhere was bewildering. Take, for example, a five-hundred-pound Jordanian in keffiyeh and robes, dancing in patent leather Gucci loafers as nimbly as a tiny whirling ballerina, while also wielding a four-foot scimitar in flashing arcs like a skipping rope to the rhythm of ten dour Arabs beating drums, plucking ouds, wailing tunelessly, clapping out of time, and all of them following the lead of a grinning sheikh who sat cross-legged howling at the moon. I wouldn't mind managing the Jordanian Sword Dancers: they had distinct star potential.

The Ishtar, now at 100 percent occupancy, thronged day and night with people living in a perpetual Halloween. Crossing the lobby, exiting elevators, packing the restaurant were Cossacks, medieval princesses, Babylonian harlots, Turkish pirates, Balinese chieftains, Ukrainian dandies, and a whole animated encyclopedia of international folk traditions. Everyone else was a secret police officer.

"This is a weird trip," was Rob's first indication that he felt something like the way I was trying to pretend I didn't feel. "Nothing makes sense, man. Do you ever get the feeling that there's two of everything here? Two answers to each question; two versions of every story. In fact —" He scratched his head and frowned. "— There are two people inside each person you meet. One minute you like them, the next you can't stand the sight of them. They're friendly, then they're fucking unbelievably rude. I dunno, dude. Something's *wrong* here . . ."

"But you don't know what it is, do you, Mister Howard . . . ?"

"I just told you I didn't know, *ape brain!*"

"It's a line from a song, *bitch!*"

"Yeah? By who? Neal Diamond, no doubt."

The banter had a bit of a sharp and rusty edge to it — not something it ever did before — and we were both conscious of the unease grinding our words into swords, ready for battle. We just wanted to leave, to go home, home to what we loved and whom we loved and where we were also loved. We hoped. It all seemed so far away suddenly. Even Amman seemed so unattainably far away. The thought of never seeing home again, of life ending here in Baghdad with some squalid form of death — *this* was awful. And it hatched still more awful thoughts, making even trivial incidents pungent with terror.

We confessed our feelings in the car Hassan had arranged for us to hire, driven by the man he'd also arranged for us to hire with it, Faisal, whose lazy good humor, John Travolta smile, and almost nonexistent command of English proved to be the Halloween costume concealing a ruthless and talented Mukhabarat officer. Of course, this doesn't mean anything remotely like a Baghdad James Bond. Even London has never contained any of those. In Iraq it meant a poorly paid state thug with a high IQ and a grade 4 education, who did what he was told to do — and *whatever* he was told to do — with mechanical efficiency. In Faisal's case, it also meant possessing a gift for not seeming remotely like the person he really was, a genuine knack for presenting himself as a simple soul of goofy affability, a driver more than content with the thought of a lifetime's driving ahead of him, and with whatever modest tip in U.S. dollars he was given.

In a sense, he even *was* this humble driver. But he was also that other person, the one who had looked on dispassionately, perhaps, while his colleagues broke the bottle they had just shoved up someone's ass; the one who had possibly stubbed his cigarettes out on the face and torso of a man left hanging from a meat hook for three whole days and nights. Faisal was maybe also the person who had delivered a coffin containing the corpse of a brother/father/son to the next of kin some months after a strange disappearance, telling tear-streaked faces about the man's unfortunate "accident," even — conceivably — adding his own official sorrow to theirs. Then requesting immediate payment for the coffin and burial arrangements that the state had so kindly taken care of for them. Then finally leaving with the cash and the certain knowledge that these poor people were grieving over and burying an empty box: for he had personally disposed of the man that the box was supposed to hold, or rather, what was left of that man after his long season in hell.

Such tales are common in Iraq, both well-documented from the past and also in progress, being composed just as energetically while I write about them as they will probably be when you read about them. Such men as Faisal are common, too, chauffeuring businessmen or diplomats to and from meetings, sitting idly yet attentively in hotel lobbies, or just watching TV monitors showing activity on the streets through the eyes of cameras concealed on rooftops, in doorways, or in statues. The primary task these men are trained and paid for, however, whatever they seem to be doing, is to make sure no outsider, no foreigner, ever meets the kind of Iraqi he or she shouldn't meet: the kind of Iraqi who, like the Ancient Mariner, cannot choose but speak of the torments whose cruel tides have carried him to a place where he no longer cares whether his journey will continue or not, because there is no longer anywhere to go, any reason to go there, and nowhere to return, let alone anyone to return for.

The sign warned those entering to abandon hope, but by the time they were close enough to read the words it was too late: the gates had slammed shut behind them. *Check your fear and cowardice at the door, sir. We've arrived at the place I promised: where you'll see the truly wretched, those whose minds can no longer perform any good . . .*

GRIEF FINDS A BARRIER WHERE THE EYES WOULD WEEP

No one knows who anyone really is in Baghdad anymore — it's an axiom. Fathers don't trust sons, sons suspect fathers, brothers are wary of each other, and daughters have been known to save their own skins rather than a father's life. People have been executed for crimes they were accused of intending to commit, crimes that had not yet actually been committed at all.

This was the tenor of our discussion behind Faisal's head, as he drove us to an area Rob found promising as subject matter. We assumed Faisal barely understood a word, but, since we had not done anything wrong, we were not especially worried whether he or anyone heard us.

This confessional of fears and feelings was also cleansing, I found. Our moods had turned around and, hey, the night looked like fun again. It was even difficult to recall what it was that had bothered us so profoundly. Such about-faces of the mind, I gradually noticed, were frequent, and still more frequent in the Iraqis I managed to spend any time with alone. For it *was* possible to meet the kind of Iraqi who foreigners are not supposed to meet. It was *possible*, but it was not sensible — but then I've never been very sensible. My mother told me so.

Rob felt he had hit pay dirt when we stumbled across the Juma Shuaie Coffee House, a vast antique where neither clientele nor contents appeared to have changed much since 1850, although the place had only opened in 1941, according to Mohammed, manager and grandson of the man who had opened it. Sheikhs and soldiers sat side by side on crude wood and string benches, playing dominoes or backgammon — in their original forms — on buckled old tables. It may have been called a coffee house, but I never saw anyone drinking coffee. They all drank tea that arrived on saucers in small glasses with an inch of sugar silting at the bottom. Besides tea, Mohammed provided narghiles, water pipes where marinated tobacco burned upon a small bed of charcoal, its smoke sucked down through water and into the throat via a flexible tube with a pipe-stem mouthpiece. You had to inhale rather than puff, which, for a novice like me at least, flung a cloud of what felt like acrid soot straight into my lungs. I'd tried it once in Cairo and had spent twenty minutes coughing my innards out. My eyes still looked as if they'd been boiled two hours later. I could never understand how anyone ever got past this initial experience and persevered on to the pleasure stage, let alone addiction.

How the place turned a profit with just tea and pipes, and a staff of some twenty or more to pay, was also a mystery. Eight teas cost around a cent, and, unlike us Western hogs, most customers spent three hours over one glass.

Between many breaks to sip tea, Rob slowly set up his tripod and started adjusting the jumbo cameras and fiddling with light meters. This way he managed to win the trust of initially wary customers and was soon asking if they minded having their portraits taken.

An hour later he was besieged by sheikhs, clerks, corporals, majors, and minors, the entire gamut of downscale society in blue collar Baghdad — all anxious to be captured for posterity. Another humdrum night at the Juma had suddenly become an event.

Looking on, I gradually came to appreciate how vain these characters were. The regal old sheikhs, with their gold-braided, see-through abayas and cascading folds of keffiyeh — they knew damn well how elegant they looked beside men in mere shirts and pants stained from a day's work. The soldiers were similarly aware of a uniform's distinct advantages over civilian dress. As Rob squinted and focused, clicked and wound, everyone was smoothing down hair, arranging folds, adjusting lapels, and checking themselves out in the nighttime window's vast mirror.

This was a man's world, too, as I recalled thinking an age earlier. Iraq had men blessed with perfect bone structure, dark pools for eyes, slim yet accentuated lips, proud chins, delicate hands with long slender fingers, and a posture that made their walk a stately tour rather than the usual scramble. This was nothing unusual, of course, just genes and luck; but what was uncommon, to me at least, was this self-conscious and somewhat aimless vanity. There wasn't a woman in sight, so they were either preening for themselves or each other. Or both — which was probably the truth.

I had to tell Rob to shoot the manager whether he wanted to or not. Poor Mohammed had been growing more and more anxious as the minutes passed and he watched as customer after customer gained the camera's rapt attention. Soon he was pacing, patting down strands of shining hair seeped in oil and black henna, pretending to instruct errant employees, but really just edging closer in the hope of igniting the photographer's interest in himself, *The Manager*. At one point he enlisted a translator to announce that our tea was on the house. At his prices, that seemed always to be the case, however. The gesture was, of course, deeply appreciated.

After much goading, Rob relented and Mohammed's turn finally came. He sat on the throne behind the cash register, lord of the bazaar, and was unashamedly delighted when Rob ordered the cousin or nephew who'd leapt over three men to sit beside him to move away: Mohammed was all the camera wanted. The manager screwed a fresh Rashid Filter into his foppish holder, fingers perched upon its stem like a flautist, streamers of smoke escaping through gold-capped teeth displayed in a smile he could not terminate. He was a page from some Victorian street photographer's album: "Coffee House Manager, Baghdad, 1855." Only the Batman bumper sticker on his till, once I'd noticed it, would have fixed the scene in its time.

Faisal seemed unnaturally pleased that the evening had turned out to be such a success. Rob was the highlight of the Juma Shuaie's week, perhaps its decade, and it took half an hour to shake enough hands to be able to leave courteously. He wanted to come back, though. The place was a "goldmine." I suggested that there were probably a hundred similar or even better places in the city. In fact there weren't.

That night, I sat up until 3:00 a.m. talking with Dusan Dimitrijevic, Serbian director of the Serb-Arab Association in Beograd. He had a low opinion of U.S. foreign policy, and he also believed, like Saddam and Noam Chomsky, that a conspiracy lurked behind the American media's reporting of news. In other words, Serbs had been getting bad press lately, and it pissed him off. I suggested that evidence revealing mass murder rarely *improved* anyone's media image.

"*Allegations!*" he yelled.

"OK: Alleged evidence of alleged mass-murder . . ."

"The Bosnians are just as bad," he protested.

Perhaps they are. This seems to be the rule with most violent squabbles.

"If the U.S. just kept out of other people's business," Dusan suggested, "things would resolve themselves."

Serbs would resolve Bosnians, seemed more likely. I hadn't cheered the Serbs when they were getting better press than the Bosnians, though, and I felt no different now that the situation had reversed. Yet it was interesting to hear how things looked to them. After two hours of hearing how things looked to Serbs, I was invited to spend Christmas in Beograd as Serbia's guest so I could see how things looked to Serbs myself. In Serbia. Apart from Baghdad, I couldn't think of anywhere else I'd rather *not* spend Christmas — or any other day of the year — than Beograd. My memory of the city is mingled with images of Mayhew's London and the aftermath of Stalingrad's siege, for some reason. I do, however, recall that there were about a thousand people dressed in rags, the old, the young, whole families, all asleep in a draughty open hall of the city's railway station — and they were not waiting for the trains.

Little wonder Dusan did not find Baghdad especially depressing. He did find Saddam somewhat undesirable, though, but ascribed his impressive tenacity to the CIA.

"They put him there; they keep him there," he summarized. "They could have taken him out after 'Desert Storm' but they let him go. Just like his supporters, CIA believes Iraq will fall apart without the iron hand ruling it."

"It's falling apart *with* the iron hand ruling it. No one would notice any difference."

He agreed slightly, muttering about Kurds being more trouble to Kurds than Saddam was; then about Iraqi Shi'ites being unlikely to merge the South into an Iranian empire, since they were Arabs and Iranians hated Arabs as much as Arabs hated Iranians. They shared a branch of a religion, true, but then so did Germany and Britain in 1939, 1914, and numerous other dates receding into the Middle Ages.

"True," I kept saying. "True."

He went on to produce about fifty similar examples from Africa over a mere decade.

Then I recalled Faw and its battling "human frogs," pointing out that Saddam's interest in the South had nothing to do with religion; it had to do with water. Iran's interest was also not related to faith; it was related to trying to thwart Saddam's interest. Iraq had to have access to a major port, and major ports rarely exist anywhere away from major seas, and since the only sea in Iraq also happened to be in the South, no power on earth would persuade Saddam — or any Iraqi leader — to let the South go its own way. Especially since that way led to Iran, which would not give up the chance to deprive its Arab neighbor of all sea access and anything else that would wreck its economy (if there still was one to wreck).

"True," said Dusan, concluding that America was to blame for everything too complicated for us to resolve in three hours.

"Come to Beograd," he urged, as I staggered away. "You will see for yourself the way things are."

"Right. Thanks."

If seeing reality in all its pristine purity involves going to Beograd, I'll have to be satisfied looking at it for the rest of my days through a glass darkly — whatever *that* means.

The next morning two things happened: Firstly, Rob and I were assigned another "guide," a young woman named Ala,* from the labyrinthine Ministry of Culture and Information. She replaced Hassan, who was now overloaded with clients, but she merely reinforced Faisal. Secondly, we found ourselves booked on a tour of the Iraq Museum, that seemed to be impervious to cancellation. This was all the more puzzling since we were the only ones on this tour — along with our new guide and driver, of course.

"How come fifty people have Hassan on his own for a guide, yet we have a guide each?"

"Good question. Maybe because we're big tippers?"

As we both knew, the answer was really because we weren't deemed trustworthy enough to be allowed the opportunity of evading

---

* Note: This character's identity is so heavily concealed that any attempts to discover his or her identity will be futile.

surveillance for a second. I'd kept quiet about being on assignment for *The New York Times*, but obviously not quiet enough.

Still buoyant from the previous night, we got petulant instead of nervous at the attempt to shrink-wrap our freedom, deciding to give our keepers a run for their money by splitting up and each taking cabs to a different part of town. This was a stupid move if ever there was one.

As I watched Rob's cab speed away and started hailing my own, Ala materialized at my side. After five minutes of chat, I'd been persuaded that Iraq's premier museum was well worth my time, ending up with Faisal and Ala in the car heading for what was supposed to be a morning's worth of cultural artifacts. However, 99 percent of the museum's exhibits had been removed to its cellars for safety in the event of another U.S. bombing jamboree. What was left on display would have fitted inside my bedroom closet — with the exception of a five-thousand-year-old basalt lion from Eridu, which probably could withstand anything but a direct hit, and was also far too heavy to move three inches, let alone half a mile through a maze of cellars.

The other version of this story — backed up by objects appearing in European auction houses — is that the general in charge of safeguarding Iraq's national heritage shipped the best of it out to be sold on his behalf.

However, as it is with most countries that have a history old enough to embarrass the superpowers — whenever they try to recall what *their* people were up to as others were inventing alphabets and constructing buildings of such size and complexity no one could even reproduce them now with modern technology — most of Iraq's past is already in European museums. The Germans, for example, somehow managed to carry off from Babylon to Berlin the entire Ishtar Gate. Although compared with the British Museum, which still contains half of Egypt and ancient Greece, most nineteenth-century treasure hunters were mere amateurs.

Ala complained about this cultural crime at some length, as we strolled past displays of carved rubble and cases of the coins that Greeks and Romans appear to have strewn all over their world like seeds or garbage. Never had any nations lost so much small change in so many places as these two. Only recently did I realize that this was because inflation had even hit the Roman Empire. Thinking it would be a good scam to dilute the coinage's silver content a bit, one of the later Roman emperors took it down to 96 percent. Within a century, though, silver coins only contained 3 percent silver. It took a financial genius to work out that the short-term profits of this outrageous rip-off were hardly worth the long-term losses: all taxes were paid to the emperor in the same worthless coins. Since Rome made nothing except money, everything else was imported; but the denizens of empire weren't the dolts Rome took them for. No one would accept money for goods, only gold or silver. People weren't losing coins: they were tossing them away. With money, forms change but the substance remains the same: unless it is made of something that's worth something, money is ultimately worthless.

Ala knew a fair bit about ancient history, I realized, and even more about Iraq's staggering span of vanished years. She carefully presented the endless saga of invading Turks being replaced by invading Persians, with brief spells when some indigenous megalomaniac managed to hold his own in Baghdad by forming an alliance with the Turks and punishing the Persians, or by forming an alliance with the Persians and punishing the Turks, either of which resulted in a severe backlash from the punished party as soon as its army had regrouped or replenished itself. Then Persians would stamp Baghdad into dust once more, proceeding on to attempt the same with Turkey; or, alternatively, Turks would stamp Baghdad into dust once more, proceeding on to attempt the same with Persia. The "proceeding on" part rarely met with much success, but Baghdad being stamped into dust was a constant. There was generally enough time to glue the city back together before another alliance with either Turks or Persians — whoever seemed stronger — was required, and the city returned to "Go."

Iraq's occasional attempts at putting an end to this tedious cyclical process sounded like a soccer referee, disgusted with players on both sides, deciding to form a third team to play the other two, with new rules permitting him to join up with one of the teams *if he felt like it*. But the new rules also allowed both former teams to ignore him if they chose, playing each other while his boys lay in the mud beneath them. Inevitably, the referee would concede that soccer with three teams was unworkable. Then the entire process would start over.

In this scheme of things Saddam was in a brief interlude. The Turks were on very cordial terms with Iran lately, too.

"Maybe your Leader will have to close up shop soon, then?" I suggested to Ala, making it sound as much like a joke as possible.

"I hope," she replied, simply.

It stunned me.

THERE, WEEPING KEEPS THEM FROM WEEPING . . .

"How old do you think I am?" Ala asked.

"Thirty-seven . . . or -eight . . ."

I was thinking *forty-five* or *fifty*.

"I am twenty-six."

Two hours later we sat in the Ishtar's restaurant. Faisal had felt it safe to go off for lunch on his own, although it wasn't at all safe. Ala told me in ever-deepening tones of despair about the reality of her life, until, seeing the tears brimming up in her eyes, I grasped that this was someone at the end of her tether, someone who had to tell her tale of woe before it devoured her from the inside out.

She had ten brothers and sisters, only one of whom worked, meaning that, with her parents, there were thirteen people living on 6,000 dinars a month brought home by two wage earners between them. This sum had the buying power of two dollars now.

They had sold most of their furniture, she explained, and they did without all luxuries like sugar and milk.

"Sugar and milk are *luxuries*?"

They were. So was medicine for her sister's ten-week-old baby, born with jaundice and some other infection requiring antibiotics that, if you could find them, cost as much as a second-hand car.

For the dessert that did not exist in the Ishtar, I offered her a chocolate bar. She bit off a tiny piece and promptly began to cry. "I don't feel right eating it myself. Do you mind if I take the rest back for my brothers and sisters?"

Chocolate was not something they'd seen in a long while. That candy bar would cost her over three weeks' wages. She didn't even *think* about such luxuries anymore. But the biggest luxury in her life was her job: thirteen people depended on her 3,000 dinars a month for half their basic needs. One sister's husband had been killed "in the war"

(I didn't ask which one); another sister appeared to be a single mother; and besides an unaccounted-for brother, all the other siblings were too young to work. Her father had "given up looking for a job." Once he'd owned a construction business and they'd lived in "a nice neighborhood," but now they were down to selling off furniture, and her father had seemingly just lost the will to go on.

"Please," she said, half an hour later, "this is between us, yes? If they find out, I am finished."

I knew I wasn't supposed to be hearing any of *this* version of Saddam's Iraq. But I'd heard nothing yet. Ala had spent too much time alone with me already, she said. She had to go home now, but she managed to persuade Faris to push through a permission for us to drive to Kerbala the next day. She had relatives there — she was a Shi'ite, I realized — and it would be "nice" for me to meet them, just as it would be "nice" for her to see them and to "get out of this awful city."

"Guess what, darling."

"What, darling?"

"Cool," Rob decided when he'd heard the tale. "Maybe I can do a cover shot for *The New York Times* magazine?"

"Yeah, that's a good idea: they can run a banner across it saying THIS WOMAN IS NOW DEAD BUT WE'VE GOT THE STORY. Somehow I don't think *The New York Times* is going to want this story."

They wanted a story about Uday Hussein. It would have been more fun: *Uday on Girls, Cars, and Murder: Iraq's First Son Tells All.* But that wasn't the story. What we were putting the Iraqi people through was the story. We were punishing the criminal's abused family because we couldn't get to the criminal. And I was right: *The New York Times* didn't want *that* story. It wasn't what Americans wanted to hear. Americans wanted to hear more tales of Beelzebub and His Son, more justification for the war and the subsequent attacks on Baghdad and other places. Justification for an embargo that was slowly starving 20 million people for the crimes of 2,000. The Iraqis should just get rid of Saddam if they didn't like him.

"Why don't you go over there and explain how it's done — they'd love to hear," was the reply this fatuous statement elicited.

◈

That night Rob wanted to go back to the Juma and shoot some more portraits for what had now became a major opus: *The Tea House Suite*.

We decided, since we knew Ala was at home, that it would be fun to see what Faisal would do if we split up. He could take Rob to the Juma and I would see if I could get away in a cab on my own. There was a bazaar I needed to visit — since shopping is my whole life — and I'd meet Rob later. This was only inadvertently very stupid, though.

I managed to slip out unobtrusively, I thought, and hopped in a cab.

"My people very angry with you," the driver announced, after some minutes of sullen silence.

"Me?"

My heart pounded.

"Why you hate Iraqi peoples? Why you planes bomb Iraqi city?"

Oh that! I nearly said. *I thought you were Mukhabarat . . .*

I had to convince him that I was Canadian, not American, that my planes hadn't bombed Iraq's cities. Canada didn't have any planes.

He softened. "Why they make this embargo, hmm? Why they make us suffer?"

After I'd paid him and he'd left, I realized I was at the wrong bazaar and walked straight through it to hail another cab at the other end. Failing to find the bazaar with this cab, I noticed we were passing the Juma, so I decided to abandon my search and get out. There was no sign of Rob or Faisal inside, however, but, greeted effusively by Mohammed, the Manager, I figured I might as well have tea and wait to see if they showed up. No sooner had I sat down than a nervous, scholarly old man in the remains of what was once a good suit asked in French if he could join me.

His name was Wathik,[*] and he'd been educated in France. He rhapsodized about Paris in the old days for a while, then recounted his life as a teacher in Baghdad. Now he was retired, with a pension of 300 dinars a month. I thought I'd misheard — that's about 10 cents — but he nodded in anguish, saying that a pack of cigarettes cost him 600 dinars (I was being ripped off). He'd sold all his furniture, sold all his posses-

---

[*] Note: This character's identity is so heavily concealed that any attempts to discover his or her identity will be futile.

sions, in fact, and now lived "like an animal." He'd seen us in the tea shop the day before, he claimed, and hoped we might come back.

"*Pourquoi?*" I assumed he was about to request a loan.

"You must be my voice," he said, suddenly frightened and desperate.

I offered him my cigarettes and asked how much money he needed. He thanked me profusely, pushing the cigarettes back and taking out a pouch of hand-rolled ones.

"I am used to these. I don't want to remember what a good cigarette tastes like." He drew closer. "We don't have long. I want nothing for myself, you understand? I want you to tell the world what is going on here . . ."

I thought of the Sudanese man, the monsoon-cloud-colored man in that Jordanian refugee camp years earlier. *You must help us, sir. We have no voice in all this world. You must be our voice, please. You must tell this story, or world never going to hear . . .*

"This government is a sham," Wathik was saying. "They are criminals, bank robbers, men with no education. Now it is like an animal in a cage, this leadership. It is frightened and dangerous. *Look around you!*" He gestured at the hubbub of backgammon players, tea slurpers, and narghile puffers hunched on wooden benches. "They are *sheep*! Saddam has destroyed the education system; everyone is stupid! And they feed on each other like cannibals! That is what this criminal has done to our land! With his hundreds of palaces and his Swiss bank accounts . . . Please!" He grabbed my hand. "You must carry my words around the world. So people *know* . . ."

I told him that no one imagined Iraq was Shangri-la, or that Saddam was the Wise and Bounteous One.

"We must be careful," he warned in a whisper. "The tea shop manager is a *detective*."

I assumed this meant "spy." And, right on cue, Mohammed came over and offered me a tour of the premises. He spoke only Arabic, so Wathik trailed along as translator.

"He says the place has been open since his grandfather started it in 1941."

"Tell him it looks it. And he told us that yesterday."

Mohammed proudly showed me into a sulfurous room where the tobacco for narghiles was being prepared in clay cones. It looked like shit and straw.

"It is the *worst* tobacco," Wathik muttered. "Only sheep smoke it."

When I'd done enough dutiful marveling at the tea shop's wonders, and the Manager had made sure his customers had all seen him showing the honored guest — the Canadian Minister for Tea Houses, perhaps — around his domain, I managed to return with Wathik to our table alone.

"You have heard of this General Hussein Kamel?" he asked.

Kamel was one of Wathik's nephews. I was about to say he must be pleased about the defection, but he grabbed my hand and squeezed it hard, saying, "No one should trust Hussein Kamel. He and Saddam plotted this together so they can crush the opposition. He is an evil man, this Hussein Kamel, a mass murderer. In Kerbala he had all the houses about Imam Hussein's mosque bulldozed so that no one could see inside, where he was slaughtering thousands. Sixty, seventy thousand . . ."

Nephew or not, Wathik wished the general dead. Wathik had been cut out of the family years ago, but did not want a cent of their "blood money." There were further dire indictments, and listening to them, I became aware of a certain change in the Juma's atmosphere. The Manager was on the phone, and a few serious military types had entered and seated themselves not far from our table, watching us rather than behaving like customers. Wathik was the kind of Iraqi whom foreigners are not supposed to meet, I realized. It was a very bad idea to be seen talking with him — bad for both of us.

Just then Rob showed up, but not with Faisal. I gestured for him to ignore me.

"Oh, I thought you were swatting flies, darling," he explained, when I asked him why he wasn't ignoring me.

I muttered enough to have him scurrying to the back of the tea house to set up his equipment alone.

"You've got to leave right now," I told Wathik.

I walked him out and down the dimly lit streets for a few hundred yards, hearing more — too much, in fact — about the infernal misery Saddam Hussein will some day be held accountable for creating. Slipping Wathik a hundred-dollar bill wrapped in a 100 dinar note (so he'd *accept* it), I told him to take care, that I'd sponsor him to leave if he could, that he should write to me. And I promised I'd do my best.

I wish it were more.

"I am too old to leave," he said. "And I love this country. I will die here. But I hope . . . not before *he* is gone . . . *Je vous en prie!*"

No sooner had I returned to the Juma when Faisal came ambling in. His easygoing facade was still there, but slightly askew. He was rattled.

And no wonder. Rob had given him the slip, too, finding another driver, who took him to the wrong tea house, where he'd shot some rolls then managed to find his way here. Faisal must have been frantic, looking for both of us — and perhaps getting conflicting reports about where we were, since we weren't together. He tried telling us it was dangerous for us to be out at night alone.

"Faisal, Manhattan's *dangerous* and I —"

"And although he's Canadian from Toronto, he's been to New York once or twice as a tourist. So he knows. *Don't* you, Robert?"

"Yeah. Don't be a pussy, Faisal. We're big boys . . ."

Rob did a good job of diffusing the situation, then an even better one of convincing Faisal we were at the Juma just to shoot *The Tea House Decades*.

"You know, it really *is* boring watching you take photographs, darling."

"Yeah, it's even boring me having you looking so bored there."

"Let's take Faisal out to dinner and see if we can buy his loyalty."

Three hours later, we did. And he showed us a fabulous restaurant, too; one where he, a humble driver, was clearly very well-known. One where half the customers also knew him — and looked just like him.

Only later did it occur to me that my actions had been ludicrously suspicious. Changing cabs at the market must have looked like a premeditated plan to lose anyone tailing me — and someone obviously was — and then running into Wathik the moment I entered the Juma must have seemed like a prearranged meeting.

My room had been searched, too. I'd expected this from the start and thus employed all the usual tricks learned from James Bond movies for seeing if someone has rifled your belongings. No one had until that night, though.

A cold fear set in. Rob and I took a midnight walk along the Tigris, mainly to talk freely. A whole darkened strip consisted of restaurants that roasted huge fish from the river on open pits of charcoal. It was one of Saddam's favorite meals. For tourists there would have been considerable charm in these ancient traditional Baghdad establishments; but the country's facade had been stripped away, and all I could see now, wherever I looked, was the Iraq that Ala and Wathik described. It was utterly sinister.

> On we went,
> to where frost roughly swathes a people who,
> Instead of downward, turn their faces up.
> There, weeping keeps them from weeping — for as they do,
> Grief finds a barrier where the eyes would weep
> But forced back inward, adds to their agonies:
> A crystal visor of prior tears fills the cup
> Below the eyebrow with a knot of ice.

— DANTE, INFERNO, CANTO XXXIII

THE MAN OF FRUIT FROM THE EVIL GARDEN

The heart of Shia Islam it may well be, but Kerbala was just another dusty, dirty, worn-out wreck of a town to me. Only the mosques were beautiful, and the shrine of Imam Hussein, grandson of the Prophet, was pungent with the aura of centuries of piety. Martyred on this spot while journeying to accept a caliphate that had already slipped from his grasp in the internecine strife that followed his grandfather's death, Hussein is really the true founder of Shia Islam, and the reason it places such a high price on martyrdom to this day.

Kerbala was also where General Hussein Kamel, assigned by Saddam to put down the Shi'ite rebellion in the months following Desert Storm, rounded up hundreds of rebels in the holy mosque itself and slaughtered them, ordering the houses surrounding the shrine to be bulldozed so no one could see what was going on. The houses still lay in piles of rubble. Bloodstains were even still visible on the inner courtyard's marble.

Although Faisal was our driver, he found Rob enough of a distraction to leave Ala and me alone. She was cautious in his presence, but she knew how to manipulate Iraqi men, quickly changing topics and flirting with him if he approached. Most of the time, though, she was free to talk. And talk she did, as if everything that came tumbling out had been long bottled up and, toxic as it was, at least became diluted and rendered a little less harmful by this release. Like many Iraqis, she was a shattered soul, though, a poor, bare, forked animal scarcely clothed in sufficient sanity to pass as fit for work. As for play, there was none. She had grown old without ever being young.

The unaccounted-for brother she'd mentioned, I discovered, was in prison. He'd originally been charged with what struck me as the non-crime of borrowing money for his business from someone who'd stolen this money. That was how the brother had explained it, I presumed, though he'd probably stolen the money himself. Yet as a defense it was pitiful. Surely he could have come up with something better. It was this very pitifulness, however, that eventually convinced me the story was just as she told it.

Ala had gone to the police station to bail her brother out the day he was arrested. The police chief had a better idea: she would become his third extant wife and her brother would skip out of jail a free man. But Ala was already engaged. When she told her father what had happened, he hit the roof and marched down to the prison to give the police chief a piece of his mind.

"Fine," the chief apparently said. "You'll never see your son again."

A whole catalogue of spurious charges was suddenly added to her brother's original sin, and within a week he'd been sentenced to twenty-six years in the Baghdad pen.

Ala didn't need to convince me that prison in Iraq was not quite the same as prison the way we know it. The first time she visited her brother he'd been strung up on a meat hook with his arms tied behind his back for three days. Hundreds of cigarettes had been stubbed out on his chest and legs. There appeared to be no reason for this punishment besides the fact that it had struck someone as a good idea. Currently he was sharing a cell designed to hold two people with twenty-three others. The floor was the only toilet facility available; and the only food he got to eat was what his sister and mother brought in on the two weekly visits they were allowed. The only possible way out of this hell involved lawyers and money — far more money than anyone could now dream of ever having.

I assumed Ala would soon hit me up for this cash. But she didn't. She also seemed a bit embarrassed that her brother was in jail, as if it reflected on her. Over the next few days I gradually came to learn that her embarrassment was related to something else altogether.

At eighteen she'd been raped by Lieutenant General Hussein Kamel. When Ala's fiancé discovered she wasn't a virgin, he broke off the engagement, leaving her that worst of all possible creatures in the Arab world: a woman of questionable reputation, a woman no man worth marrying would ever marry.

At this point we were walking through the rubble that surrounded Imam Hussein's shrine, the rubble that had been homes until Hussein Kamel came along. It occurred to me that she might have been making up the rape story, but her tears were too real, and no Arab woman in my experience would make up such a story about herself. And there was more.

Ala had been one of Uday Hussein's *girls*, and she owed her current job to his intercession. She'd met the president's son a few years earlier as a guest at one of his notorious parties.

"He has a palace out by the lake," she told me. "And there were twenty girls all driven out in convertible Cadillacs — for *show*, you understand?"

There was live music and dancing, then toward the end of the evening Uday would traditionally pick one or two girls he wanted to take to bed. He called Ala over.

"You're *black*," he said.

Color, as I've noted, still means much in Iraq. By the pink standards of the Iraqi hierarchy Ala was dark-skinned.

"But you have nice eyes," Uday continued. "And a nice nose."

She was apparently embarrassed by this and stood looking down.

"Do my remarks offend you?"

"You are our leader's son," she replied dutifully, "and I appreciate your comments."

He asked if he could kiss her goodnight; she offered her cheek.

"That's not my way," he announced, seizing her shoulders and kissing her lips roughly. "Now I will drive you home."

Ala managed, she said, to get out of this by promising to return with friends. But Uday had his secretary call her daily, demanding a date.

"You should not refuse him," the secretary confided at one point. "He can make your life very hard."

Ala didn't refuse for long, and her job was her reward. Uday's secretary still called, but now it was to order her to bring girlfriends to his parties. Times were so tough that parents even urged their daughters to go to these events, knowing full well what could happen. A man like Uday — no matter what his reputation — was worth knowing, worth having on your side, and a daughter's duty was to help her family in any way she could.

Some of Uday's girls "disappeared," however, or so I'd heard.

"Yes, it's true," Ala said. "He's just like his father. A woman does something to offend him and she's taken out into the desert by his guards. Then they throw her onto the road and run her over many times with the car. It's reported as an accident."

She also confirmed another story I'd heard about Uday. He liked to cruise the city looking for attractive girls. When he saw one he fancied, he'd order his guard to fetch her. Knowing the consequences, no one refused. Once he'd been passing a hotel where a wedding was taking place and the bride and groom were posing for photographs on the steps up to the lobby. Uday took a great fancy to the bride, telling his guard to bring her to the suite he keeps at the Rashid Hotel. After Saddam's son had finished with her, the bride calmly put her wedding dress back on and jumped from the balcony twenty floors to her death.

"She was the cousin of my best friend," Ala stated, "so I know it's true. He is a terrible man."

But these were terrible times, and people did what they had to do in order to survive. The reason for the recent ban on drinking alcohol in public was, in fact, according to Ala, an attempt to curb the soaring rise in prostitution. Every woman had lost a father or a brother or a husband — a *provider* — in the wars, and many were now forced to provide for vast extended families themselves in any way they could.

This suddenly made more sense of the importuning women in veils I'd come across. I wasn't irresistibly cute after all.

There were two Mukhabarat agents outside my door every time I looked now, and you could tell by the faint stir in the lobby every time we walked through it that someone was very interested in our activities.

And our activities became very low key.

DEMOCRACY IS COMING

"I have arrange meeting for you with the Meenister of Information hisself," squeaked Hassan.

"Oh, great, Hassan! That's fabulous!"

"You're a dude, Hassan. Did you know that?"

"A drood?"

"You can be that, too. It's okay if Hassan's a druid, isn't it?"

"Not a problem, Hassan. Be what you want to be . . ."

"*And do watcha wanna do-hoo-hoo . . .*"

"You have a great voice, Rob. You should have been a major star, did anyone ever tell you that?"

"Yeah. All the time . . ."

"But you rebelled?"

"You got it! Dude."

Better everyone thought we were nuts than that we were trouble.

Another little pink man, General Hamadi entered the room briskly in a beige leisure suit. The interview turned out to be more like a lecture by the general, with me seated at a hundred-foot-long table below the judicial-bench-like desk raised on a dais where he sat flanked by portraits of Saddam and flags of the nation and its ruling Ba'ath Party. It's *only* party.

Like a mad old man with a surgical walker, Rob moved his massive tripod from spot to spot, shooting hundreds of flash pictures. Without any film in the camera.

I asked an innocent question, only to be cut off mid-sentence by a translator repeating what I hadn't yet said to his boss. The minister then cut off the mortified translator, announcing, "We will speak in English. This fellow is a terrible translator."

His English was flawless, which, since he'd been educated at Oxford (and was, indeed, the only member of the government to have a university degree), wasn't particularly surprising. Unfortunately, however, it allowed him to speak uninterruptedly for two hours, while I sat like a fish moving my lips with silent questions in the hope that I'd be allowed to voice one. It was a predictable, if eloquent, tirade: U.S. "fury" and "threats" had no influence on Iraq; sanctions were the only weapon we had, and these were causing unnecessary distress.

The way Hamadi told it, it sounded as if the sanctions were also unnecessarily petty. For example: Iraq had ordered 100,000 pencils from Pakistan for schoolchildren only to find the request rejected by the UN sanctions committee on the grounds that the graphite in these pencils could be used to manufacture casings for missile warheads. Hamadi laughed at the absurdity, while I wondered if graphite could serve such a purpose, because if it could there was no doubt that Saddam would have had five thousand people shaving off pencil wood the moment the shipment arrived.

Frozen assets were another sore point. Hamadi next recounted how his government had requested that a mere $10 million of the $480 million held in Saudi Arabia and the $1 billion held in the United States be unfrozen to finance the printing of Korans — again for schoolchildren. The Iraqis even agreed to let UNESCO supervise the printing operation. That was in 1993, the minister announced, and they were still waiting for a reply. Newsprint had by now been reduced to 10 percent of previous consumption, so textbooks were priced out of reach. This explained why photocopying done by the hotel had turned out to be on the back of old correspondence.

Even the importation of a calendar from Scotland had been denied (he didn't say why, though, and I speculated about military applications for spiral binding, and about why Iraq needed calendars from *Scotland* in the first place). Most petty and pathetic, however, was a request for research material made to the British Library by an Iraqi student named Sheda Salman. Hamadi read me the letter that Helen Parnaby of the British Library's Customer Services division had written in reply. It said that regretfully Ms Salman's request had to be denied on account of trade sanctions, but that once these sanctions were lifted, the library would be happy to be of service to her. Since this particular deprivation could be checked out — and is, in fact, true — it did strike me as preposterous. Is the trade in knowledge and ideas also capable of coming under UN sanction?

The West was trying to create another Rwanda in Iraq, Hamadi theorized, but the plan wasn't working because of the Iraqi people's indomitable will. Deaths from leukemia had risen 700 percent since the war, he claimed, on account of pollution from depleted uranium used by U.S. armor-piercing shells and now scattered all over the South. (Ala was to tell me that after the war everyone developed a strange skin rash that no medicine could relieve. They'd been told to wash everything in the house — clothes, floors, furniture — and wear masks while doing it. No explanation was given, but the rumor persisted (and was later repeated to me by a U.S. soldier) that America had tested a new low-range nuclear device during Desert Storm. Iraqi soldiers also reported being blinded and deafened by something that, after exploding, threw out a massive shock wave that scattered people and trucks in its path. They were ordered to keep quiet about what they'd seen, in order not to scare the other men.)

Finally, Hamadi launched into what I felt was the real purpose of this meeting: the referendum. The Ba'ath Party had come to power in 1968, the minister said, in a reverential tone. Before that there had been the monarchy, and before that the Ottomans, and before them the Abbasid caliphs. Since most exiled Iraqis I'd spoken with privately wanted the monarchy back, and since life under Turks or caliphs could hardly have been worse than life under Saddam, Hamadi's point was lost on me.

What the country had apparently been trying to do since 1972, I now learned, was to move from "Revolutionary Legality" to "Constitutional Legality." What was hindering this process? Well, by 1979, it seems they had arrived at what Hamadi termed "Multiplicity"; this basically means that non-Ba'athists — like the Kurds — were able to get nominal government representation, which has not done them much practical good. Although the Great Progress toward the revolution's real goal continued, alas, it had to be "postponed" because of the Iran-Iraq war. After this was over, in 1989, a "new constitution" was formulated. Then, alas, came the "Gulf Crisis," so the Great Progress had to be postponed yet again. After this came sanctions, as we well knew. Yet this time nothing was going to hinder Iraq from embarking upon — in the minister's favorite phrase-of-the-day — a "New Political Life."

I tried asking how he hoped to achieve a "New Political Life" with a referendum capable only of endorsing the old one, but Hamadi replied that the voting process would be scrupulously fair — and that if I didn't believe him I could observe it myself.

"No one would dare vote against Saddam," Ala told me, as we walked the ruins of old Babylon. "Even if the ballot is fair, Iraqis believe the Mukhabarat will know how they vote . . ."

It was what people believed, not what was, that counted. It is everywhere. As things turned out, Saddam was endorsed as president by a staggering 98 percent of the vote. The other 2 percent was probably lopped off to make it look good.

"Oh, waycool! Babylonian-Bauhaus . . ."

"No, Robert! No! No photographs of *that*!" Ala yelled. "It is forbidden!"

High on a hill beyond the Marduk Temple — beyond the city itself — was Nebuchadrezzar's Palace.

"Okay, okay! No pictures. It's cool." I could see him clicking away surreptitiously. "But why, Ala?"

"It is the Palace of Nebuchadrezzar."

"So, what is it — holy, or something?"

"I will get into very bad trouble."

"I gotta tell you, but where I come from, this is a *house*, not a palace. Sorry."

"It is also Palace of Saddam Hussein. He . . . likes to be here, in Babylon."

It was *one* of Saddam's palaces: he has scores of others scattered around Greater Baghdad. Thirty-seven were pointed out to me, and two more under construction. Apparently he doesn't like to spend more than two nights under the same roof. Or woman.

Every brick of the new Babylon has stamped upon it "The Babylon of Nebuchadrezzar Rebuilt During the Reign of Saddam Hussein."

"The *reign*?"

"Yes. Saddam had himself crowned king — have you not heard that?"

"No. We didn't hear *that* . . ."

It appears to be a persistent (thus probably state-sanctioned) rumor in Iraq to this day.

Every brick of the old Babylon also had stamped upon it cuneiform information along the lines of "I AM NEBUCHADREZZAR, KING OF

KINGS, LORD OF BABYLON. LOOK ON MY WORKS YE MIGHTY AND EAT YOUR HEARTS OUT."

"Look, sir! See?" asked Babylon's own Official Guide (Ala wasn't allowed to show us around on her own). He'd just levered up one of the stones in Nebuchadrezzar's Processional Path with an improvised crowbar to show me the bird's feet runes of its cuneiform inscription.

I assumed the message pecked into this ancient slab of brick did not say MADE IN IRAQ.

"You *like*, sir?" the Official Guide inquired.

I examined the rock more intently, nodding. I wondered how the Ministry of Ancient Stuff felt about him digging up one of the world's most important archaeological sites.

"You *take* it, yes? One dollar Amerkan. Okay?"

I now have eight cubic inches of Nebuchadrezzar's Babylon — a signed first edition — helping to quiet a dreadful, geriatric rattle in my fax machine. For less than a hundred grand I could probably have had Marduk's Temple in my garden.

It's sad.

Approaching the third week now, we'd had enough. We were weary. It was when Faisal offered to drive us back to Amman for a quarter what anyone else was charging that we got worried. Clearly he'd been ordered to drive us — somewhere. You didn't just decide to do things like that on your own in Baghdad. The images of us lying squashed and bloody on the highway were haunting, as were the official government telegrams dispatched to our homes: *There has been an unfortunate accident . . .*

We attended so many Babylon Festival events that I even started to think I might pursue folk dancing as a hobby. The Russian Cossacks were great; so were the Mongolian Throat Singers. Best of all, though, was Hattam, Iraq's Elvis — only still alive. We even got to hang out with him, although this was disappointing, since there's no copyright law in Iraq and all audio cassettes are bootlegs, so Hattam wasn't very rich. Performers made money by singing privately.

"Who for?"

"Uday."

"Just Uday?"

"Well, heeze fader, our pressident, he geeve me zeese." It was a wrist-watch hewn from a nugget of diamond-studded gold.

"Cool, Hattam. Really *smokin'*."

"Tasteful, too. Did he give you any of his old neckties? I'd kill for one of those."

Uday had given Hattam a silver and pearl Luger, which he wore in a shoulder holster.

"That's cool, too. Do you shoot many people, Hattam?"

We left before dawn, in a cab hired furtively and at great expense.

It seemed a bargain.

I never thought I'd come to see Jordan as a little paradise, but when my passport was finally handed back by an Iraqi official and I was waved on, out of Saddam's grim republic and into the other Hussein's bright desert kingdom, I felt like an exiled soul finally forgiven and summoned back to Life and Light.

> *There is below,*
> *As far from Beelzebub as one can be*
> *Within his tomb, a place one cannot know*
> *By sight, but by the sound a little runnel*
> *Makes as it wends the hollow rock its flow*
> *Has worn, descending through its winding channel:*
> *To get back up to the shining world from there*
> *My guide and I went into that little tunnel;*
> *And following its path, we took no care*
> *To rest, but climbed: he first, then I — so far,*
> *Through a round aperture I saw appear*
> *Some of the beautiful things that Heaven bears,*
> *Where we came forth, and once more saw the stars.*
> — DANTE, INFERNO

Epilogue

It is hard to think of those who still wait so patiently to see the stars once more, who wait for the privilege of being summoned back to Life and Light. It is harder still to watch as our governments make their hell more hellish. According to a recent UN survey, nearly half of the babies born in Iraq now have birth defects caused by malnutrition. We are the ones punishing the innocent, poisoning the wombs of the unborn.

In mid-January 1996, I received a letter from Ala. It was unsigned and there was no return address. She left spaces for the English words she did not know. "Pleese," she wrote in the last paragraph, "I knoweing not ware to turn and now no job. It is very bad now . . . can you helpp us Mister Paul . . ."

> Today, like every other day, we wake up empty
> and frightened. Don't open the door to the study
> and begin reading. Take down a musical instrument.
>
> Let the beauty we love be what we do.
> There are hundreds of ways to kneel and kiss the ground.
>
> ***
>
> But there's a difference with this dream.
> Everything cruel and unconscious
> done in the illusion of the present world,
> all that does not fade away at the death-waking.

It stays,
and it must be interpreted . . .

The world is that kind of sleep.

The dust of many crumbled cities
settles over us like a forgetful doze,
but we are older than those cities . . .

Humankind is being led along an evolving course,
through this migration of intelligences,
and though we seem to be sleeping,
there is an inner wakefulness
that directs the dream,

and that will eventually startle us back
to the truth of who we are.

— Jelaluddin Rumi (thirteenth century)
(translated by Coleman Barks with John Moyne)

End Notes

Part One: The Paradise

1. From Samir al-Khalil (Kanan Makiya), *Republic of Fear* (New York: Pantheon, 1990), p. 21.

2. Saddam Hussein, *Al-'Iraq wa al-Siyasa al-Duwaliyya* (Baghdad: Dar al-Hurriyya, 1981), p. 164.

3. See Hanna Batutu, *The Old Social Classes and the Revolutionary Movements of Iraq* (Princeton: Princeton University Press, 1978), p. 1065.

4. See Samir al-Khalil, *Republic of Fear*, p. 48.

5. This speech was published as a pamphlet called "Kul shay' min 'ajl al-ma'raka" (Baghdad: Ministry of Education and Information, 1970), pp. 6–7. Apart from words like "exploiters," "rabble," "riffraff," and "fifth columnists," Bakr is evidently very fond of certain words that defy translation, such as *al-mashbuheen* ("those who are suspected and suspicious") and *al-mutala'ibeen* ("ones who toy frivolously with the national interest").

6. See Lorenzo K. Kimball, *The Changing Pattern of Political Power in Iraq: 1958 to 1971*, (New York: Robert Speller & Sons, 1973), p. 361.

7. Ibid., p. 148.

8. Quoted in Samir al-Khalil, *Republic of Fear*, p. 36.

9. British Foreign Secretary, Lord Curzon, in a speech to the House of Lords, June, 25, 1920.

10. The Encyclopedia Britannica Online.

Part Two: The Purgation

1. Quoted in Ronald Lewin, *Hitler's Mistakes* (London: Secker & Warburg, 1984), p. 68.

2. Quoted in John Bulloch and Harvey Morris, *Saddam's War: The Origins of the*

Kuwait Conflict and the International Response (London: Faber & Faber, 1991), pp. 104–5.

3. "The Confrontation" (transcript released by the Iraqi Ministry of Culture and Information), Baghdad, May 1990, p. 17.

4. U.S. State Department Records (Iraq, unclassified), April–July 1990, p. 241.

5. Ibid.

6. See John R. MacArthur, *Second Front: Censorship and Propaganda in the Gulf War* (New York: Hill & Wang, 1992). This frightening book documents in vivid detail the behind-the-scenes activities by the U.S. and Kuwaiti governments, as well as the media's own cooperation when its rights to observe, question, and report were increasingly limited. MacArthur shows how the press corps was treated more like a fifth column than as representatives of a free people, and he demonstrates how, despite the torrent of words and images from the Persian Gulf, Americans were systematically kept in the dark about events, politics, and simple facts during the entire Gulf crisis.

7. *The New York Times*, April 27, 1997.

8. Quoted in Bullock and Morris, *Saddam's War*, p. 24.

9. Quoted in *F.D.R. Meets Ibn Saud* (New York: American Friends of the Middle East, 1954), p. 34.

10. See *The Holy Quran*, translated by A. Yusuf Ali, sura xvii, 4, p. 695.

11. VeZoth HaBerakhah/Deuteronomy 34, translated by Rabbi Aryeh Kaplan and the author from *The Living Torah*.

12. From the papers of Sir Henry McMahon, July 1915–February 1916 (Cairo High Commission: British Foreign Office Archives).

13. Ibid.

14. Ibid.

15. From the British Foreign Office Archives (London); Balfour, Nov. 82.

16. From the British Foreign Office Archives (London); Balfour A., state papers, 1919.

Part Three: Inferno

1. See Samir al-Khalil (Kanan Makiya), *Republic of Fear* (New York: Pantheon, 1990), p. 68.

2. "The Code of Hammurabi" (Iraqi Ministry of Culture and Information, 1987).

3. Talk on January 19, 1988, in "Saddam Hussein on the Application of Justice" (Baghdad: Dar Al-Ma'mun for Translation and Publishing, 1988), pp. 22–23.

4. "Fao — The Gate of Victory in the Gulf War" (Iraqi Ministry of Culture and Information), p. 5

Index